Education and the
Industrial Revolution

E. G. West

Education and the Industrial Revolution

Second Edition, Revised and Expanded

E. G. West

Liberty Fund

Indianapolis

Education and the Industrial Revolution was first published by B. T. Batsford Ltd., London and Sydney, 1975. "Literacy and the Industrial Revolution" first appeared in August 1978 in *The Economic History Review*. Reprinted with permission.

05 04 03 02 01   C   5   4   3   2   1
05 04 03 02 01   P   5   4   3   2   1

Library of Congress Cataloging-in-Publication Data

West, E. G.
    Education and the Industrial Revolution/E. G. West. — 2nd ed., rev. and expanded.
        p.   cm.
    Includes bibliographical references and index.
    ISBN 0-86597-309-1 (alk. paper)   ISBN 0-86597-310-5 (pbk.: alk. paper)
    1. Education—Great Britain—History—19th century.   2. Industrial revolution—Great Britain.   3. Education—Economic aspects—Great Britain—History—19th century.   4. Industry and education—History—19th century.   I. Title.

LA631.7.W47 2001
370'.942—dc21

                                                                    00-048131

LIBERTY FUND, INC.
8335 Allison Pointe Trail, Suite 300
Indianapolis, Indiana 46250-1684

Contents

    10   Tom Paine's National System   143

    11   The National System to Promote Order:
         The Benthamite Prescription   152

    12   A System to Complement Poor Law Legislation:
         Senior and Chadwick   168

    13   John Stuart Mill's National System and the
         Problem of Liberty   181

    14   A Homogeneous National System: Horace Mann   198

    15   W. E. Forster and Robert Lowe versus the
         Birmingham League   209

Part 4   The Economic Realities of Intervention   215

    16   The Public/Private Displacement Mechanism:
         Did Education Grow Faster or Slower?   217

    17   Legal Compulsion: Logic and Reality   245

    18   Free Education: Who Benefited?   267

    19   Education and Industrial Growth: Did Victorian
         Britain Fail?   285

         Bibliography   299

         Index   309

Foreword to the Liberty Fund Edition, Revised and Extended

This volume was first published in 1975 by B. T. Batsford Ltd. And thanks are due them for permission to produce this second edition. As indicated in the first preface, the book originally focused exclusively on education in the nineteenth century, the main reason being lack of systematic evidence for the period immediately prior to 1800. Since writing the first edition, however, important sample data has been published relating to literacy changes in the late eighteenth century. The availability of this material has now made it possible to extend the discussion to the whole of the Industrial Revolution period, conventionally taken to refer to the years 1760–1840. Analysis of literacy in the early part of the Industrial Revolution now appears as Chapter 5, which reproduces our article "Literacy and the Industrial Revolution" published in 1978.

As explained in the original edition, the title of the book allows two major interpretations. The first is an investigation of the significance of education as an ingredient of economic growth. The second is its place in the debate about changes in the standard of living. Several versions of hypotheses relating to the growth theme are discussed in Chapter 19. As emphasized there, it is important to avoid dogmatic and untested assertions to the effect that education is the exclusive key to economic growth. It is not surprising that subsequent literature has pursued the same cautionary approach (see especially Blaug, 1970; Mitch, 1990 and 1992; Coulson, 1999).

The first simple question is whether or not the unprecedented surge

levels that were exactly optimal for the time. We make no such claim, however. Indeed to some extent the book is an examination of the work of others (such as Kiesling himself) who implicitly or explicitly argue that social optimality was reached only after intervention, or that education levels were substantially suboptimal before. In contrast, our book's general finding is that, down to the mid-1970s at least, the typical historian of education had seriously underestimated the extent of nongovernment education in the laissez-faire period.

By all standard measures used today, Britain was an underdeveloped or developing country right down to the later part of the nineteenth century. In the light of this it is relevant to compare three prominent findings concerning developing countries today. They are as follows:

- The growth of education combats the Malthusian spectre of over-population—that the population would grow (geometrically) faster than production (arithmetically).

- Education growth leads to increases in *per capita* incomes which, in turn, improve health and lower mortality; and since these improvements enhance the pay-off to human capital investment, the growth in education becomes cumulative or, at least, self-enforcing.

- As *per capita* incomes increase, parents voluntarily spend more on education.

These findings pertain to a systematic study of the records of over 100 developing countries since 1960 (Becker, 1995).

Consider now the presently developed countries England and Wales in their developing years. With a population of nearly twelve million in 1818, and no "public" (government) schools, about one in seventeen were attending private schools paid for largely by working parents. There were no government subsidies to private schools and no laws for compulsory schooling. By 1858 the proportion of the population found in fee-paid schools had increased dramatically (almost doubled) to approximately one in eight. And by this time the percentage annual growth rate of population had fallen to 1.21 from 1.40 in 1818. This relationship between population and education is consistent with the first of the three "modern" findings concerning the twentieth-century developing countries reported above: the growth of education combats the threat of over-population. And at that time it was education without the state.

Next, we have seen that the annual growth of *per capita* income in the years 1801–71 was just over 1 per cent while the annual average growth rate of day scholars was well over 2 per cent. This combination of circumstances is consistent with the second of the three findings from twentieth-century developing countries: education growth is associated with, or leads to, increases in *per capita* incomes. Moreover, it is pertinent that in Britain the years 1801–71 witnessed a drop in mortality rates, a factor that increased the yield from human capital investment.

Finally, since in Britain's case it was education largely without laws of compulsory education, we have the strongest possible support for the third finding from today's developing countries: parents voluntarily spend more (directly, from their own pockets) on education as their incomes rise. Indeed, the nineteenth-century figures for England and Wales show that the income elasticity of demand was particularly high: or, in other words, the desire for private education rose much faster than incomes.

This is not to deny, of course, a potential role for government. Furthermore, the book emphasizes the important distinction between two types of intervention that were eventually provided in nineteenth-century Britain. The first was the allocation of subsidies (after 1833) to non-government schools and in proportion to enrolment. The second type, introduced after 1870, was the provision of government schools, referred to in the U.S.A. as "public schools." The comparison made in the book happens to be very pertinent to the debate about educational choice at the beginning of the twenty-first century. The 1833 method of allocating subsidies according to enrolment, in fact, had similar consequences to those intended by modern education voucher advocates. Just as in the case of today's formal education voucher, under the nineteenth-century subsidy mechanism the parent triggered an incremental portion of the school grant whenever he or she chose one school over others. Government funds followed the child just as they do today where vouchers exist. And for this reason we can expect vigorous competition as a consequence.

This is not the place, however, to rehearse the whole modern debate about vouchers versus other forms of government provision. The main point being advanced is simply the fact that the period of history studied in this book offers pertinent material to modern scholars who are genuinely seeking real-world evidence about the effects of alternative government policy instruments.

One final word needs to be offered concerning data sources. Critics who find themselves surprised at the extent of nineteenth-century education provision reported in this book, are tempted to question the quality of the data. The extreme version of data criticism, however, is nihilistic. It denies that anything useful can be concluded from the available evidence since it is asserted to be unreliable. But if this is true then no proposition at all can be entertained from any quarter. This means that all the histories of education that have argued retrospectively, for example, about the urgent need for nineteenth-century government intervention, must all be disqualified on the grounds of inadequate evidence. For this reason most writers do not want to go so far as to dismiss the data sources outright. But apart from some rare exceptions the sources they rely on are the same as those investigated in this book. The main controversy, therefore, comes to focus on data interpretations. And the interpretations herein have attempted to be balanced, reasonable and consistent.

The debate continues on what remains to be a fascinating subject. It is hoped that this new edition will provide a further contribution.

Edwin G. West

September 2000

References

Blaug, M. 1975. "The Economics of Education in English Classical Political Economy: A Re-Examination." In A. Skinner and T. Wilson, ed., *Essays on Adam Smith*. Oxford: Clarendon Press, p. 595.

Blaug, M. 1987. "Where Are We Now in the Economics of Education?" *The Economics of Education and the Education of an Economist*. Aldershot, Hants: Edward Elgar Publishing.

Bowman, M. J., and Anderson, C. A. 1963. "Concerning the Role of Education in Development." In C. Geertz, ed., *Old Societies and New States*. Free Press of Glencoe.

Greenwood, M. J., and McDowell, J. M. 1986. "The Factor Market: Consequences of U.S. Immigration." *Journal of Economic Literature.* 24 (4).

Kiesling, H. J. 1983. "Nineteenth-Century Education According to West: A Comment." *The Economic History Review* XXXVI, No. 3, August.

Mathias, Peter. 1969. *The First Industrial Nation: an Economic History of Britain, 1700–1914.* New York: Scribner, p. 522.

Mitch, D. 1990. "Education and Economic Growth: Another Axiom of Indispensability? From Human Capital of Human Capabilities," in Tortella, 1990, pp. 29–45.

Mitch, D. 1992. *The Rise of Popular Literacy in Victorian England. The Influence of Private Choice and Public Policy.* Philadelphia: University of Pennsylvania Press.

Nicholas, S. 1990. "Literacy and the Industrial Revolution," in Tortella, 1990, pp. 47–68.

Seldon, Arthur. 1996. *Re-Privatising Welfare: After the Lost Century.* I.E.A. Readings 45, Institute of Economic Affairs, London.

Tortella, G., ed. 1990. *Education and Economic Development Since the Industrial Revolution.* Valencia, Spain: Generalitat Valenciana.

West, E. G. 1994. *Education and the State,* 3rd ed., Indianapolis: Liberty Fund, Inc.

Preface to the First Edition

The primary aim of this volume is a study of the relationship between education and the process of industrialization during the nineteenth century. Our use of the term Industrial Revolution does not coincide with—although it overlaps—the conventional period. The book relates to industrialization in the nineteenth century exclusively. The term "education" is used in the special sense of popular or "mass" education. Whilst the modern economics of education has produced several hypotheses about education's role in underdeveloped countries, there has been little previous attempt to test them in the context of Britain's nineteenth-century relatively underdeveloped economy. The present book contributes to this field primarily by searching and establishing the relevant facts. In addition there is a preliminary attempt to arrange the facts in the conventional perspectives of the modern quantitative approach. One main example of this is our attempt to estimate the proportion of national income devoted to education in 1833, 1858, and 1882 and to compare it with other countries.

Questions about the role of education in nineteenth-century economic growth are treated directly in Parts 1 and 2 and in the concluding chapter. Parts 3 and 4 can be regarded in one sense as an indirect approach to the same problem. They are concerned with the increase of government intervention and the difference in the growth of education that resulted. These parts of the book bring us into contact with other types of "revolution" that occurred. In these sections, the phrase "Industrial

Revolution" in our title acts as a broad surrogate for many other rapid changes or revolutions that were occurring. We discuss, for instance, the nineteenth-century political "revolution" associated with the extension of the franchise in the Reform Act of 1832, and more especially the Act of 1867. Although we do not concentrate upon the issue of educational method, we do make some substantial study of the educational "revolution." We thus examine changes in educational techniques that involved the monitorial methods of the 1820s and 1830s, the pupil-teacher training system, the Sunday School as a new agency for mass literacy, the various forms of apprenticeships, industrial schools, mechanics institutes and the literary and philosophic societies. Finally we examine the "literacy revolution"—the great surge in literacy that began between 1790 and 1800 and reached full strength in the 1830s and 1840s.

In an investigation of the changing methods of government intervention we focus upon the administrative "revolution"—the growth of an official inspectorate of schools, and the evolution of a central department of education that was only weakly accountable to Parliament. Our approach here attempts an application of one of the newest branches of economics—the "economics of bureaucracy."

Part 4 examines the "public finance revolution"—the striking changes in the method of public finance especially after 1870. It demonstrates the crucial economic significance of the special type of public finance of the new board schools that were introduced by the 1870 Act to "fill up gaps" in the voluntary system. The ability of these new types of schools eventually to capture the main part of the growing educational "market" will be demonstrated in the context of the political "revolution" in education in late Victorian Britain. Our analysis here includes some retrospective application to the nineteenth-century data of the type of "economics of politics" that has developed in the last fifteen years. From such criteria we examine anew the precise arguments of the various campaigners of the period—those who consciously wanted and welcomed the new changes—and those who did not. The debate will be shown to have centred upon arguments about the need for what they called "national systems" of education or what contemporaries now call the need for "social cohesion."

In some ways this book is an extension of our earlier *Education and the State* (1965, second edition 1970, third, Liberty Fund edition, 1994). This was an exploration of the basic political economy principles of state intervention in education. In the course of writing this earlier volume, we developed a growing interest in the history of the subject. The two or three historical chapters in it indeed foretell the present work. Thanks are due to the Institute of Economic Affairs, London, for allowing reproduction of some parts of the historical chapters in *Education and the State* as points of departure. We wish also to thank the editors of the *Economic History Review* for permission to draw upon two of our recent articles published in the early 1970s and the editor of *Explorations In Economic History* for a similar privilege.

Helpful assistance was provided by the following libraries: The British Museum (State Papers Room), the library of the University of London, the Goldsmith Library, the Bodlean Library of Oxford, the University of Newcastle-upon-Tyne Library, Carleton University Library, the library of the University of Kent, the library of the St. Osyth's Teacher Training College, Clacton-on-Sea, and the libraries of the University of California at Berkeley.

We also express gratitude for the valuable comments of numerous students and the stimulating discussion in seminars presented at the Colloquium in Economic History at the University of California Berkeley, in 1974, and the Graduate History Workshop at Carleton University in 1973. We have benefited considerably from discussion with Mark Blaug, William Niskanen, Albert Fishlow, Max Hartwell, Carlo Cipolla, Michael Bordo, from correspondence with W. G. Armytage and A. C. F. Beales, and from contributions from Karen King, Research Assistant at the London Institute of Education. Acknowledgements are due to the Canada Council for a research grant in the summer of 1972 and for facilities provided by the University of California Law School (Childhood and Government Project) during a sabbatical leave there in 1974.

Finally this volume would not have been completed had it not been for my wife, Ann, who not only patiently typed and retyped several versions of many chapters, but also offered much sound editorial comment.

E. G. West

Carleton University, Ottawa

Part 1 · The Statistical Framework and Basic Hypotheses

1 · Traditional Measures of Nineteenth-Century Educational Deficiency

Most discussions on the economic history of British education usually reach a consensus that the spread of industrialization in early nineteenth-century Britain was accompanied by educational stagnation if not deterioration. In other words the Industrial Revolution exposed not the effectiveness of education, but the serious lack of it. To some this might appear paradoxical. For the same writers who adduce little connection between industrial growth and education in the early nineteenth century in Britain stress its importance in the later years of the century in America and Germany both of which then "overtook" Britain. On this reasoning therefore, Britain enjoyed a rapid growth *despite* the lack of education in the early period and slow growth *because* of the lack of it later. The relationship between education and growth is a complex one and we shall endeavour to resolve the above paradox in our final chapter. Education in the nineteenth century is usually treated as an indicator of social condition; as a consumer good rather than a producer good. This is, of course, another valid property of education, and it is the one usually adopted by historians.[1]

---

1. Lawrence Stone in particular takes this view in his article "Literacy and Education in England 1640–1900," *Past and Present* No. 42, Feb. 1969. Welcoming the fact that the "standard of living debate is now shifting . . . to an examination of the *quality* of urban life in terms of housing, sanitation, living space, community sense . . ." Stone contends (p. 126) that: "The decline of literacy in the cities, if it can be proved beyond

Many conventional histories tell us that the period of Industrial Revolution brought for the workers such precarious economic circumstances and moral degradation that, as a consequence, education was among the important human (consumer) provisions, or social services, to decline. It is because hardship and ignorance are believed by some to have grown hand in hand with industrialization, that education has been automatically linked with one side of the nineteenth-century standard of living debate.

Some of the most strongly expressed versions of this verdict are contained in J. L. and B. Hammond's conclusion that in the new manufacturing towns of the Industrial Revolution:

> . . . all diversions were regarded as wrong, because it was believed that successful production demanded long hours, a bare life, a mind without temptation to think or remember, to look before or behind.[2]

> The ruling class argued . . . that with the new method of specialization, industry could not spare a single hour for the needs of the man who served it. In such a system education had no place.[3]

> . . . politicians were prepared to leave the nation to a hopelessly inadequate provision made by voluntary societies, and it was not until 1833 that education received any help from the public funds.[4]

Usually associated with this kind of view is an implicit or explicit allegation of inefficient or inhumane governments and insufficient or tardy legislation in England and Wales in contrast with Scotland. W. H. B. Court referring to the belated recognition of the value of public education in England observes:

> Education was a vital concern of the new manufacturing districts for two different reasons: first, because of the concentration of population there and the neglected state of the children, which made organised

---

doubt, would add a further dimension to the discussion and would tend to support the pessimists."

2. *The Rise of Modern Industry*, 5th Edition, 1937, p. 229.
3. *Ibid.*, p. 231.
4. *Ibid.*, p. 231.

primary education a necessity; and secondly, because of the growing perception of the need for technical training. . . .[5]

G. M. Trevelyan writes: "Only about half the children in the country were educated at all and most of these very indifferently. England, for all her wealth, lagged far behind Scotland and several foreign countries." Only by the passing of the 1870 Act did England obtain: ". . . better late than never, a system of education without which she must soon have fallen to the rear among modern nations."[6]

Similarly Sir Arthur Bryant: "In 1869 only one British child in two was receiving any education at all."[7] Impressions similar to those of the Hammonds and W. H. B. Court are repeated in the works of specialist historians of education S. J. Curtis[8] and Frank Smith.[9] As a final example of a particularly strong expression of the viewpoint above outlined, consider Richard D. Altick's book published in 1957. Referring to the new industrialism's attraction of the early-nineteenth-century population to the "sprawling new factory towns" he gives his reason for the common conclusion in one all-embracing and graphic sentence:

> The occupational and geographical relocation of the people—the total disruption of their old way of life, their conversion into machine-slaves, living a hand-to-mouth existence at the mercy of their employers and of uncertain economic circumstances; their concentration in cities *totally* unprepared to accommodate them, not least in respect to education; the resultant moral and physical degradation—these, as we shall see, had significant consequences in the history of the reading public. (our italics)[10]

In our attempt to reassess the nineteenth-century position we shall draw upon the same major sources of evidence that most of the above writers have used. In addition, for both England and Scotland we shall use ma-

5. W. H. B. Court, *A Concise History of Britain,* 1967, p. 258.
6. *British History in the Nineteenth Century,* pp. 354–5.
7. *English Sage* (1840–1940).
8. S. J. Curtis, *History of Education in Great Britain,* 1965, p. 224.
9. Frank Smith, *A History of English Elementary Education,* 1931, Ch. 1.
10. Richard D. Altick, *The English Common Reader,* The University of Chicago Press, 1957.

terial that so far does not seem to have received its due attention. Our review of the evidence will be continually related to the two prominent implications in the popular verdict; first, that there was serious educational
underconsumption; second that lack of legislation was the chief cause of
this deficiency. Whether on the question of underconsumption or underinvestment clearly it is first necessary to obtain as accurate a picture
as possible of the precise quantity of education in the period. We antic-
ipate one problem straight away however. From previous experience we
expect from some readers the same prompt reaction when evidence is
produced which shows in some cases that the early-nineteenth-century
enrolments were not so "bad" as we have been led to expect. Some will
impatiently insist that such a conclusion may be quite true with regard to
the quantity, but it says nothing about the deplorable *quality* of schooling.
Conversely, if one starts by a re-investigation that shows that the quality,
relative to nineteenth-century economic development and to twentieth-
century achievement, was often not as "bad" as had been thought, or as
has been described to us by prejudiced observers, many readers will want
to switch to the problem of *quantity*. We should emphasize in advance
therefore that questions of quantity and of quality will both be given due
attention; but at the appropriate time. Chapter 2 will be devoted to quantity and Chapters 3 and 4 to quality. The way that investigation is hindered when we continually try to jump from one dimension to another,
will be illustrated in Chapter 2 with our report of the vacillating response
given by the witness James Kay to the searching questions put to him in
a Royal Commission enquiry by Mr. Gladstone in 1838.

Predominant in many reactions will be the belief that however widespread and strongly expanding was the supply of schools before 1870
they suffered so much from one particular quality failure that it is questionable whether they deserve association with the name of "school" or
even with the process called "education." The "deficiency" will be related to the fact that the schools in question did not belong to an inte-
grated "national system." It is not made sufficiently clear that what many
a historian of education is recording with primary weight when he speaks
of the "belated progress" in education in the nineteenth century is not so
much the growth of education as the growth of the centralized political

control of it. Since it is easy for the unwary to confuse the two the impression is frequently established, without demonstration, that "education did not really start" until it was "organized," until it became "public" or until a particular nineteenth- or twentieth-century Parliamentary Bill was passed. This confusion is much more deep-seated in the subject of education than in others. No one believes, for instance, that because it is only now in the twentieth century that serious legislative attempts are being made to weld transport into "one co-ordinated system of public transport" that it did not seriously exist in the nineteenth century.[11] Neither does any one believe that because there was not a "public system" of food or housing that they were not provided. Conventional histories lead on to the belief that no substantial progress could have occurred without legislation. In this book this will be treated as an hypothesis to be tested.

We could test it if we could compare, for instance, the progress of another country which established educational legislation and a "public system" before 1833 with that of England which did not, but which was identical in all other respects. Fortunately there is one such opportunity available. Scotland had educational legislation before England. Moreover some parts of Scotland received the full impact of the new industrialism while others did not. What difference then did industrialization really have within Scotland? Data on the various degrees of educational success among these different areas are amply available and will therefore be useful to test the hypotheses of the above mentioned writers that industrialism was detrimental to educational progress. Chapter 6 will be devoted to the Scottish case with these questions in mind. Chapter 7 will

11. See again the above reference to G. M. Trevelyan and his emphasis upon the crucial attainment in 1870 of a "system of education." Notice also W. H. B. Court's use of the word "organised." Historians C. Birchenough (*op. cit.*), G. R. Porter (*The Progress of the Nation,* 1912) and S. J. Curtis (*op. cit.*) make estimates of children who were "not provided for" in the nineteenth century without clearly specifying that they meant not provided for in the public sector of education. For further details see E. G. West, *Education and the State,* 3rd edition, 1994, p. 148. Writing in 1969, Lawrence Stone (*op. cit.,* p. 127) asserts without much argument that: "The major advances in elementary education in Scotland seem to have taken place in the late seventeenth and eighteenth centuries, when a *national education system* was set up by legislative action." (our italics).

consist of a critical survey of the same primary sources of information on English education in the period, upon which most writers previously mentioned have hitherto depended, and again bearing in mind that Scotland had legislation while England did not. As a final application of the comparative method we shall, in this same chapter, make some brief comparisons between educational attainments in the industrial areas in England and those in the non-industrial areas.

2 · The Quantity of Education:
Key Issues

In this book we endeavour to produce fully representative evidence by scrutinizing nearly all the data that is available; and in particular by examining closely the same primary sources that are used by most writers in the field. Thus our evidence on the first half of the period in England is gleaned from such varied sources as the Manchester Statistical Society, the Statistical Societies of London, Bristol, Hull, Birmingham and other big towns, Hansard, Horace Mann's Census Report on Education in England and Wales 1851; The Government Return of 1833; Select Committee Reports on Education; Henry Brougham's private statistical surveys; Factory Inspectors' Reports; the National and the British and Foreign School Societies and the Reports of the Committee of Council.[1]

The biggest area of statistical contention comes in fact not from choice

---

1. Not surprisingly it is impossible to find a sufficiently comprehensive single source of compiled documentary evidence on early-nineteenth-century education. The data is extensive and it would be difficult to compress into one publication. The valiant attempt by J. Stuart McLure, *Educational Documents England and Wales 1816–1968*, Methuen, 1965, is very helpful yet shows the problems involved. McLure's book confines itself to *official* documents. It therefore excludes abstracts and references to many important and rarely accessible *private* sources. Thus it has to omit such important evidence as that contained in the Reports of the Statistical Societies (most especially those of the Manchester Society), and the Reports of the British and Foreign School Societies. Even from the list of official sources there are important omissions. There are for instance no extracts from the "Kerry" Return for 1833, The Report of the Select Committee on the Education of the Poorer Classes 1838, the 1851 Census Report by Horace Mann, the Factory Commissioner's Reports and the Factory Inspectors' Reports.

of figures but from different views as to their interpretation. On this we shall have much to say and as a preliminary we produce in this chapter the most important general points.

Defining the School-Age Base

The early nineteenth century was still in the pre-statistical age, not so much in their enthusiasm for the collection of numbers, which indeed shows considerable Victorian zeal, but in their systematic processing, analysis, and application. The outstanding error consisted of the mis-identification and misapplication of the "school-age" population base.

Educational "deficiency" can be produced by arbitrary variation of this base: To explain: suppose that today there are seven million pupils at school in England and Wales. Now select a base of "population of school-age" that we assume to consist of people between the ages of 5 and 20. Suppose next that the Registrar General reports ten million in this category in the population census. For a social statistician to conclude that there are three million "who never see the inside of a school" is, in the twentieth century, to invite immediate resistance, even from laymen. For it is first of all obviously not reasonable that the school population age "ought" to extend to as late as 20 years. Second, even if it was considered "proper" it is illogical to conclude that three million do not in fact receive any schooling; if the *de facto* average school leaving age is nearer 15, nearly everybody *will* receive a schooling. Obviously by simply varying the base we can vary the supposed educational deficiency. The latter can be increased "mechanically" for instance by placing an extra year on either end to make 4–20 or 5–21.

It would be unnecessary to dwell upon such simple points if it were not for the fact that the work of nineteenth-century statisticians has misled many people for the reasons stated. They typically used 5–15 years as the definition of school-age over a century ago and used it as the bench-mark for attendance deficiencies. Yet as late as 1922 only 31 per cent of the 14 year olds were attending school.[2] At this rate there were significant

2. *The Education of the Adolescent,* (The Hadow Report) 1927, p. 46. In 1913 40 per cent of the children left school at the age of 13 years.

enrolment deficiencies after half a century of State education. In 1972 average schooling in England began at 5 years and ended at 15 years. It is surely unrealistic to assume that a similar 10 year schooling was also an appropriate definition of the base "population of school age" a century and a half before. Yet this in fact was the practice by nineteenth-century investigators when measuring schooling "deficiencies" even as early as the 1830s; and it was used by Forster's advisors on the eve of the famous Act of 1870. The same investigators made comparisons between countries, moreover, without drawing attention to or explaining the importance of the fact that school age bases were different in each country. Consider the conclusion of its Report on the Borough of Manchester in 1834, by the influential Manchester Statistical Society. It observed that, if Manchester afforded a fair average, English education presented "a painful and mortifying contrast" to that of some of the countries on the Continent:

> That while in Prussia, and several of the German states, all children of every class, between the ages of 7 and 14, are obliged by law to attend school; and it is shown by statistical returns that they actually do so; it appears by this Report, that in Manchester not quite two-thirds of those between the ages of 5 and 15 years are receiving even nominal instruction.

The German school base of 7 years to 14 years was a 7 year one. That applied in Manchester, 5 years to 15 years was a 10 year. It is obvious to modern readers that comparing a 7 year base with a 10 year one has serious dangers. Very important assumptions are necessary before we conclude that substantially more were educated in Germany than England—even if we accept the Manchester Report's belief (which others do not) that the policing of attendance in Germany *was* 100 per cent successful.

Confusion of Quality with Quantity

The question of whether the Industrial Revolution was associated with progress, stagnation, or decline in schooling can be tested by an enquiry whether the industrial towns in England fared worse in school provision than the other, non-industrial, areas. On this issue historians use as a main reference the *Report from the Select Committee on Education of the Poorer Classes* (presented to the House of Commons July 13th, 1838). This body was set up specifically "to consider the means of providing useful Education for Children of the poorer classes in large towns throughout England and Wales." Among its members were Sir Robert Peel, Lord Ashley and Mr. Gladstone. The chief witness was Dr. J. Philip Kay. The only available national figures on education were those provided by the Government Return of 1833 (The Kerry Report). Because it accepted criticisms of the Manchester Statistical Society the new Select Committee of 1838 dismissed the official (Kerry) returns as unreliable. It did not, as it should have done, attempt to adjust for errors. Instead the committee adopted a negative approach and regretted that on such an important matter there existed no sources of information in any department of Government. "Until recently the subject appears to have entirely escaped the attention of Government. There appear to be no Returns to Parliament of any authority on this point, *nor indeed are there at present adequate means of making them.*"[3] (our italics). Nevertheless the Committee announced its firm opinion, much of which was obviously subjective, that education was in a pretty destitute state. More precisely it concluded:

1. That the kind of education offered is lamentably deficient.

2. That it extends (bad as it is) to but a small proportion of those who ought to receive it.

3. That without some strenuous and persevering efforts being made on the part of the Government the greatest evils to all classes may follow from this neglect.

Whilst the 1838 Select Committee dismissed the official Returns of national education it paid more attention to the figures of the case study of Manchester in 1834. It attached especial importance however to the pessimistic remarks about quality. Although we shall later examine the problem of educational quality separately it will be useful here to stress one point. Lack of "character-training" and "proper religious instruction"

3. *Towns Report,* p. 1.

was the strongest criticism of quality of education made by those who advised early nineteenth-century governments. Thus the Manchester Statistical Society objected in 1834 that in the common schools, "Religious instruction is seldom attended to beyond the rehearsal of 'a catechism,' and moral education, real cultivation of the mind and improvement of character, are totally neglected."[4] Twentieth-century historians may or may not have views as to the effect of Bible knowledge, religious discipline and recognition of one's "proper station in life" in satisfying the true needs or preferences of nineteenth-century families. Many moderns indeed seem to take the other side and champion the nineteenth-century secularists against the "inefficient" religious schools. But whatever their own opinions, those of them who seek to measure the relationship between education and economic development should note the degree to which the early official concepts of "efficiency" in education meant primarily a schooling which scored high marks in divinity and morality. Some of the schools were often written off by the statistical societies as worthless largely on account of failure in these respects.[5]

The increase of secular education and the new emphasis on the "three Rs" was provided by the schools in clear and direct response to parental wishes. By this time the Establishment was clearly fighting something of a rearguard action against the new expression of popular educational preferences. Not that there was a serious decline in the demand for religious instruction, but in the parents' opinion the teeming Sunday schools catered for that quite well; on week-days families were demanding education in more "practical" matters. In some places even in Sunday schools parents took the initiative. Arguing that these institutions had in fact a considerable influence on literacy, Professor Harold Perkins has observed that although the church was often reluctant to teach writing (as distinct from reading) it often took place. He cites the case of a group of cotton operatives in Glossop, Derbyshire, who sought instruction for

4. Manchester Statistical Society Report on Manchester, 1834, p. 10.
5. Today there is general agreement that religious and "moral" education is still one of the least satisfactory parts of British education. The founder members of the Manchester Statistical Society, and the 1838 Select Committee, would undoubtedly be at least as critical of today's "religious instruction."

their families. Unable to persuade the existing Sunday schools to teach their children to write, they "founded their own, and met, for lack of other accommodation, in the largest local public house."[6]

In the 1830s, the religious establishments, now on the defensive, were joined by new and unexpected partners, the Utilitarians. In the heyday of enthusiastic Benthamite blueprints for the reform of society it was argued that the "greatest happiness" could be achieved only after middle-class Utilitarian leaders had exercised temporary empire over the minds of men. In the words of Roebuck when (successfully) presenting his Education Bill to Parliament in 1833, "The people at present are far too ignorant to render themselves happy."[7]

Gladstone and J. Kay

The anxiety of the Utilitarians to obtain pedagogic influence was aptly reflected in Dr. James Philip Kay's replies to the 1838 Select Committee's questions. Kay, the colleague of Bentham's disciple Chadwick, had been appointed, on Nassau Senior's recommendation, as an assistant Poor Law Commissioner. At this time keenly occupied with the building of large experimental Benthamite schools in pauper settlements, he was eager to spread what he was convinced to be their advantages to the general public and to see them supersede the smaller private establishments which free choice was fostering. While Bentham himself was anti-religion, Benthamites often saw their main chance through alliances with the clergy and its spokesmen. Kay's answers[8] to the 1838 Select Committee as chief witness certainly demonstrated the strategic appeal of the religious aspects of education to his contemporary peers. In the following

---

6. H. J. Perkins, "The Origins of the Popular Press," *History Today*, VII (1957), p. 428. For an account of the parental demand for the 3 Rs in Nottinghamshire, see J. D. Chambers, *Nottinghamshire in the Eighteenth Century*, (1966), pp. 308–9. For the case of Scotland see below, Chap. 6.

7. Hansard, *Parl. Debates*, x cols 139–66, 30 July 1833. The sentence well represents the central message in James Mill's essays "Education" in the *Encyclopaedia Britannica*. Roebuck was one of Bentham's protégés. Bentham spoke of him to John Bowring: "But I have a new tame puss. I will make Roebuck my puss for his article on Canada; and many a mouse will he catch." J. Bentham, *Collected Works*, 1843, XI, p. 81.

8. Kay was a churchman. See Smith *op. cit.*, p. 178.

quoted dialogue the reader will understand our temporary digression on the "quality" of education.

The exchange between Gladstone and Kay strikingly illustrates the difficulties in obtaining straight answers on the subject as well as the erroneous nineteenth-century uses of the school-age population base. The committee, simply wanting to know how much education existed in the towns, in 1838 asked Kay, via (the devout) Mr. Gladstone, the direct and apparently innocent question: "Can you form an estimate of the amount of deficiency in the means of education in any given district, say for instance, the district of Manchester?" Promptly diverting attention to quality and away from quantitative facts (which contained much potential surprise for those prepared to probe), Dr. Kay replied: "If by education I am to understand what I have previously described, sound religious instruction, correct moral training, and a sufficient extent of secular knowledge suited to their station in life, I should scarcely say that it exists within the limits of my observation." Chairman: "You think it is not afforded by any schools at present efficiently?" Dr. Kay: "Not efficiently." [9]

It was this kind of "evidence" which led to the Committee's conclusion that though generally in the towns the proportion of the total population receiving education was 1 in 12, about a half of it was of little use. The conclusions of the Manchester Statistical Society's Report, which seem to have been presented in increasing order of importance, finish with a comparison with German schools. While none of the latter was "allowed to *exist*" which did not effectively teach Religion, the Report's last two sentences protest:

> . . . in this town, on the other hand, and generally throughout this country, the acquisition of Reading, Writing and Arithmetic seems to be considered as constituting the finished education of the children of the lower classes of the people . . . and that the real improvement of the character, instruction on moral and religious subjects, and all the more valuable *objects* of education, are totally neglected and forgotten.[10]

Kay, a utilitarian enthusiast for large scale economies in schooling, had an almost doctrinaire dislike of small schools, which were usually the en-

9. *Report* paras 100 and 101.
10. *Report,* p. 19.

tirely self-supporting establishments called "common day schools." The large monitorial Lancastrian and National (Charity) schools were among his favourites in 1838. In reaching their conclusions as to the quality and quantity of schooling, the 1838 Committee relied heavily on Kay's evidence, and that of the Manchester Statistical Society of which he was treasurer and a founder member. That it was particularly in the small private schools that poor quality teaching was complained of by this body is therefore not too surprising. But to return to the exchange with Gladstone; in his anxiety Kay obviously confused questions of quality with those of quantity in his answers. But Gladstone seems to have been the only member to have grasped this. Consequently he further questioned the information on Manchester that was being presented to his Select Committee. His subsequent dogged cross examination of Dr. Kay brings out not only the weakness of the statistical inferences but also the distinct evasiveness in this chief witness: [11]

> *Gladstone:* "Separating from your view at present all those considerations which appear to attach rather to the quality than to the quantity of education, and looking simply to the question of quantity, can you form an idea of what number of children there are in the town and neighbourhood of Manchester, upon any given population, that are entirely without education of any kind, however defective?"

> *Dr. Kay:* "The Report of the Committee of the Manchester Statistical Society states that one-third of the children between 5–15 are not receiving instruction of any kind whatever; [12] and the report also proceeds to state, that the education given in the common day schools and

11. The following dialogue is reported in paragraphs 102–113 of the 1838 *Select Committee Report.*

12. Actually the edition of the Manchester Report that was published in the previous year had cautiously stated in a footnote with very small print that the Committee "have not drawn the inference which various commentators have attributed to them, that this proportion of the youthful population continued *permanently destitute of schooling.* . . . The Committee possess no data for stating what number of children have never enjoyed the advantage of attending school." (italics in original) Report p. 18. Despite this rider the Society persisted with the habit (subsequently echoed in innumerable educational reports) that the difference between the numbers found by surveys to be in schools and the census of the 5–15 year olds represented the numbers who were "receiving no instruction in schools whatever"—to use the precise words (p. 3). The Committee eventually purposefully estimated the numbers permanently destitute of school-

dame schools, and certain other schools appears to be either altogether inefficient or very indifferent."

Gladstone: "In reference to the first part of your answer, do you imagine that they have arrived at that statement by calculating the number of children between 5 and 15 in the population, and then ascertaining the number of children who attend schools, of any kind, and given the difference as the amount of deficiency which exists?"

Kay: "Certainly."

Gladstone: "Do you imagine that the average number of children who attend schools in Manchester continue in attendance for anything like the period of 10 years?"

Kay: "In the Sunday Schools the great mass of the children continue pretty regularly in attendance; and I have personal experience of the quality of instruction conveyed in the Sunday schools of Manchester which, as far as religious instruction is concerned, may be stated to be the best instruction which exists of this nature."

Gladstone: "But do you think that the generality of the children who go to school at all in Manchester continue at school, week-day or Sunday, for anything like so long a period of 10 years?"

Kay: "I think the great portion of the Sunday scholars do."

Gladstone: "Do you think that any considerable proportion of the day scholars continue at school for 10 years?"

Kay: "I do not think that any very considerable proportion of day scholars do."

Gladstone: "Then will not the calculation be inaccurate if it has been upon the supposition, that those who are at school continue at school from the age of five to the age of fifteen?"

Kay: "Certainly; it can only refer to the number who were at school at the period when the calculations were made. . . ."

Gladstone: "Looking at the nature of the employment of the manufacturing population in general, do you think that it can be reasonably ex-

---

ing in their intensive report on the Salford township of Pendleton in 1838 and found it very small indeed.

pected, with a view not to what is desirable, but to what is practicable, that the mass of the children should attend daily school from the age of 5–15?"

Kay: "I think that from the age of 5 to 13 is not only desirable, but perfectly practicable."

Gladstone: "To keep them in attendance upon daily schools?"

Kay: "Yes."

Gladstone: "Do you include in that answer a supposition that, during the years from 9–13, they are to work for a part of the day in factories?"

Kay: "I suppose that their industrial employment in the factory should go along with their training, for a certain number of hours in the day."

Gladstone: "Do you happen to have estimated the number of children, upon the population of Manchester, which there are between the ages of five and thirteen?"

Kay: "I am not prepared to answer the question at the moment, though, of course, it is a matter of mere statistical detail, which might be resolved from calculations of the mortality of various ages, and returns of various persons living at the respective ages in the last population return."

Gladstone: "Do you think that the daily instruction at this moment provided in Manchester is sufficient to supply all the children of Manchester between the ages of five and thirteen?"

Kay: "*If the instruction conveyed were of the quality that I would desire,* I should say that its extent was insufficient for that purpose." (our italics).

There is no reason to suspect that Kay was wrong in his estimate that most of the Sunday scholars (half of the total of scholars reported by his Committee) went to Sunday school for 10 years. Nevertheless if Gladstone had pressed still further he would have elicited that on the modified criterion to which Kay now conceded for day schooling, eight years of schooling instead of ten years, and assuming for the sake of rough approximation that there were consequently one fifth less children in the Census base figure, an arithmetical revision of the Manchester Statistical Society's figure of day school pupils would reveal, on their own basis for calculation, about an 80 per cent schooling instead of their original 66 per cent, i.e. a deficiency of only 20 per cent. Curiously enough Gladstone did not press his challenge.[13] His colleagues were similarly reluctant to do so when, a few days later in the investigation, Kay was again quietly assuming a "normal" school life of ten years.[14]

Even on Kay's criterion of 8 years as the correct (i.e. the "desirable") schooling life the shortfall of 20 per cent between the census count of the 5–13 year olds and the numbers found by the survey to be at school still does not imply that 20 per cent never had instruction. To find this proportion we need, not an idea or official (target) figure of "proper" school age, but a specific survey to elicit the *de facto* school entering and leaving ages. This crucial information did not appear until after the 1838 Towns Committee had reported. It eventually came in 1839 from the results of an intensive house-to-house survey in 1838 of Manchester's neighbour—Pendleton, a typical town of the Industrial Revolution. It is reproduced in Table 1 which represent Tables v and vi in the Report.

The Committee had at last, in the Pendleton case, found one of the most appropriate methods of reporting a more accurate and comprehensive picture of educational quantity. It concluded "That not more than 2 to 3 per cent . . . of the juvenile population are at present left entirely destitute of instruction. . . ." Of the school-goers, ". . . one-third appear to remain less than three years; one-third from three to five years; and one-third remain above five years" (Report page 74). These facts seem to have been carefully obtained. The investigators acknowledged the difficulty of checking the accuracy of the personal statements from each household, "but wherever anything in these statements threw upon their report the slightest suspicion of inaccuracy, the cases have been classed as not ascertained" (p. 73).

13. It is interesting to speculate whether Gladstone, a man of religious solemnity, was more swayed by the accusation of poor quality (i.e. amoral) teaching rather than poor quantity.
14. For an account of the same kind of statistical error in the measures of the "gaps" in schooling on the eve of the 1870 Education Act, see West, *Education and the State*, 1965, Chap. 10.

Table 1. Manchester Statistical Society's Report

Length of Time Which Minors Now at

AGE	Less than $\frac{1}{4}$ of a year	$\frac{1}{4}$ and less than $\frac{1}{2}$ a year	$\frac{1}{2}$ and less than 1 year	1 and less than 2 years	2 and less than 3 years	3 and less than 4 years	4 and less than 5 years
Under 5 years	40	34	49	39	4	..	..
5 and under 10	20	33	43	126	144	142	111
10 and under 15	1	3	3	9	23	11	28
15 and under 21	..	1	1	7	8	1	1
Total	61	71	96	181	179	154	140

The majority of those who are now at a

Manchester Statistical Society's

Length of Time Which Minors Not Now at Day

AGE	Less than $\frac{1}{4}$ of a year	$\frac{1}{4}$ and less than $\frac{1}{2}$ a year	$\frac{1}{2}$ and less than 1 year	1 and less than 2 years	2 and less than 3 years	3 and less than 4 years	4 and less than 5 years
Under 5 years	..	4	..	4	..	..	..
5 and under 10	1	2	7	45	35	18	8
10 and under 15	..	10	17	26	88	73	91
15 and under 21	..	1	..	23	65	64	83
Total	1	17	24	118	188	155	182

The majority of those who have attended day or evening

Day or Evening Schools Have Attended

5 years and up- wards	Time at School not ascer- tained	Total now at School	Regularly instructed at home	Have been or are at Sunday School only	Not now attend- ing any School	Not ascer- tained	Total
..	11	177	25	18	1101	2	1323
64	76	759	52	104	223	5	1143
176	55	309	26	97	596	13	1041
7	16	42	19	130	610	204	1005
247	158	1287	122	349	2530	224	4512

day school also attend a Sunday School

Report on Pendleton (Salford)

or Evening Schools Have Formerly Attended

5 years and up- wards	Time at School not ascer- tained	Total not now at School	Regularly instructed at home	Now at School	Have been, or are now at Sunday School only	Have never been in- structed	Not ascer- tained	Total
..	19	27	25	177	18	1074	2	1323
2	68	186	52	759	104	37	5	1143
136	111	572	26	309	97	24	13	1041
206	143	585	19	42	130	25	204	1005
344	341	1370	122	1287	349	1160	224	4512

schools have also attended, or are now attending, Sunday Schools.

The 1833 Government Return

The Return (the Kerry Report) of 1833 reported that 9 per cent of the total population were found to be in day schools while the proportion of children between 5 and 15 years old was 24 per cent. It is probably this Report which has misled most writers, especially those referred to in Chapter 1. To take a recent example, Phyllis Deane, supporting her hypothesis that lack of education delayed the organization of labour in the 1830s and 1840s observes: "The Education Returns collected in 1833 showed that only one out of three of the children of school-age were receiving any kind of daily instruction. . . ."[15] The phrase "children of school age" as we have seen means those between 5 and 15 years. On the experience of Pendleton the majority of children left school around 10 years old. If this was typical one should conclude not that only one out of three children ever received instruction, but that probably well over 90 percent *did*. In addition we must note that according to the statistical societies the unreliability of 1833 Government Return was in the direction of serious *underestimate*. But most important it is clear that if we want a precise measure of the "deficiencies" in the quantity of nineteenth-century schooling we must concentrate mainly, not on the number who *never* received it (which was very small), but on the "shortness" of the number of years of schooling of those who did; and on an argument that 4 or 5 years' schooling was inadequate and that another year or so would have made all the difference.

It is interesting that Hull, which was surveyed by the Manchester Society in 1839 and showed a marginal lead over Pendleton in the length of average school life, showed more than proportionate advance in literacy attainments. Out of 2,798 children who had left school in Hull:

131	had remained at school after reaching the age of 13
1,108	left at 12 and 13 years of age
964	left at 10 and 11 years of age
595	left before 10; about half of whom had been removed before they were 9

15. Phyllis Deane, *The First Industrial Revolution*, 1965, p. 150.

Only one-third of one per cent of ascertained cases among adults in Hull had never attended a day school compared with 2 per cent in Pendleton. The differences in educational attainments were more pronounced: while nearly the same proportion (90 per cent) of adults could read in Pendleton as in Hull only one-third could also write and cipher in the former town compared with two-thirds in Hull.[16] The figures suggested that the ability to stay at school until the age of 12 years was the most critical variable as far as writing was concerned and 9–10 years for reading. But this was only 1838 and there was an upward trend in schooling. Towns such as Pendleton were clearly on the threshold of full majority literacy in the last two years of the Industrial Revolution period.

16. Phyllis Deane, *op. cit.*, quotes the "low" schooling figures of the 1833 Return in support of the proposition that workers were prevented from organising themselves into trade unions successfully because of literacy disabilities. But where 90 per cent could read, as in Pendleton, this would seem to be refuted. This seems to be the case too where one-third could also write.

3 · The Quantity of Education:
The One-in-Six Rule

Nineteenth-Century Policy-Makers' Targets

The target of all policy-makers in the second half of the nineteenth century was a schooling of one in six of the population.[1] There is no precise evidence as to how or from where this originated. One possibility is that it was at first a figure frequently mentioned by officials in the Education Department and then adopted by habit by politicians and ministers. It seems odd to a twentieth-century observer that a population ratio was used rather than an age group. It seems curious too that there was no precise agreement on deductions necessary for the sick and handicapped. What is most surprising of all is that there was no consideration of the need to adjust the figures because of a change in the age structure of the population. These points are brought out strikingly by the fact that today the school population has still not reached one-sixth of the total population (it is about 1 in 6.4).

Clearly such "targets" must be treated with considerable caution in attempting to make retrospective judgements on whether or not there was educational "failure" in the nineteenth century. The targets of policy-makers in Britain since 1945 have included a school-leaving age of 16 years. This has been continually postponed, however, on the grounds that the growth of national output had not yet made the "reform" pos-

---

1. For details see Gillian Sutherland, *Elementary Education in the Nineteenth Century*, The Historical Association, London, 1971, p. 11.

sible.[2] If there was educational failure in the nineteenth century because targets were not attained, the same is true of the twentieth century. One can be sure that in any debate as to the "correct" proportion of the national output that "should be" devoted to education (or to any other service), those most involved in supplying the service (teachers, administrators, education bureaus and pressure groups) will be prominent. They will always produce the highest figure and will invariably complain that the present one is insufficient. Yet it is from these sources that the most conspicuous and most quoted targets always come. These groups protest today that "not enough" is spent on education; their counterparts did the same in the nineteenth century. We shall show in Chapter 5 that in terms of the share of primary schooling in the national output there was actually little difference in the two centuries.

Meanwhile one must treat with reserve the accounts of those historians who implicitly or explicitly adopt as a criterion of nineteenth-century educational failure the target figure of one in six merely because it was used by contemporaries. These "contemporaries" were often selected voices only; and usually they had no idea as to the origins of the target they were using.[3]

Possible Origins of the One-in-Six Rule

Official respect for the ratio of "one in six" probably originated in the 1851 Census Report's special section on education. Horace Mann, the Registrar General's assistant in charge of this section (not to be confused with Horace Mann of Massachusetts), subsequently explained:

"The object was to show that, as there is no valid reason why a sixth of

2. A Conservative Government announced in 1964 that the leaving age was to be raised in 1970. It could not be done before that because of "lack of resources." In 1970 a Labour Government had to postpone the "target" year for similar reasons in circumstances that were aggravated by a devaluation; it was reached in 1973.

3. It is surprising that Gillian Sutherland, who acknowledges most of the above criticisms of the one-in-six target (*op. cit.* footnote 23), proceeds to judge educational achievement throughout the century upon it. Her explanation is that "it seems simplest to use the one crude measurement of school supply—one-in-six—which contemporaries agreed on and used." We strongly disagree; such a course begs the very question that is at the root of our problem.

the entire population should not be constantly at school, it would not be proper that the community should rest satisfied until, by the exercise of various influences, that proportion should be brought there and retained there."[4]

The 1851 Census Document on Education, which was written by Mann, concluded that there were three million children requiring education compared with approximately two million found to be at school. The method used by Mann to obtain this figure was different from the alternative procedure of fixing upon the "proper" or minimum limits of school age (e.g. 5 or 6 years of schooling) and applying such an assumed average to the census figures of population. Mann's method was to take the number of children between what he took to be the school limits of 3 years to 15 years and to analyse the members of this selected group with respect to their incidence of employment. This was done "in order to eliminate all the impediments to school attendance, and thus ascertain the number that might, without inconvenience to themselves, or their parents, be found at school."[5] Employment was not the only "admissible cause of absence" from school. The complete list included (1) sickness, (2) home education, (3) employment of any kind, whether remunerative or merely domestic, and (4) "the mere pleasure of the parents as to the matter with regard to all children under 5 and above 12 years of age."

The above process generated the following results:

Census population between 3 and 15		4,908,696
From which there would have to be deducted		
(1) Physically incapacitated by sickness	95,435	
(2) Educated at home	50,000	
(3) Occupied at home or for wages	1,000,000	
(4) Kept at home by parents, etc. without any stated cause		
Under 5	574,611	
Above 12	73,245	1,893,291
		3,015,405

4. The Commission appointed to inquire into the State of Popular Education in England [*the Newcastle Report*]: minutes of evidence taken on 6 December 1859; Horace Mann Esq., examined.
5. *Ibid.* (p. 120).

The final figure of 3,015,405 happened to be one-sixth of the total population. The same figure was claimed by Mann to represent the number "which might, so far as any reasonable hindrance could be ascertained or conjectured, be constantly found upon the school books." Since only about two-thirds of this number were found to be at school the implication was that there was a serious shortfall from the "target" (of one in six of the total population). Mann's statistics were not published until 1854— three years after the year of the census. In many quarters they caused considerable alarm. Robert Lowe told the House that if public education was to be provided for three million children it would require an "army" of 200 inspectors, 18,000 school-masters, and 40,000 public teachers. Other observers estimated that the current expenditure on education (£761,000 in 1858–9) would have to be trebled or quadrupled.

Nobody seems to have questioned Mann very closely on his criteria. His findings implied that roughly a million children were being kept from school without any "obvious causes."[6] This meant simply that many of his questionnaires had not elicited from the parents any precise reason for school absence. This does not necessarily mean, however, that the parents did not really have any reason; only that they refused to articulate one. No doubt many parents would have treated with suspicion official requests for explanations why their children were not at school at the particular time of the Census. Others probably did not fully understand the questionnaire. Despite these fairly obvious possibilities Horace Mann simply concluded that, where there was no explanation, or none that fell under his very wide category of "admissible causes of absence," the children concerned might, without inconvenience to themselves or their parents, be expected to be able to attend school. There might indeed have been considerable inconvenience to many large but poor Victorian families. These would have been too independent to explain in detail the economic value to them of domestic and indirect labour services rendered by the children aged ten and above.

To many people, Mann's criteria will appear even more curious. Consider again his concession to that parental declaration that a child's occupation at home or for wages should qualify as an admissible cause for

6. Mann's answer to Question number 849.

school absence. Supposing his questionnaires had shown 3 million instead of 1 million children declared occupied in domestic or outside work. In this case the residual number "requiring education" would fall to 1 million—which is 1 in 18 of the total population. Suppose also that one million children (or 1 in 18 of the population) had been found to be in schools. On Mann's reasoning the target of attendance would be 1 in 18 (instead of 1 in 6) and there would have been no cause for further government action. At the furthest extreme of all, if children above five had been declared employed, the target of school attendance would fall from 1 in 6 or 1 in 18 to zero! It is certainly unlikely that the Education Department or Mann himself would have found his criteria and these lower targets acceptable.

Horace Mann versus Nassau Senior

An alternative method of measuring school accommodation deficiency was first to fix upon some practical target based upon a typical school duration—say 6 years' minimum schooling—that parents were likely to demand voluntarily, and then to observe any *de facto* shortfall. This was the approach adopted by the political economist Nassau Senior, a member of the Newcastle Commission. Prior to Horace Mann's examination by the Newcastle Commission in 1859 "Senior" sent him a memorandum that forewarned him that his 1851 census figures on education were to be challenged. In the memorandum Senior disputed Mann's apparent opinion that public education should be provided for 3 million children. Senior urged that a target of six years' schooling for all was the best starting point for discussion. On this basis only 1,200,000 children of the working class needed to be in *"public* education." This conclusion took into account that nearly 1¼ million of such children were in entirely independent schools (*"public* education" simply embraced those schools that were subject to government inspection—a majority of which were receiving a partial government subsidy).

In his subsequent replies before the Newcastle Commission Horace Mann acknowledged that there were two possible methods of estimating—his and Senior's. He also retreated somewhat by emphasizing that the estimate in his Census Report was an estimate of the proportionate number of children who *ought to be* at school, not of the proportionate number who might be *expected to be* there in the short period. He agreed with Senior that the Privy Council need only have a short-term target of about 1⅕ million; but only if one made the assumption that the prevailing proportion of ⅔ths of the whole number of working class children at private (i.e. non-inspected) schools was to continue. He thought, however, that this assumption was unrealistic: it was not likely that private and independent schools would positively increase with the increasing population. More likely they would be "either destroyed by the unequal competition to which they would be exposed, or themselves [become] included amongst the recipients of Parliamentary aid." This was one of the first explicit recognitions of the displacement effect of private by public schools. There was no discussion of alternative methods of intervention that might avoid or reduce such effects. Mann's opinion seems to have been that this was inevitable.

Proceeding to alternative estimates on the assumption of positive displacement effects Mann concluded, for example, that if the absolute numbers in private and independent schools were to remain the same when population expanded (i.e. their relative share to fall), the numbers expected to be in the public sector schools would be 1,338,735. On the same set of assumptions but applying the one-in-six rule (which Mann agreed was not likely to be attained "for some years if at all") the number in public sector schools would be 1,727,674. He admitted that the one-in-six rule would mean an average of seven years' schooling for the whole population and more than six years' for the working class.

Working Classes' Voluntary Attendance for Nearly Five Years on Average in 1851 and Nearer Six Years in 1858 (Horace Mann)

It should be remembered that the 1851 Census recorded 2,144,378 day scholars. To find the average years' schooling for the working class and the rest, certain assumptions had to be made concerning class distribution. When asked how many years working class children were (voluntarily) in school on average Mann thought that it was certainly above 4 years.[7]

"At the time of the census we found that assuming the children of the upper and middle classes to be at school for only six years, and to constitute one-fourth of the population, the children of the working classes would actually then have been at school for four and two-thirds years on an average. . . ."[8] He expected that the improvement by 1858 was such that six years was by then a suitable maximum estimate.[9] He was satisfied that six years was the average school duration for the upper and middle classes in 1851, provided that one could assume that one-fourth was their proper share of the total population. Mann does not seem to have seen the implication here that on the one-in-six "target" of his Census Report, the upper and middle classes were as "negligent" as the working classes; for he had admitted that the one-in-six rule called for an average of over seven years for the upper and middle classes (and an average of seven years for the *whole* population).

The 1851 Census on Education in Retrospect

How can the twentieth-century observer, in retrospect, treat the 1851 Census in view of all the above variations and interpretations? One statistic more than all the others deserves full attention: this is the total figure of 2,144,378 day scholars. This figure, it must be emphasized, was not an estimate—it was a census figure. It can be seriously faulted only if (a) the house-to-house enumeration can be proved to have been mismanaged; (b) the quality of many of the schools was such as to bring into question the value of the numbers recorded. So far as we know significantly serious errors in the enumeration have not so far been demonstrated. The question of the quality of schooling is the subject of the next two chapters. Meanwhile it is interesting to compare this one raw statistic with achievements in underdeveloped parts of the world today.

7. Minutes of evidence 6 December 1859, Q Number 833.
8. *Ibid.*, p. 120.
9. *Ibid.*, p. 121.

Modern data on underdeveloped countries gives percentages of children of primary school age attending school. Primary school age is defined as 6 years to 14 years. We know that in 1851 the population between 3 years and 15 years was 4,908,696. This age span is 12 years compared with the eight years span between 6–14. We shall therefore multiply 4,908,696 by $\frac{8}{12}$ to obtain a first crude approximation of the 1851 census of school population. We find that the latter represents 66 per cent of the estimated 6–14 year population.

Modern figures of enrolments in underdeveloped areas are obtainable from the UNESCO Statistical Office and are not entirely comparable with our 1851 English figures since the latter include a proportion of school children between 3 and 5 years (although it is possible that some UNESCO figures do include a proportion in this age). Nevertheless the numbers of under fives are not likely to have been large—not much more than 5 per cent of the total. At the same time one should keep in mind that the average English child in 1851 had the bigger advantage of access to Sunday Schools which were important agencies in the nineteenth-century teaching of reading. Finally, the UNESCO figures relating to the overestimation invariably include "by accident" many of the "individuals over 14 years." With these cautions and qualifications we now present, in Table 1, the comparable figures.

Table 1. School Enrolment Ratios

Region	Year	Percentage of children of primary school age attending school
Africa	1961	34
Latin America	1961	60
Asia	1961	50
Arab States	1961	38
World Total	1961	63
England & Wales	1851	66

Source: UNESCO Statistical Office

The figures show that in England and Wales in 1851, the percentage of children at primary school was already in excess of the world total reached in 1961. The nineteenth-century English figure was nearly twice that of Africa and the Arab States in 1961 and about 30 per cent bigger than that of Asia in 1961.[10] The Victorians of 1851 were also ahead of the figure reached in Latin America in 1961 (although the latter region has now 75 per cent of its primary school population at school). It should be noticed that it is arguable that any possible qualifications about faulty enumeration or "doubtful" quality of schooling in the English situation of 1851 are likely to be at least as strong when applied to the underdeveloped countries today.

Clearly the case of nineteenth-century Britain comes out well in these aggregate comparisons. What may be more remarkable to some is that the British schooling was entirely voluntary and almost entirely fee-paying.[11] In contrast, schools in the underdeveloped countries of the twentieth century typically operate with compulsory laws and are usually "free." Finally there remains the question of the *distribution* of the schooling between families within the social classes—which is distinct from the question of *aggregate* achievement of these classes. The more widely dispersed the incidence of schooling (the bigger the variance) the more was the apparent need for compulsory laws to protect the minorities at the end of the family distribution scale.

10. Excluding China (mainland), Democratic People's Republic of Korea, and Democratic Republic of Viet-Nam.

11. Where Parliamentary grants were received by the schools these covered less than half the school costs in 1851. The parental contribution was the biggest source of finance.

4 · The Quality of Education

Two important aspects of the debate on the quality of early-nineteenth-century education have already been touched upon in the previous chapters: the quality of belonging (or not belonging) to a national system and the quality of belonging (or not belonging) to a religious fellowship or denomination. We have already placed them in the category of "qualities" upon which there are perpetual and perhaps irreconcilable differences of opinion. Many of those who were the most vociferous agitators for a "public" system (such as the members of the Birmingham League) were predominantly out to reduce the educational influence of the "Church" system (supported by the National Education Union). Although history shows that on balance the victory has gone to the secularists and nonsectarians, in these days of high levels of juvenile crime and persistent illiteracy the debate about moral, religious, and educational leadership seems to have been rekindled. We shall proceed to other criticisms of educational quality that the careful historian can re-examine and pronounce upon more positively. These include allegations first, that the schools did not really teach anything but were large child-minding institutions; second, that the teachers were too few and too poorly paid to be efficient; third, that the schools were used to produce docile workers for nascent capitalism; fourth, that daily attendance was poor; fifth, that parents could not choose schools of good quality; sixth, that the education was too "mechanical." Chapter 5 will examine the criticism that many teachers were unqualified.

Child Minding

Historians have often quoted contemporary official enquiries that suggest that parents sent their children to school not to receive instruction but, in effect, to obtain a "child-minding" service. It is important to avoid unbalanced impressions however. Consider the following from the Statistical Society of London's Report on Westminster in 1837: ". . . a very large proportion are sent (to school) avowedly 'to do nothing,' the injunction from the parents being, that they are not to be worried with learning. . . ." Such comments are easily quoted out of context. They come in fact from a small section of the Report dealing with Dame Schools. These schools contained 759 scholars out of the total of 7,755 day scholars investigated (less than 10 per cent). Of the 759 scholars, 379 were under five years old. It should be remembered that in those days children were sent to Dame Schools sometimes as early as two years old. It is important also to remember that it is a matter of complaint today that the problem of illiteracy calls for more nursery schools that socially and emotionally prepare children for infant schooling.[1] Yet, unlike the first half of the nineteenth century the under-fives in Britain today (and the under-sixes elsewhere) find very limited provision. In the schools that do exist at this level today, we find concentration primarily upon social education and the avoidance of forcing upon three- and four-year-olds systematic instruction in reading and writing at an age when they are usually not ready for it. From the standpoint of some modern educationalists the "large proportion" of parents in the 1830s requesting that their three- and four-year-olds were not to be "worried with learning" seems therefore to have been expressing views that were in advance of their time.

While the "creche function" of some (minority of) schools in the nineteenth century may be dismissed, as it usually is by some historians, it is of considerable economic significance in its own right. For some time it has been attracting the attention of modern economists (and should now presumably alert that of economic historians). Prof. B. A. Weisbrod treats

---

1. Dr. Joyce Morris in a TV programme on the growing problem of illiteracy. "Panorama," 17 July 1972.

the child-minding function of twentieth-century schools as a substantial external economy.[2] Schools make it possible for parents, who would otherwise be supervising their children, to do other things. Weisbrod examined the case of the three and a half million mothers in the United States with children of six to eleven years of age. On the assumption that as few as one million of these mothers would not work except for the schools, and on the reasonable additional assumption that $2,000 were the early 1960's earnings of each mother during the school year, the value of the "child-minding" services of elementary schooling was estimated at about $2 billion per year, a significant portion of the national income. The need for similar assessment of the nineteenth-century Dame Schools is overdue. In addition to their economic significance they had important implications for other kinds of education. Child-minding can be viewed as a major product, and education (especially social education) can be treated as the by-product. It must have allowed a considerable amount of education of other sorts. Young parents would have been enabled to undertake many types of education, such as that associated with on-job training within firms. This would be especially so where "specific training"[3] was concerned. In this case, where improvements in worker productivity are peculiar to particular firms, the managements have a special incentive to provide free training. In these circumstances the full wages, representing some reflection of both present and anticipated future productivity, would be earned immediately. These same wages could simultaneously have provided more than sufficient means for paying for child-minding or schooling services.

Low Teacher Incomes

Another common criticism is that the quality of schooling was poor because school teachers were "being left behind in the race for higher standards of living" and that their annual income was "a smaller sum than

2. B. A. Weisbrod, "Education & Investment in Human Capital," *Journal of Political Economy,* LXX (1962), pt. 2 (supplement), 106–23. (An external economy refers to the public, as distinct from the private, benefits that a family receives from the schooling of its children.)
3. G. Becker, *Human Capital,* 1964.

common industry would procure for them in many mechanical and manufacturing employments."[4] The difficulty with this argument is that it
seems to be asserted for all conditions at all times, and it continues to as-
sert itself today. Yet the fact that employees in one service industry get
less than employees in other industries does not imply that the productivity of the former is zero, otherwise we should be receiving zero education today! Indeed, the distinction between quantity and quality in
discussions on education can be a misleading one. When competition
prevails, differences in the quality of schooling can largely be resolved in
terms of differences in the quantity of resources (books, buildings, teachers). If quality is strongly related, for instance, to the size of building it
can improve by an increase in quantity of expenditure on construction.
Where national income is steadily rising the quality of services will also
rise because more resources are automatically available. Today "quality"
has improved in proportion to the "quantity" of expenditure. Education,
while still "imperfect," is less "imperfect" than previously.

With respect to the criticism that in the nineteenth century the teachers were too few we should notice that if anything, lower student/teacher
ratios existed than now. The number of scholars per teacher at common
day schools was on average 26.8 in the 1830s in the six towns, Bury, Salford, Liverpool, Manchester, York and Birmingham.[5]

Schooling a Docile Proletariat

Let us consider the claim that the quality of education was constrained
by the fact that education was used to make the working class more
docile.[6] First there is a question of internal logic. If the working classes
were passively receiving from their superiors "conditioning" kinds of
education, how did it succeed when education was neither compulsory
nor free? Perhaps all that is being suggested, however, is that the ruling

4. J. S. Hurt, "Professor West on Early Nineteenth Century Education," *Economic History Review,* 1971.
5. *Jnl. Stat. Soc.* London, III (1840) p. 33.
6. Hurt (*op. cit.*), also M. Vaughan and M. Scotford Archer, *Social Conflict and Educational Change in England and France 1789–1848,* C.U.P., 1971, ch. 5.

classes expressed their motives wherever they could by complementing parental and ecclesiastical effort with subsidies. But if this is the interpretation we should expect to find bigger subsidies in the new "proletariat" areas than in others. Yet the Manchester Statistical Society reported that 80 per cent of the schooling in Manchester was paid for entirely by parental fees, a much bigger proportion than in country areas such as Rutland and in cathedral cities such as York.

School Attendance

High absentee rates affect the quality of schooling. The 1851 Census report stated that in private schools the number of children attending on any particular day was 91 per cent of the number belonging to such schools. In "public" schools the figure was 79 per cent. Public and private schools were officially distinguished by the fact that the former comprised schools receiving a subsidy from *any* source, whether it was the church, the state or private philanthropy. These figures refer to one particular census day and the authorities were clearly assuming that this day was a typical one in the year. If the chosen census day (Monday, March 31st, 1851) was not typical, the bias could have been either way; it could have overstated or understated the true average attendance. There seems to be no reason to suspect that it was not typical however.

One can easily be given the impression of an excessive frequency with which children changed school. Consider for instance the fact that about 38 per cent of the children at school in 1859 were thought to have attended the same institution for less than a year (see Table on p. 112). Remember however that the average school life in those days was around five years. Typically a child would spend, say, one year in a Dame School and four in a common school. It would therefore be not unusual for over 50 per cent of the pupils in a Dame School to consist of those who have attended for less than a year. With a typical common school, and an average school life of four years per pupil, one would expect that 25 per cent of the scholars, on average, would fall into the category of having attended for less than a year. Any greater percentage (such as the 38 per cent realized) could well be accounted for by two prevailing circumstances: (a) a mobile population associated with the new industrialism; (b) the exercise of choice in a competitive and expanding education market. None of this is to suggest that excessive frequency of change was not a problem in some cases. The point is that there is a need to correct exaggerated impressions.

In several nineteenth-century government reports the observation was made that school attendance was most erratic, especially in rural areas at harvest times. One must guard against the temptation of applying too readily twentieth-century English standards to a nineteenth-century English setting. It must be remembered that in those days national income per head was much lower and agriculture was a relatively more important source of ordinary livelihoods. It is now a recognized world-wide phenomenon that absenteeism from schools is more common in agricultural areas, whether their education is compulsory or not, and whether they have state schooling or private schooling. Thus Professor T. W. Schultz, the American economist, observed in 1963:

> The average daily school attendance of children from farm homes tends to be lower than that of children from non-farm homes. There is much work on farms that children can do and many farm families are relatively poor which makes the value of the work that children can do for them by missing a few days of school now and then rate comparatively high.[7]

Periodic absence from nineteenth-century schools was thus not necessarily a sign of parental negligence. It could have been the result of a judicious weighing of the expected sacrifice in family income against the expected educational benefits. This would have been a rational assessment, in other words, of what Professor Schultz considers to be an educational cost (opportunity cost) which is particularly important today in low income countries. It is significant that after education was made compulsory special holidays were frequently granted at harvest times. It is interesting too that in some Socialist countries in recent years school children were actively encouraged, and sometimes compelled, by gov-

7. T. W. Schultz, *The Economic Value of Education*, Columbia University Press, 1963, p. 30.

ernment authorities to help with the harvest. Indeed all kinds of work on farms was often made part of the normal educational curriculum in these countries and was then of course included in the national statistics of education.

Parental Choice and Quality of Schooling

The next question is whether the parents, many of them uneducated, would choose the best quality available. Strictly the question is whether fallible parents would choose at least as well as fallible public officials. Obviously mistakes were made but the increasing practice of choosing among schools was improving parental judgement.

The evidence of Assistant Commissioner Mr. Coode, to the Royal Commission on Popular Education (1861), showed how in his district, ordinary parents were ready to use the good schools and to withdraw their custom from the bad. But similar reports came from other districts and the 1861 (Newcastle) Commission in its overall reference to parents declared:

> they prefer paying a comparatively high fee to an efficient school to paying a low fee to an inefficient one. . . . There can be little doubt that a school which combined high fees with a reputation for inefficiency would soon lose its pupils.[8]

On this evidence it follows that there was a built-in mechanism ensuring that inefficient schools were already being weeded out. Parents were their own inspectors and, compared with official ones, they were not only much more numerous but exercised continuous rather than periodic check. Moreover the sanction exercised by the parents was of much more financial significance to a school than was an unfavourable inspector's report. For if parents withdrew their children, the school lost not only the government capitation grants but the parents' fees payments as well.

The supply of education was certainly not homogeneous; sometimes because of low standards, parents may have kept their children away from

8. *Newcastle Report*, 1861, p. 74.

school with good reason. Mr. Coode reported in the same Newcastle Commission Report of 1861:

> It is a subject of wonder how people so destitute of education as labouring parents commonly are, can be such just judges as they also commonly are of the effective qualifications of a teacher. Good school buildings and the apparatus of education are found for years to be practically useless and deserted, when, if a master chance to be appointed who understands his work, a few weeks suffice to make the fact known, and his school is soon filled, and perhaps found inadequate to the demand of the neighbourhood, and a separate girls' school or infants' school is soon found to be necessary.

Mr. Coode gives several instances of this. In one case a school-master began with three pupils and raised the number in 15 months to 180. Even when a strike took place and reduced the colliers to great distress:

> . . . such had now become the desire of the children to remain at school and of their parents to keep them there, that the greater number remained during a time when the provision of the school fees must have encroached in most of the colliers' families on the very necessaries of life.[9]

"Mechanical" Education

The so-called mechanical nature of rote learning in some Victorian schools will be examined and assessed in the next chapter. Suffice it to say here that with the persistence of some illiteracy and the alleged lack of sufficient attention to the teaching of reading in English schools the judgements of an increasing number of observers on Victorian methods are becoming less harsh. True there is more than one contemporary school of thought on the learning problem. But in the 1970s Dr. Joyce Morris looked with apprehension on the fact that the British system had become one of the "most relaxed and indulgent systems in the world."[10] In view of serious failure rates in the teaching of reading in this period, the key questions, according to this same authority, were: "Has the pen-

9. *Newcastle Report,* 1861, p. 175.
10. Dr. Joyce Morris. TV programme "Panorama," 17 July 1972.

dulum swung too far?" and: "Should the children be taught or go on at their own pace?" Declaring that reading is an "unnatural activity," Dr. Morris's opinion was that children had to be *taught;* they could not pick it up as if by "osmosis"—however psychologically attractive and conducive the school environment.

Such specialists are likely to be impressed with the task that faced the nineteenth-century educators and their "crash courses" for a rapidly growing population. Discussion of teaching methods however will probably never cease to be controversial. Meanwhile some proof of the pudding is in the eating. Most Victorians did manage to become literate; and long before the 1870 Forster Act.[11]

Religious tracts enjoyed a large circulation in the early period, while

11. In E. G. West, *Education and the State* (1970) surprise was expressed at the failure of historians of education to explain the remarkable achievements in literacy in the nineteenth century prior to the establishment of State education. Professor Mark Blaug has since measured the extent of this neglect. Conventional histories of education have recently disposed of this "problem," he observes, by simply ignoring the evidence on literacy. None of the following books, he tells us, even mentions the word "literacy" in their index:

J. W. Adamson, *English Education 1789–1902,* Cambridge, 1930;

F. Smith, *A History of English Elementary Education,* London, 1931;

C. Birchenough, *History of Elementary Education in England and Wales,* London, 3rd ed. 1938;

B. Simon, *Studies in the History of Education 1780–1870,* London, 1960;

H. C. Barnard, *A History of English Education from 1760,* London, 2nd ed. 1961;

W. G. Armytage, *Four Hundred Years of English Education,* Cambridge, 1964;

S. J. Curtis, *History of Education in Great Britain,* London, 6th ed. 1965;

S. J. Curtis & Boultwood, *An Introductory History of English Education Since 1800,* London, 4th ed. 1966;

M. Stuart, *The Education of the People. A History of Primary Education in England and Wales in the Nineteenth Century,* London, 1967;

D. Wardle, *English Popular Education 1780–1970,* Cambridge, 1970.

Some of them, such as Simon and Curtis, do discuss the problem of literacy rates from Tudor to Victorian times (Curtis *op. cit.,* p. 196). A few specialist studies do weave the new evidence in their story but turn it around so as to allow for expressions of dismay that as much as a quarter of the working class was illiterate around 1850 (J. F. C. Harrison, *Learning and Living 1790–1960. A Study in the History of the English Adult Education Movement,* London, 1961, p. 42.) However, G. Sutherland, *Elementary Education in the Nineteenth Century,* London, The Historical Association, 1971, now makes up for all the rest. M. Blaug "The Economics of Education in English Classical Political Economy: A Re-examination" in *Essays on Adam Smith,* Clarendon Press, Oxford, 1975.

the reading of the Bible at home was, of course, traditional. Beyond this, there was an extensive market in popular literature from the "penny magazine" and serialized fiction such as *Pickwick Papers* down to almanacs, ballads and last dying speeches. The innovation of steam printing in the 1830s caused revolutionary cost reductions in the production of newspapers, which then began steadily to increase their sales despite the restrictive taxes. The most rapid increase in newspaper sales, therefore, did not come until after the removal of the taxes; the advertising duties were removed in 1853, the stamp taxes in 1855 and the excise taxes on paper in 1861. That a mass newspaper-reading public was largely in existence well before 1870 is now firmly acknowledged by specialist writers. Mr. Perkins writes: "no historical myth dies harder than the belief that the modern popular press grew up in direct response to the introduction of state education."[12] Similarly Mr. Raymond Williams: ". . . there was no sudden opening of the floodgates of literacy as the result of the 1870 Education Act."[13]

Statistical Estimates of Literacy

In the more formal or statistical evidence of literacy in the nineteenth century, the first thing that stands out is the consistency of its testimony that the ability to read was always in advance of the ability to write. The schools generally taught reading before writing and this reflected the relative contemporary demand. Ordinary people wanted to read in order to enjoy the new excitements of magazines and newspapers, whereas they did not have quite the same need for writing and writing materials were expensive because of taxes upon them.[14]

Two sets of figures to demonstrate the extent of literacy have been used by educationists since the Victorian period. The first were the records of educational qualifications of criminals published by the Home Office from 1835. The second were the figures showing the number of persons signing the marriage register with marks.

12. *Op. cit.*, p. 425.
13. *The Long Revolution*, Chatto and Windus, 1961, p. 166.
14. The introduction of the penny post in 1840 gave a vigorous boost to letter writing.

As an example of the first type of figures consider the researches of Mr. R. K. Webb.[15] Of the persons committed for trial between 1837 and 1839 44.6 per cent were reported to be able to read and write. Such tables, however, obviously suffered from not being properly representative of the whole population. Furthermore, since such averages mix older with younger persons they do not adequately intimate the current education standards of juveniles. Criminals aged about 30 and over, for instance, would have been of school age in the difficult period of the Napoleonic war.

Webb's information can be supplemented with data relating to another public institution—the workhouse. A good sample of this can be obtained from the 1838 report on the Training of Pauper Children in workhouses. The following Table[16] taken from the report, refers to the children maintained in the workhouses of Suffolk and Norfolk:

Table 1. Workhouse Children in Norfolk & Suffolk, 1838

Youths from 9 to 16 years	Who can read – well	206
	– imperfectly	217
	Who cannot read	62

Thus 87 per cent of these children could already read to some extent. It is true that a smaller proportion of them could write but even this was 53 per cent.

It is interesting to compare this evidence with the extent of literacy as measured by UNESCO in some countries in 1950: Portugal 55–60 per cent, Egypt 20–25 per cent, Algeria 15–20 per cent. The UNESCO figures are percentages of the adult population, whereas the English example refers only to pauper children between 9 and 16 years.

Table 2 giving estimates of literacy among miners in 1840 appeared in the report of an inspection into educational standards in the mining districts of Northumberland and Durham.[17]

15. R. K. Webb, "Working Class Readers in Early Victorian England," *The English Historical Review*, 1950.
16. From the Report on the Training of Pauper Children, 1838.
17. Minutes of the Committee of Council on Education, 1840–41, Appendix III, p. 138.

Table 2. Literacy among Northumberland and Durham Miners, 1840

Colliery	No. of pitmen employed	No. who can read & write	No. who can read only	No. who can neither read nor write
	843	445	220	178

Such early Victorian figures show that 79 per cent of these miners were already able to read; also more than half of them had learned to write. This attainment must have been largely independent of State help which started in 1833, when most of these pitmen would have left school. In any case state subsidies were very small in the 1830s.

The reports from the Assistant Handloom Weavers' Commissioners in 1839 indicated that handloom weavers were even more advanced. For instance, according to one inspector only 15 of 195 adults (shoploom weavers) in Gloucestershire could neither read nor write. A special survey of the reading and writing abilities of the people of Hull in 1839 found that of the 14,526 adults (people over 21) 14,109 had attended day or evening school and that only 1,054 of them could not read; in other words over 92 per cent *could* read.[18] Again hardly any of these people could have benefited from State subsidies to day-schools since the average school-leaving age in those days was eleven at most; most of these adults, therefore, were at least 15 when the State first began to subsidize schools in 1833.

A more important test of success in educational self-help in a developing country faced with an unprecedented population problem is the *rate of growth* of literacy compared with the growth of the national income per head. The period we are most interested in is that immediately before 1870. Mr. Webb's general opinion of literacy in the late 1830s was:

18. "Report on the State of Education in the Borough of Kingston upon Hull." *Journal of the Statistical Society of London*, July 1841, quoted by R. K. Webb, *op. cit.* See this same source for similar findings in Bristol and the Manchester areas. Refer also to pp. 19–20 above for an account of literacy in Pendleton.

In so far as one dare generalize about a national average in an extraordinarily varied situation, the figure would seem to run between two-thirds and three-quarters of the working classes as literate, a group which included most of the respectable poor who were the great political potential in English life.[19]

By the middle of the 1860s the proportion was probably nearer nine-tenths. Professor Mark Blaug (*op. cit.*) observes: "When we consider that the world mean literacy rate in 1970 is about 60 per cent and that of the whole of Tropical Africa, the Middle East and large stretches of Latin America fail to attain even 40 per cent, the statistics . . . for adults in Britain in 1840 and working-class at that, are nothing short of extraordinary."

The appreciable rate of growth in literacy is reflected in the fact that young persons were more and more accomplished than their elders. Thus a return of the educational requirements of men in the Navy and Marines in 1865 showed that 99 per cent of the boys could read compared with Seamen (89 per cent), Marines (80 per cent), Petty Officers (94 per cent).[20]

If we accept Mr. Webb's estimate that at least two-thirds of the working classes were literate round about 1840, how far are we to attribute the improvement of much of the remaining third to government intervention from that time down to 1870? It is certainly true that state subsidies played an increasing part at this time. Even so, as late as 1869, two-thirds of school expenditure was still coming from voluntary sources, especially from the parents, directly or indirectly. Even the state subsidies were derived from a tax system which was largely regressive, falling heavily as it did on food and tobacco, so it is not easy to demonstrate that had the state not raised the money through taxation to subsidize the schools the total expenditure on them would have been lower, or that the great impetus in the growth of literacy already established before state help would not have continued.

19. R. K. Webb, "The Victorian Reading Public" in *From Dickens to Hardy*, Pelican, 1963.
20. *English Historical Review*, 1959, p. 214.

Marriage Signatures

Not everybody is willing to accept the marriage signature test of literacy. Some object that if for instance 60 out of 100 sign their names on this one important occasion in their lives, the figure may include many who perform the feat only as an isolated once-and-for-all gimmick designed to win social prestige. In other words we cannot be sure that many of the 60 could write more than their signature. Nevertheless, it is useful to apply this test to a time series of such statistics. If, for instance, with the passage of say 20 years it was found that the figure had increased from 60 to 80 out of 100 of people signing their names it would be far more difficult to attribute such an increase to a growth in the average propensity to perform gimmicks. The following Table shows the actual increase of male marriage signatures in the nineteenth century as well as figures of population increase to remind readers of the contemporary circumstances against which the educational enterprise had to struggle.

Table 3. Literacy and Population in Great Britain 1841–1901

(1) Percentage of Literates (Males) Registrar General's Returns		(2) Percentage Increase	(3) Population Increase (percentage)	
1841	67.3 ⎫	2.0	12.5	
1851	69.3 ⎭			
1861	75.4	6.1	11.1	
1871	80.6	5.2	12.7	
1881	86.5	5.9	13.9	
1891	93.6	7.1	11.2	
1900	97.2	3.6	12.0	
			10.3	(1901–11)
			4.6	(1911–21)
			4.7	(1921–31)

Sources: (1) and (2) R. D. Altick, *The English Common Reader,* University of Chicago Press, 1957, p. 171.

(3) P. Deane and W. A. Cole, *British Economic Growth 1688–1959,* Cambridge University Press, 1962, Table 75.

Commenting on the Registrar General's figures Professor R. D. Altick concludes:

> . . . the Forster Act did not significantly hasten the spread of literacy. What it did was to insure that the rate at which literacy had increased in 1851–71 would be maintained. Had the State not intervened at this point, it is likely that the progress of literacy would have considerably slowed in the last quarter of the century, simply because illiteracy was by that time concentrated in those classes and regions that were hardest to provide for under the voluntary system of education. In short, the Forster Act was responsible for the mopping-up operation by which the very poor children, living in slums or in remote country regions, were taught to read.

Even Professor Altick, however, seems to be claiming too much for the Forster Act. For one thing, such figures of literacy refer to people who were getting married and in their late twenties, not to young people of school-leaving age; in other words they over-estimated the size of the "mopping-up" operation which was called for from school provision. Further, he gives no evidence to show that "mopping up" was in fact a complete success. Even by 1948 there were still in England and Wales 5 per cent of 14-year-old school-leavers officially classified as nearly or completely illiterate and by the criterion not of writing but of reading ability (the easier of the two).[21]

21. According to Professor J. L. Williams there was in 1870 almost universal literacy in Wales, the Sunday School having played a particularly important part. It was however literacy in Welsh. What the new board schools did after 1870 was to change this for literacy in English. *Times Educational Supplement*, 22 May 1970.

5 · Literacy and
the Industrial Revolution

I

Sharp differences of judgement appear to persist on the precise extent
and timing of literacy changes in eighteenth- and nineteenth-century
Britain and their relationship to economic growth. This chapter will explore the exact nature of the differences and will attempt to resolve some
of the main issues.

Recent research among British historians seems to have been sensitive
to the seminal work of the American economists M. J. Bowman and C. A.
Anderson in 1963.[1] From statistics of cross-sectional comparisons of literacy rates in the 1950s they generalized that a literacy rate of 30–40 per
cent was a necessary condition for a country to make a significant break-
through in *per capita* income. Several British historians seem to have
been uneasy about Bowman and Anderson's inclusion of eighteenth- and
nineteenth-century Britain as one of the many "industrial and literacy
success" examples. Their critical response to the American authors has
included the following three arguments: first, that literacy deteriorated
in the Industrial Revolution; second, that growth produced literacy, not
vice versa; and third, that private educational activities were inadequate.

This response has probably been conditioned by the long-established

---

1. M. J. Bowman and C. A. Anderson, "Concerning the Role of Education in Development," in C. Geertz, ed. *Old Societies and New States* (New York, 1963), pp. 247–79.

tradition in British history that the Industrial Revolution, especially in its early stages, was generally inimical to reasonable *material* comforts, let alone educational improvements, among the working class. Typical of the originators of this tradition, for instance, were the Hammonds. See above p. 4. Richard Altick, one of the upholders of this tradition, summed it up in one sentence:

> The occupational and geographical relocation of the people — the to-tal disruption of their old way of life, their conversion into machine-slaves, living a hand to mouth existence at the mercy of their employ-ers and of uncertain economic circumstances; their concentration in cities totally unprepared to accommodate them, not least in respect to education; the resultant moral and physical degradation — these, as we shall see, had significant consequences in the history of the reading public.[2]

The supporters of this traditional view, nevertheless, have had to face the challenge not only of Anderson and Bowman but also of the new empirical work of writers (including the present author) who claim that education did not decline.[3] The response to this challenge has been in-teresting. Some historians, whether traditionalists or not, have reacted by concentrating on intensive surveys of particular localities that suggest apparent exceptions to the rule of progress. Sometimes, too, the "new sceptics" have challenged the reliability of the statistical sources used in recent work, but then they have proceeded, regardless of the inconsis-tency, to rely themselves on the same sources, but with their own particu-lar interpretation.[4] More important, the sceptics have concluded that the

2. R. D. Altick, *The English Common Reader* (Chicago, 1957), p. 207.
3. R. K. Webb, *The British Working-Class Reader, 1790–1848* (1955); V. E. Neuberg, *Popular Education in Eighteenth-Century England* (1971), who argues (p. 139) that there was a "mass reading public" by 1800; D. Robson, *Some Aspects of Education in Cheshire in the Eighteenth Century* (Manchester, 1966); T. W. Laqueur, *Religion and Respectability: Sunday Schools and Working-Class Culture, 1780–1850* (New Haven, 1976); Lawrence Stone, "Literacy and Education in England, 1640–1900," *Past and Present*, XLII (1969); E. G. West, *Education and the State* (1965); M. Hartwell, *The Industrial Revolution* (1971).
4. This was a central point in my reply to J. S. Hurt, "Professor West on Early Nine-teenth-Century Education," *Economic History Review*, 2nd ser. XXIV (1971).

verdict that the Industrial Revolution period (which most participants in the debate seem to take to be 1760–1840) was favourable to educational growth is, at best, appropriate only for the last few years of the period.[5] They base their main argument on large-scale sample data on eighteenth-century marriage-register signatures, first published in 1973. Previously scholars had been limited to national figures from 1839 in the Registrar's annual reports, and to one or two small local samples.

This chapter takes the opportunity to examine the new data. I shall argue that, on correct interpretation, they do not support the sceptics.[6] The chapter will also consider the latter's claim that wide regional variations in nineteenth-century literacy throw doubt on any generalized conclusion on the relationship between industrialization and educational growth. The main focus will be on the regional example that is so often cited, the case of Lancashire. It will be argued that here some important variables have been missing from the discussion. Finally, it will be shown that, in reaching their conclusion, the sceptics have gone from figures of literacy to figures of schooling, and that, in this latter field, their argument is equally unconvincing.

The discussion begins in section II with a re-examination of the Lancashire case. Section III analyses the new data on eighteenth-century literacy and discusses the current interpretation of it. Section IV links the evidence of changing literacy with that of changing educational institutions, and especially the innovations of "free," "compulsory," and publicly provided schools, in a way that tests hypotheses about such linkage that are commonly employed by the sceptics but not efficiently tested by them.

II

It is generally agreed by all participants that people were more literate at the end of the Industrial Revolution period, 1760–1840, than they

5. See, for instance, Michael Sanderson's review of my 1975 book in *Econ. Hist. Rev.* 2nd ser. XXIX (1976).
6. These were not available at the time of writing my 1975 book. On the same reasoning the opinion of Sanderson, *ibid.*, that "the recent debates on literacy" render some of the conclusions of my book "seriously outdated," will be rebutted.

were at the beginning. Michael Sanderson's survey of Lancashire, however, has suggested to him initial decline or stagnation that only reversed
itself after over one-half of the period was over.[7] Sanderson based his
survey on a selection of what he believed to be fairly representative instances of the industrializing centres in the country.

After adding further data, Thomas Laqueur, using the same measure
as Sanderson—marriage-register signatures—also pointed to an early
decline in literacy in Lancashire. The low point was 48 per cent of men
and 17 per cent of women able to sign their names in 1814–16.[8] Laqueur,
however, rejected Sanderson's suggestion that the low point might have
been *caused* by the introduction of large-scale factories using steam-
power in the 1790s which, according to Sanderson, was the beginning of
real social dislocation. This is unproven, Laqueur insisted, because the
downward literacy trend had by then already been in progress for forty
years. Sanderson's argument, moreover, could not explain the beginning
of a long-term rise in the literacy rate which Laqueur placed at around
1800, when the full influence of the factory system was beginning to
be felt.

> In fact, it appears that the Industrial Revolution reversed a downward
> spiral of working-class literacy which began in the mid-eighteenth cen-
> tury . . . By the time the full effects of the factory system came to be
> felt, literacy was once again on the rise.[9]

Laqueur emphasized that the marriage literacy test reflected an education that ended about twelve to fifteen years before, as, for instance,
with a marriage age of 25 and a school-leaving age of ten. It was for this
reason that the correct date for the improvement in literacy was around
1800. Laqueur's article also stressed that the adult literacy rates in the
same Lancashire towns were below the national averages just *before* the
Industrial Revolution.

In his reply in 1974, Sanderson did not satisfactorily meet Laqueur's

7. Michael Sanderson, "Literacy and Social Mobility in the Industrial Revolution in England," *Past and Present,* LVI (1972), 75–104.
8. Thomas W. Laqueur, "Literacy and Social Mobility in the Industrial Revolution in
England," *Past and Present,* LXIV (1974), 96–107.
9. *Ibid.,* 100.

point that the downward trend in literacy had been in progress for forty years before the introduction in the 1790s of steam-powered factories, and that the latter were not therefore the obvious cause of the low point in literacy in 1800. Instead, Sanderson shifted the debate to the latter end of the period. He argued that his own figures of literacy in Lancashire at the time of marriage did not show a "consistent" upturn before 1820.[10]

The graph of his data,[11] however, shows that there *was* a distinct upturn before 1820, as Laqueur argued. First, Sanderson's nine-point moving average curve rises steadily from its first point in the year 1817. Second, and much more importantly, his graph needs an adjustment lag to account for the interval between school and marriage. Sanderson (1974) accepted Laqueur's argument that literacy records in marriage registers reflected a schooling of twelve to fifteen years earlier. On the assumption that schooling creates literacy (which all participants accept), his nine-point average curve of literacy should, on his own concession, start twelve to fifteen years before 1817, that is in 1802–5. Third, neither Laqueur nor Sanderson gives the source for his belief that the lag was twelve to fifteen years. My own research (1965, p. 133) suggests that on the average it was about seventeen years. On this estimate, Sanderson's graph reveals the rise in literacy starting in 1800, as Laqueur argued on the basis of his own data. Notice that the argument that the full effects of the large-scale factories in 1800 caused a social dislocation that was inimical to education requires evidence that literacy *declined* at this time. Sanderson's evidence shows instead that the period around 1800 was the beginning of an *increase*.

The question whether industrial change in the past hindered or helped literacy is much more complex when other substantial changes were occurring. The most dramatic change in the late eighteenth and early nineteenth centuries, apart from the Napoleonic War, was the unprecedented expansion of population. The true test of the question is whether literacy rates would have fared better if the same late-eighteenth-century population explosion had occurred in the pre-factory environment. Even

10. Michael Sanderson, "Literacy and Social Mobility in the Industrial Revolution in England: A Rejoinder," *Past and Present*, LXIV (1974), 108–12.
11. Sanderson, loc. cit. (1972), 87.

if we ignored the previous criticisms, this consideration would make Sanderson's argument much more hypothetical. Laqueur mentions a 60 per cent increase in the Lancashire population between 1781 and 1800. Not only was the natural increase well above the national average but so was the rate of immigration. The combined (natural plus migration) increase in population was four times the national average. According to rough estimates, just under half of the increase between 1781 and 1800 was by immigration (126,319 increase by immigration and 146,852 by natural increase).[12] This means that if the typical immigrant family consisted of two adults and two children, then for every two "local-born" children there was about one immigrant child needing education over this period. The more that immigrants consisted of young single adults, the more the early marriage signatures would be represented by them. Also relevant is that between 1801 and 1831 population increase reached its peak in absolute numbers, 637,543, as did the natural increase, 474,009, and immigration, 183,543.[13] The ratio of immigrants to natural increase, however, was evidently falling by this time.

Because a considerable proportion of the immigrants were low-income Irish, and since by all accounts they had the poorest of educations,[14] the growth of Irish arrivals relative to the local-born Lancashire population must have had a significantly depressing effect on the local literacy records, especially between 1781 and 1800. According to Arthur Redford, Lancashire contained a greater number of Irish settlers during the period than any other county, and the majority of them settled in the Industrial Revolution towns.[15] In 1835, Dr. J. P. Kay estimated that the Irish and their immediate descendants in Manchester had grown to about 60,000. This was between one-quarter and one-third of the town's total population.[16]

It is surprising that, in the works cited above, neither Sanderson nor

12. Phyllis Deane and W. A. Cole, *British Economic Growth, 1688–1959* (Cambridge, 1962), p. 109.
13. *Ibid.*
14. West, *Education and the State*, pp. 113–14.
15. Arthur Redford, *Labour Migration in England* (New York, 1968), p. 154.
16. B. R. Mitchell and P. Deane, *Abstract of British Historical Statistics* (Cambridge, 1962), p. 24.

Laqueur connects the Irish immigration with the relatively low literacy rates in the Lancashire of the Industrial Revolution. Indeed, Laqueur argues the possibility that the immigrants were typically the more accomplished and literate. Clearly, the data produced by Sanderson and Laqueur would benefit by a re-examination and search for a correlation between Irish settlement and literacy rates in the various parishes so far studied. Their investigations are surely significantly incomplete without it.

If the explanation of a depressant effect by immigrants holds up, the view that literacy had no major connexion with economic growth in the period would be even weaker.[17] The quickening of economic activity in the Industrial Revolution stimulated the demand for new construction of houses, port facilities, canals, and roads. This in turn increased the demand for general labourers, the literacy among whom, it is generally agreed, is not of the strongest relevance to their particular productivity. As Redford observes:

> Much of the work done by the Irish in Great Britain was of the same general manual nature as their harvesting and agricultural labour . . . An immense number of Irish were employed as hodmen in Lancashire . . . By 1833 there were at least seven hundred Irish hod-carriers working in Liverpool, and two years later it was said that four-fifths of the bricklayers' labourers in Stockport were Irish.[18]

Such a picture is quite consistent with a situation of significant "threshold" literacy among the indigenous population enabling them better to concentrate in "key" growth areas, like manufacturing, where literacy *was* of more consequence. But even if this were not the case, insofar as the literacy of the immigrant Irish improved, compared with its normal attainment at their place of origin, we can still speak of this as a growth in education; and one that was associated with industrialization. The positive association could still prevail despite the stagnation or even decline shown in Lancashire marriage signatures in particular localities. This kind of explanation too could give its own kind of support to a

17. See the view of R. S. Schofield, in section III below.
18. Redford, *op. cit.*, p. 154.

"threshold"-type argument similar to Bowman and Anderson's. And it is noteworthy that, at the end of his recent debate, even Sanderson comes to reconcile his position with theirs: "Yet I find credible the notion that pre-industrial Britain had already crossed a threshold of literacy sufficient for industrialization and that, however much it fell during early industrialization, it did not regress beyond that threshold." [19]

III

One other modern specialist, R. S. Schofield, still rejects the "threshold" theory. After referring to Bowman and Anderson's association of literacy with growth he observes: "Inferences sometimes drawn from this association are that an illiteracy rate of about 60 per cent is a threshold above which economic growth is unlikely. . . ." Schofield then objects:

> Although it is true that the national male illiteracy rate had crossed the 60 per cent threshold before 1750, the female rate only crossed it definitely around 1795, and female illiteracy was very high in areas of high female industrial employment; for example, it was still 84 per cent in Oldham in 1846. [20]

These objections do not stand up. First, the threshold described by Bowman and Anderson is not 60 per cent, but between 60 and 70 per cent; [21] and it is relevant that these authors also suggested from their data that within the range from 30 to 70 per cent literacy there was "remarkably little" increase in income with rising literacy rates. [22] Schofield's figures show that the national rate for women was about 37 per cent in 1755, rising steadily to 40 per cent around 1795, and still rising thereafter. Clearly, this was well within Bowman and Anderson's relevant threshold.

Second, Bowman and Anderson's figures refer in any case to the *adult* literacy rate (men and women combined). In England according to Scho-

19. Sanderson, loc. cit. (1972), 111.
20. R. S. Schofield, "Dimensions of Illiteracy, 1750–1850," *Explorations in Economic History*, X (1973), 437–51.
21. Bowman and Anderson, *loc. cit.*, p. 252.
22. More precisely this was the case in 27 out of 32 countries studied.

field's figures, this rate started well above the limit at about 50 per cent (in 1755), and rose to about 60 per cent in 1840. Finally, Schofield is misleading when he supports his argument that female industrial illiteracy was very high in areas of high female industrial employment by taking "for example" the case of Oldham with a 16 per cent female literacy rate in 1846. This was an extreme instance. The figure for industrial Lancashire as a whole, which is the more relevant one, was about 31.1 per cent.[23]

Schofield's article has the distinction of offering the strongest defence hitherto of the marriage-signature measure of literacy. His main point is that it is the most standard, direct, and inclusive. One can agree with this up to a point;[24] and one can accept, as reasonably representative, the national estimates from his random sample of 274 parishes (out of a total of 10,000) relating to the pre-1839 years, the period before the Registrar General recorded aggregate literacy. What is debatable is his interpretation of these figures.

Schofield argues that the "long period of stability" in literacy in the eighteenth century suggests that "for England, at least, the usual causal relationship between literacy and economic growth might profitably be reversed." But taking the conventional dates of the first Industrial Revolution to be between 1760 and 1840, and assuming, as Schofield does, that entry into the labour force may be taken to be fifteen years prior to marriage (i.e., at school leaving), then 1790 is the date when the long-term stability in male literacy changed to one of definite improvement.[25] It follows that, despite the unprecedented population growth after 1760, England was not only able to maintain the male literacy rate that had been constant for twenty years preceding the Industrial Revolution, but well before half the "revolution" period was over, and at a time when the population explosion was in full force, it managed to begin an upward trend. It is interesting again to notice that the date of upturn, 1790, coincided with the beginning of the large-scale factory system and the widespread commercial use of steam power.

23. Laqueur, *loc. cit.*, 99.
24. I gave almost as strong support for the marriage-signature test of literacy, but from different arguments, in *Education and the State*, p. 134.
25. Schofield agrees with this timing, *loc. cit.*, 446.

The influence of the British tradition on educational history[26] might be one factor inhibiting Schofield from drawing the central attention to the 1790 "take-off" point, and from making reference to the enormous handicap of the sudden growth of population. For such an early year suggests a growth in the *means* of literacy improvement such as private schools for all classes, while the tradition argues the impossibility of any progress (or avoidance of decline) until *public* action was taken.[27] Interestingly enough, Schofield eventually moves from his major data, on literacy, and into the evidence on schooling. Since the evidence he uses refers to the post-1830 years, we must, for the moment, shift our focus from the early (eighteenth-century) Industrial Revolution period, and from literacy, to schooling.

Schofield starts by rejecting the "rash of educational surveys" in the 1830s as being too restricted in date span to be useful for a study of trends over a long period. Yet, inconsistently, he himself eventually leans heavily on one of them; and he does this to demonstrate that schooling (over a long period) was seriously deficient. More significantly still, he here makes serious errors in interpretation and reporting.

Referring to the period 1750–1850, he argues, "*All* schools had great difficulty in securing attendance."[28] He supports the statement about this "long period" from one example of the "in-period" survey of the 1830s, the survey of education in Westminster in 1837–8. According to Schofield, this reported "that school attendance in winter was down to between a quarter and a half of the number enrolled."[29] But, to be precise, the Committee of the Westminster Statistical Society was reporting, in 1838, on a total of eight different types of school. Its comments on decreased attendance in the winter months related to only two of them; and these contained 29 per cent of the total scholars in the area.

With respect to this sub-set the Committee reported: "*In some instances* the decrease thus caused was stated to amount to one-fourth, to

26. See above, pp. 369–70.
27. The government did not intervene until 1833, and even then only with very modest subsidies to private schools.—West, *Education and the Industrial Revolution*, p. 75.
28. Schofield, loc. cit. 439 (my emphasis).
29. *Ibid.*, 439.

one third and even to one half."[30] If we take a quarter to be the proportion of scholars absent in the whole of this sub-group of schools this would amount to an absence rate of about 7 per cent of the total school population of the area—although to be realistic we should add some small rate of absence in the other schools outside the sub-group. Even this absence rate referred to part of the year (the winter) only. The annual rate of absence would have been smaller.

Next, the winter of 1837–8 was not typical. There were three causes of absence reported by the Committee. One was "the sickness of the children," the second, "the unwillingness of the parents to expose their children to the inclemency of the weather." The Committee added: "This was particularly the case during last winter, which was remarkable for its great and long-continued severity." The third cause of school absence in the sub-group was unemployment. This factor, which could have been related to the severity of the winter, obviously prevented some parents paying the fees.

Schofield mentions neither the sickness nor the severe winter. He simply deduces the general statement that the fees in most schools were an important barrier; and he does this in a way that gives the impression that they prevented the average family from buying education in the typical school. But whatever the balance of causes, the real absence rate reported by the Westminster Committee for 1837–8 would not look unusual in the English state schools of the 1970s, especially in the winter months, and more especially when sickness epidemics (like influenza) occur.

Schofield switches from his literacy figures into schooling statistics in order to support his hypothesis that education was more the effect than the cause of economic growth. His argument is that if schooling was of economic value the parents would have invested in it widely and voluntarily. Because the education that really promoted productivity was related to more practical skills, the schools, which provided literary skills

30. "Second Report of a Committee of the Statistical Society of London, Appointed to Enquire into the State of Education in Westminster," *Journal of the Statistical Society of London*, I (1838), 193–215 (my emphasis).

only, were not well patronized. This argument is difficult to accept for three reasons. First, parents did invest in education widely and voluntarily. Second, Schofield's argument does not explain satisfactorily how the literacy rates did manage to improve so strikingly. Third, he makes errors in his numerical estimates of schooling. The latter he gathers from the same single example from the independent surveys of the 1830s (apparently having forgotten that he warned readers that this route is "fraught with danger"). Referring once more, and exclusively, to the survey of education in Westminster to show that the parents wanted a practical not a literary education, Schofield concludes: "Consequently, few children were regular in attendance, and few remained at school for more than 1½ years."[31]

The incorrectness of his estimates of attendance has already been explained. The next issue is school duration. Nowhere in the Committee's report is there any statement about the typical child receiving in his lifetime a schooling of not more than one and a half years. What *is* included is an investigation of each of the eight prevailing types of school and a reference to the fact that, in three types of school, the entrances within the course of the year exceeded the number of children upon the books. This suggested, at most, a high turnover in these particular schools. But in those days of high mobility and competition between schools, the children typically accumulated several years of schooling from several schools, having relatively short stays at each. Schofield's estimate of one and a half years neglects this fact and is therefore far too low.

The Newcastle report for 1858 found that on the average for the whole country the children of the working class alone were receiving an education of 5.7 years. Horace Mann, the compiler of the special educational extension to the national census of 1851 stated that for that year working-class children over the whole country were receiving a schooling that was "more than four years, and more than four and a half years."[32] For these reasons it is difficult to accept Schofield's judgement that "the prospect

---

31. Schofield, *loc. cit.*, 452.
32. *Commissioners on Popular Education, Minutes of Evidence (Parl. Papers, 1861, XXI, pt VI)*, H. Mann, Q.833.

of upward mobility for their children did not lead many working-class parents to invest heavily in education.[33] The four and above years of schooling on the average for working-class children in 1851, reported by Horace Mann, were paid for substantially by the parents.

Both Schofield and Sanderson venture the arguments that fee paying was a significant barrier to the working class and that accordingly they had to wait for public action to provide nearly free schooling. Neither of these arguments can be accepted. According to the Manchester Statistical Society, 80 per cent of the school-children's education in Manchester in 1834 was paid for entirely by parental fees. The remaining 20 per cent was paid for partly by fees. The same study suggests that at least four out of five Manchester children were being schooled. Neighbouring Pendleton (Salford) schooled 97 per cent of its children in 1838 and, according to the particularly intensive survey of this township by the Manchester Statistical Society, one-third of the school-goers remained for three to five years, one-third above five years, and one-third less than three years (figures that are fairly consistent with the national estimate of Horace Mann).

E. J. Hobsbawm has recently given the opinion that the quantitative study of education that has made so much progress since 1963 is largely due to the study of parochial records of marriage signatures. *School* statistics (attendance and availability), Hobsbawm adds, have also been scrutinized for "optimistic" purposes, "but their value remains in serious doubt."[34] If their value is in such doubt then this would reduce confidence in much of the reasoning of Schofield and Sanderson who themselves ultimately rely on them. In the context of the precise facts reported in the Westminster statistical report, Hobsbawm presumably might describe Schofield as selectively scrutinizing the school statistics for "pessimistic" purposes.

The truth is that there are dangers in using all sources, including the parochial returns, as the earlier discussion has shown. Consider Hobs-

33. Schofield, *loc. cit.,* 415.

34. E. J. Hobsbawm, "The Standard of Living Debate," in A. J. Taylor, ed. *The Standard of Living in the Industrial Revolution* (1975), p. 83.

bawm's own conclusions. He argues that the marriage-signature studies suggest a halt or even a reversal in the long-term progress of literacy during the early industrial period, at least in industrial Lancashire up to the late 1820s. Schofield's figures, however, show that average literacy rates (males plus females) measured at the school-leaving stage were slowly rising throughout. Second, the same figures point to 1790 as a significant improvement point for men (1800 in Lancashire). Third, in all cases the trend of the *early* industrial period was about the same as the two decades that preceded it. The new industrialism therefore cannot be argued to have had a depressing effect.

It is too hasty, however, immediately to dismiss any data, whether of literacy or of schooling, the moment a difficulty or complexity arises. Usually, after some sensible expressed qualification, the information from most sources can be employed, tentatively at least; and confidence will be increased if a consistent pattern from the various sources seems to emerge.

Now, a general pattern does emerge from the various sources on schooling. Such is the case, for instance, concerning national statistics of school population, attendance, and years duration. It is not persuasive to argue against them that, in contrast, the literacy figures are preferable because they derive from an official government source, and one therefore that provides the most standard and disinterested test of education. The 1851 figures of Horace Mann on schooling also came from a central government official source and indeed from the same office—the Registrar General's. Moreover, this was an all-inclusive universal census. The marriage-signature test of literacy, in contrast, was not all-inclusive, but related only to the 90 per cent or so of the population who were ever married. And for the years before 1839 we have to rely on samples of parishes.

The 1851 census figures reported 2.14 million scholars with an average of over four years' schooling. Further confidence in these figures is encouraged when we look at their consistency with those of the Newcastle Commission for the year 1859 (with its larger population) which reported 2.54 million scholars. Horace Mann, who completed the 1851 figures for the Registrar General, encourages the same view with his

statement that "the estimate of 1859 (Newcastle Commission) is supported by the results of the previous and more extensive (1851 census)
inquiry."[35] And the Newcastle Commission reported that over 90 per
cent of children were receiving a schooling; and this long before schooling was "free" and compulsory.

When we consider the 1760–1840 period we certainly have to "reach
back" from the 1851 census and rely on a great variety of education surveys and circumstantial evidence. But if the marriage-signature specialists do the same, they cannot simultaneously object that these sources
are completely "unreliable." All sources should be carefully sifted for
what threads they have to offer, despite initial difficulties. Even the marriage-signature evidence is often ambiguous, at least in the first instance.
This is clear, for example, when we remember the questions or assumptions one has to make about migration before one can use the parochial
returns.

Obviously, the evidence on literacy and schooling is interdependent.
Those who set out to be "pure" specialists in the one invariably succumb
to the temptation to merge their findings with information they obtain
about the other. Literacy specialists usually describe figures of schooling
as "indirect evidence" of literacy. Schooling specialists, meanwhile, regard literacy as "indirect evidence" of schooling. Surely the two special-
isms or approaches can converge. And this should be welcomed, for total knowledge will progress better with competition and cross-checking
from both sides.

IV

The remaining part of this chapter will attempt to illustrate this by showing how the data on *literacy* can be used to check speculations or hypotheses about *schooling*. Schofield offered the hypothesis that a substantial number of parents did not school their children when "very few
genuinely free places were available."[36] Similarly, Sanderson argued that

---

35. Horace Mann, "National Education," *Transactions of the British Association for the
Promotion of Social Science, Bristol Meeting, 1869* (1869).
36. Schofield, *loc. cit.*, 439.

fees were a strong barrier to the lower orders.[37] Schofield's second hypothesis stated that compulsion of the law was even more important in obtaining universal investment in education and therefore literacy. A third hypothesis, which is more explicit in Sanderson, but is at least hinted at in Schofield, is that the supply of education was largely an "exogenous" event to industrialism and to individual (family) self-help; that is, it came largely from the initiative of "public agencies" whose task it was eventually "to combat . . . those adverse effects of industrialization. . . ."[38]

Consider now the latest data on nineteenth-century literacy. Schofield plotted national annual illiteracy rates (percentages unable to sign) on a semi-logarithmic scale showing percentage of illiteracy on the vertical ordinate and on two horizontal ordinates—marriage dates and school-leaving. His diagram is reproduced here as Fig. 1.

Schofield argues that "the fastest rate of improvement was amongst those . . . leaving school after about 1870."[39] In Fig. 1 he is referring to the graph that relates to the bottom horizontal axis that refers to schooling. Schofield assumes that marriage signatures reflect on the average school-leaving fifteen years before marriage. Whether he intended it or not, 1870 will trigger off in most minds the famous Forster Education Act of the same year, the most vigorous, ambitious, and celebrated piece of Victorian educational legislation, which eventually made "public agencies" supersede private in school provision. When we refer exclusively to the bottom (school) axis, both curves in Fig. 1 do indeed show a distinct point of inflexion (or kink) in the later part of the century. But Schofield is wrong in locating it at 1870. Rather it is in 1867, three years *before* the Forster Act.

The first time Forster's legislation could have had any significant influence on schooling must, in any case, have been some few years after 1870. The legislation did not pass through Parliament until after the middle of the year in 1870. It then took some time to establish school boards. When they were elected their time was initially taken up electing chairmen, vice-chairmen, finance committees, school sites and building

37. Sanderson, *loc. cit.* (1972), 80.
38. Ibid. 111.
39. Schofield, *loc. cit.*, 443.

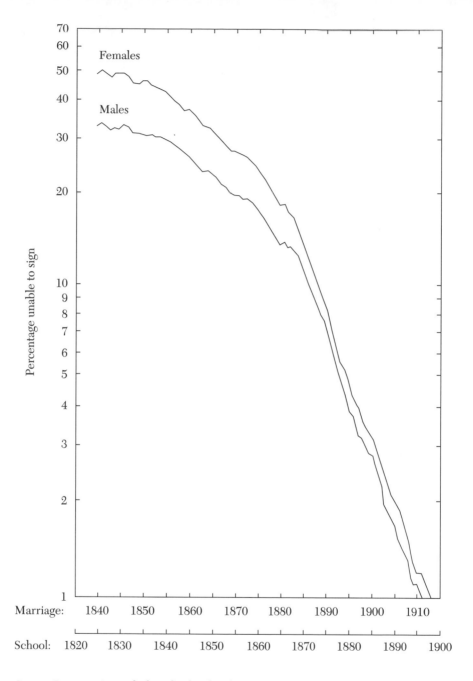

Source: Registrar General of England and Wales, *Annual Reports.*

Fig. 1. Annual Percentage of Males and Females Unable to Sign at Marriage,
England and Wales, 1839–1912

committees, school staffing committees, and education committees. The boards then had to make extensive inquiries about educational deficiencies in their areas, and this often resulted in protracted correspondence with the Registrar's Office. Where a deficiency was found, the private schools were given a period of grace to give them a chance to "fill the gaps."

After this period and, where "deficiencies" remained, the school boards had next to draw up and debate various plans, negotiate loans from the Public Works Commission, and eventually appoint architects and builders. To illustrate, the first effective school board in Northampton was elected in January 1871. But the various procedures took two years to carry out, while the first (newly built) board school was not opened until October 1874.[40] On the assumption that an efficient schooling lasts six years at minimum, the Act's effect on education and literacy in Northampton would not, therefore, begin to show until the school-leavers of 1880 who, of course, were married several years later.

Return to Schofield's assumption that the marriage registers reflect school-leaving fifteen years before marriage. (I shall not press my own preference, explained above, for a lag of seventeen years.) The point on the graph, for instance, for 1870, reading from the bottom (school) axis, represents the marriage-signature rates in 1885. This must next be qualified. If individuals were married on the *average* fifteen years after school, there would be a certain number on either side of the average. We must therefore make some qualification.

Throughout these years individuals who married under 20 years of age were under a half of 1 per cent of the total population.[41] For practical purposes, therefore, I shall take the 20-year-old grooms and brides as being "the first of the few" to appear in the nineteenth century who could possibly have benefited from Forster's Act. To give the Act the fullest chance I shall also assume that those who married youngest needed edu-

40. *Northampton Mercury*, 25 Nov. 1876. I am grateful to Victor A. Hatley of Northampton for supplying me with this source. I am aware that some boards opened schools earlier, but these were usually existing private schools that were soon taken over by them. I am only concerned here with *net* improvements in school supply which would show up in entirely new buildings.

41. Mitchell and Deane, *op. cit.*, Table 5, p. 151. The average marriage age was nearly 28 years in 1881 according to the Registrar General's Report (Vol. IV) for that year.

cation most. But even supposing that *all* school-leavers were in this category (all married ten years after school), and assuming building time lags similar to Northampton's, the first school-leavers to benefit from the Forster schooling (as in Northampton) would not appear until well to the right of the kink in the curve, say 1876 at the earliest. This point is indicated in Fig. 2. This figure is identical with Fig. 1 except for the addition of my vertical arrows with associated explanations.

If we now extrapolate the curve onwards to the late 1890s from that part of the curve between the turning-point of 1867 to 1876, the latter year, to repeat, being the first possible influence of the 1870 Act, we obtain an almost linear trend result. This pre-Forster trend shows approximately the same "success rate" as that in Fig. 1. The data in the diagram therefore do not, at least at first sight, support the third hypothesis that major literacy improvement had to wait for *public* (government) initiative. We should remember, however, that *some* intervention was operative before 1870. This was a system of subsidies to all kinds of private schools. More precisely, the diagram suggests that this mixed private and public system (dating from 1833) was just as efficient as the new apparatus of "nationalized" school intervention introduced by Forster.[42]

With respect to making education "free," the extrapolation of the trend established between 1867 and 1876 suggests that it made no difference. And even if it did, its maximum effect shown in the diagram is merely an improvement in the national literacy rate of 1 per cent—from 98 to 99 per cent. Similarly, the extrapolated trend suggests that compulsion had negligible effect. And even if it did, it could have affected literacy at most by making only 3½ per cent of the total population literate.

V

I conclude that the recent attempts to reject Bowman and Anderson's "threshold theory" of literacy, as it applies to England and Wales, have

---

42. This finding supports a central argument in my *Education and the Industrial Revolution,* an argument that Sanderson, in his review of it (1976) seems strangely to have overlooked; for he presents me as arguing simply that "state intervention was of doubtful necessity."

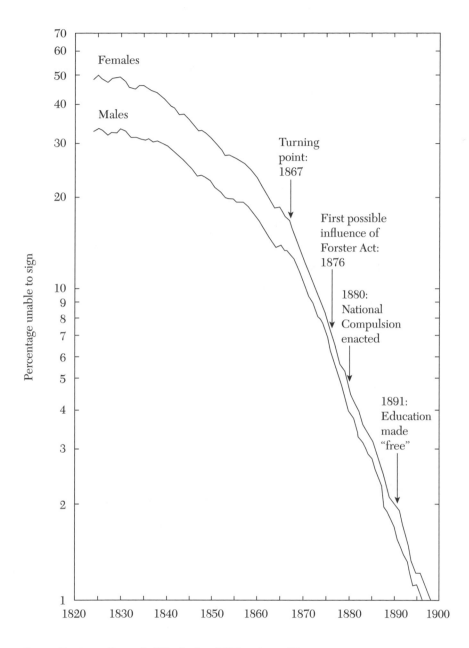

Source: Registrar General of England and Wales, *Annual Reports.*

Fig. 2. Annual Percentages of Illiterate Male and Female School-Leavers as
Determined by their Inability to Sign the Marriage Register Fifteen Years Later

not been successful; second, that available national estimates do *not* demonstrate that the Industrial Revolution depressed literacy—even if we consider the rate for males or females exclusively; third, that the date of distinct improvement in the national literacy trend coincided with the beginnings of the large-scale factory system; and fourth, that the apparent local exception of Lancashire is closer to the national trend than has been believed, and that in any case when we take Irish immigration into account, the association between education and economic growth is considerably strengthened. Finally, I have shown that, despite the attempts by historians of *literacy* and historians of *schooling* to keep their studies separate, this is not easily achieved in practice. The convergence of the two approaches nevertheless is necessary, although it is still important for the one specialist carefully to cross-check the use of his sources by the other. Evidence on literacy has its difficulties and problems, just as does evidence on schooling. But, if properly handled, both can still yield the *truest*, rather than the most "pessimistic" or "optimistic," view of eighteenth- or nineteenth-century educational progress.

6 · The Quality of Education: Dotheboys Hall and Unqualified Teachers

The death of Charles Dickens in 1870 coincided with the birth of English State schooling. The novelist shared the victory; for nobody had struggled and campaigned for popular education more than he. It seems evident to ordinary readers that Dickens the writer took every opportunity to comment explicitly or implicitly on bad social conditions wherever they occurred. Most literary critics today nevertheless would question the degree to which Dickens' writings were seriously or primarily *documentary*. Those few who see them as such, however, surely have their strongest evidence in the case of education. Where his work impinges on this topic we are in the presence of a person who transcends the literary craftsmen and becomes a social crusader. Dickens in private life was, in fact, the purposeful and vigorous reformer/agitator to whom factual evidence is meat and drink. Naturally the cause was served to good effect by presentation of the evidence by such an eminent professional. Dickens indeed left his mark on education; it is surely no exaggeration to say that his written and spoken testimony played a part in the passage of the 1870 legislation.[1]

Dickens' ideas continue to have influence in the twentieth century. The persistent hold upon our imagination about "evil" Victorian educational conditions that his works convey is understandable for some rea-

1. At the time of the First Reading of Forster's Bill in February 1870 Dickens was giving personal performances of readings from *Nicholas Nickleby* in London theatres.

sons but puzzling for others. For many years Dickens has certainly featured in school text-books as a source of colourful illustrations of early social history. His entertainment value moreover is still unsurpassed. What other classic can match the continued popularity of *Nicholas Nickleby* not only in the literature but now also on radio, film and television? For other reasons however Dickens' surviving influence is surprising. Certainly it is curious how the Dickens' impressions are to this day used without qualification in serious works in the history of education.[2] Dickens, who combined with his incomparable talents as a novelist, the zeal of the reformer, and the instincts of the newspaper reporter, should not of course be discarded as a contemporary witness. This would be mistaken even in the twentieth century when we have access to new and more efficient types of historiography. But fresh empirical verification and assessment of the Dickens verdict on nineteenth-century educational conditions in Britain is surely overdue.

Born in 1812, Dickens lived in Chatham until about 1823 and spent the next ten years in London. *Nicholas Nickleby* was first published in monthly parts from April 1838 to October 1839 and the novel was first issued in book form in October 1839. In the Preface, Dickens explains that he came to hear about Yorkshire schools when a "not very robust" child. His first impressions of them (probably through newspaper reports) were "somehow or other connected with a suppurated abscess that some boy had come home with, in consequence of his Yorkshire guide, philosopher, and friend, having ripped it open with an inky penknife." This story stuck with him ever after and he determined one day to follow it up in a report to the public at large. *Nicholas Nickleby* was commenced within a few months after the publication of the completed *Pickwick Papers.* This must have been in 1837.

Dickens insists in his Preface, that Mr. Squeers, the Yorkshire headmaster, and his school, "are faint and feeble pictures of an existing reality, purposely subdued, and kept down lest they should be deemed impossible." His evidence for his belief that he had under-written rather than over-written his story came from accounts of atrocities on neg-

2. In his *History of Education in Great Britain* (1965) S. J. Curtis uses Dotheboys Hall as an exemplar of the "terrible conditions" of the private schools (see p. 234).

lected children supplied from private quarters, "far beyond the reach of suspicion or distrust," and from past reporting of trials at law "in which damages have been sought as a poor recompense for lasting agonies and disfigurements inflicted on children." He explains that he had resolved, had he seen occasion, "to reprint a few of these details of legal proceedings from certain old newspapers." Unfortunately Dickens did not divulge much more about these private sources.

Dickens was obviously previously prepared when he made a personal visit to Yorkshire one very severe winter (probably that of 1837–8). Wishing to avoid notice as the celebrated author of Pickwick he "concerted a pious fraud" with a professional friend who had a Yorkshire connection. The friend supplied Dickens with letters of introduction in a fictitious name. They referred "to a suppostitious little boy who had been left with a widowed mother who didn't know what to do with him; the poor lady had thought, as a means of thawing the tardy compassion of her relations in his behalf, of sending him to a Yorkshire school; I was the poor lady's friend travelling that way; and if the recipient of the letter could inform me of a school in his neighbourhood, the writer would be very much obliged." After Dickens had obtained local information in this manner he returned to Kent and completed his book. At this time he was 25 or 26 years old.

The publication of *Nicholas Nickleby* in 1838 caused considerable indignation among many Yorkshire people who regarded the story as an unjust indictment.[3] At the same time it prompted public outrage and demands for immediate action in the interests of children. An intensive official survey of the West Riding of Yorkshire in the late 1850s was conducted by J. G. Fitch, the Assistant Commissioner to the Newcastle Commission. He reported: "I have wholly failed to discover any example of the typical Yorkshire boarding-school with which Dickens' *Nicholas Nickleby* has made us familiar. I have seen schools in which board and education were furnished for £20 and even £18 per annum, but have been unable to find evidence of bad feeding or physical neglect."[4]

3. A fascinating account of these reactions is contained in Philip Collins, *Dickens and Education,* 1965.
4. *Schools Inquiry Commission* (for 1858) 1861, Vol. I, p. 32.

Due regard should be paid to the fact that this government report was made 20 years after the prototype of Dotheboys Hall existed. The public shock associated with the publication of *Nicholas Nickleby* could have caused subsequent closures of the worst schools.[5] This indeed is suggested in a Preface to a later edition of his book written in 1848. Referring to the fact that the book was written ten years previously, just after *Pickwick Papers* had been published, Dickens observes in retrospect: "There were, then, a good many cheap Yorkshire schools in existence. There are very few now . . . I make mention of the race [of Schoolmasters] as of the Yorkshire schoolmasters, in the past tense. Though it has not yet finally disappeared, it is dwindling daily." If Fitch's report cannot strictly be taken to contradict Dickens' view of the 1830s it is still to be considered as an indication of conditions in the 1850s, especially in the light of Dickens' corroborative comments concerning the large number of extinctions by then of bad schools and teachers.

Whatever the validity of Dickens' account of the early-nineteenth-century schools of the "Dotheboys" kind it could never qualify as a *representative sample* of private schooling in this period—that is a representative sample of nearly the whole of early-nineteenth-century English education. The Wackford Squeers establishment was taken from one particular class of school only: the full board school. The vast majority of schools at this time were day schools.[6] The large quantity of new schools

5. In the Introduction by Charles Dickens' son to an 1892 edition of *Nicholas Nickleby* (Macmillan), there is reference to a story (in the Dickens biography by C. W. Cope) which tells of the bankrupting effect of Dickens' work. The story came from the driver of a stagecoach between Darlington and Barnard Castle. He stated that Dickens ruined a schoolmaster by the name of Shaw who was alleged to be the prototype of Squeers. The coachman himself stoutly denied that Squeers' (Shaw's) boys were half-starved and explained that Dickens obtained his story from a dismissed usher; "it was a poisoned source." Charles Dickens junior (in the same 1892 edition of *Nicholas Nickleby*) after relating the coachman's story went on to defend his father by dismissing the idea that an actual prototype of Squeers existed. He also objected to evidence from "unnamed stage-coachmen and other witnesses of similar nebulosity!" He would have been on stronger ground however if the witnesses of Charles Dickens senior were not similarly "unnamed."

6. Those schools that accepted subsidies had also to accept inspection. In this sense there was an element of "publicness" about them. In the 1851 census they were in-

which appeared in the Industrial Revolution made their biggest debut not in the remote parts of the country but in the growing towns. They did so moreover in such numbers as to encourage abundant competition and therefore rapid transit between families and others of daily information about them. The Dickens prototype moreover was a subdivision of its own class. "Dotheboys Hall" advertised "No Vacations" suggesting[7] that it was being used purposefully and specially as a place for sending from all parts of England orphans, illegitimates, and generally unwanted children—like the "suppostitious little boy" in Dickens' letter of introduction.

Despite these observations Dickens, in his writing, seems to have been speaking for English education as a whole. He did so too in a way which suggested strong Utilitarian or Benthamite overtones. In his later Preface to *Nickleby* he wrote: "Of the monstrous neglect of education in England, and the disregard of it by the State as a means of forming good or bad citizens, and miserable or happy men, private schools long afforded a notable example."[8] Dickens made no secret of the fact that his interests in education could in his own times be classed as partisan. His were the views of the Birmingham League. Favouring compulsory, "comprehensive," unsectarian, and state-provided education, he was a ready speaker to popular audiences on the subject.[9]

Whether, when he was writing *Nickleby,* the young Dickens had access to or studied closely the systematic surveys of schooling made by the Statistical Societies of Manchester and the other big industrial centres is doubtful. Had he done so his grasp of the total educational situation would have been more comprehensive and more balanced. Yet these same sources would have afforded much colourful and anecdotal mate-

---

deed classified as "public schools"; but they were still privately owned and continued to charge fees. They were entirely a different type of organization from the state schools of today.

7. Phillip Collins, *op. cit.*

8. Compare this sentence with James Mill's remark that ". . . the question whether the people should be educated, is the same with the question, whether they should be happy or miserable."

9. C. Birchenough, *History of Elementary Education in England and Wales,* 1920, p. 66.

rial upon which the fertile and creative mind of this inimitable novelist might well have worked.

There is indeed much material in the reporting of the statistical investigators upon the quality of some schoolmasters which has a considerable and unconscious "Dickensian" flavour. Quotations selected below will be taken from the Report on Manchester in 1834. In several respects Manchester was different from other English industrial towns and not least because of a significant proportion of recent Irish immigrants in its population. The fact that over one-sixth of the family heads were Irish was partly attributed by the statistical society to the circumstance that Manchester, unlike some other towns, gave relief to the Irish out of the poor rate. Proper study of the Manchester Report serves to illustrate the difficulty of steering a course between a balanced descriptive impression of typical or average school conditions and a temptation to be carried away by the more spectacular and "rumbustious" individual instances. Reports written in earnest solemnity often tell us as much of their writers as their subject. The following is an "incidental" observation placed in a footnote of the Manchester Statistical Society's Report on Manchester 1834 (p. 10).

> The Committee met with two instances of schools kept by Masters of some abilities, but much given to drinking, who had however gained such a reputation in their neighbourhood, that after spending a week or a fortnight in this pastime they could always fill their schoolrooms again as soon as they returned to their post. The children during the absence of the Masters go to other schools for the week, or play in the streets, or are employed by their parents, in running errands, etc. On another occasion, one of these Instructors and Guardians of the morals of our youth, was met issuing from his school room at the head of his scholars to see a fight in the neighbourhood; and instead of stopping to reply to any educational queries, only uttered a breathless invitation to come along and see the sport.

In another footnote (page 9) we discover our zealous and solemn Manchester investigator coolly attempting to put his questions to a master in a common school who was simultaneously in charge of a large class. The studious reporting of the result was as follows:

In one of these seminaries of learning, where there were about 130 children, the noise and confusion was so great as to render the replies of the Master to the enquiries put to him totally inaudible; he made several attempts to obtain silence but without effect; at length, as a last effort, he ascended his desk, and striking it forcibly with a ruler, said, in a strong Hibernian accent, "I'll tell you what it is, boys, the first I hear make a noise, I'll call him up, and kill entirely"; and then perceiving probably on the countenance of his visitor some expression of dismay at this murderous threat, he added quickly in a more subdued tone, "almost I will." His menace produced no more effect than his previous appeals had done. A dead silence succeeded for a minute or two; then the whispering recommenced, and the talking, shuffling of feet, and general disturbance was soon as bad as ever.

The writer does not make it entirely clear whether all 130 boys were in the same room. If this was so then the case must have been very exceptional since the Manchester Statistical Society's figures showed an average pupil teacher ratio of 1 to 34 for the 179 common schools. (The average ratio for Manchester, Bury, Salford, York, Birmingham and Liverpool was 26.8—which, as noted in the previous chapter, is a lower ratio than that in primary schools today.)

The Manchester Dame Schools for children from two years upwards afforded probably some of the most "Dickensian" examples of all. The contemporary relative poverty showed up here in several aspects. We have already shown that these schools often acted as child-minding enterprises and allowed parents the opportunity to earn bigger incomes for the family. But besides child-minding there were often *some* rudimentary attempts made at instruction—especially in reading and sewing. Many Dame Schools were found in "dirty" and "unwholesome" rooms. How much more unwholesome and dirty on average than the typical non-school dwelling of the time however is not easily discoverable. Certainly by twentieth-century standards the physical conditions of Manchester were grim.

In one of these schools eleven children were found, in a small room, in which one of the children of the Mistress was lying in bed ill of the measles. Another child had died in the same room of the same complaint a few days before; and no less than thirty of the usual scholars were then confined at home with the same disease.[10]

School furniture and books were often a luxury:

In another school all the children to the number of twenty, were squatted upon the bare floor there being no benches, chairs, or furniture of any kind, in the room. The Master said his terms would not yet allow him to provide forms, but he hoped that as his school increased, and his circumstances thereby improved, he should be able sometime or other to afford this luxury.[11]

Some of the teachers could not make a living wage out of such teaching and had to augment it with other employment such as shopkeeping, sewing and washing. Of all the graphic footnotes in the Manchester Report for 1834 the following is surely the most poignant and bizarre:

One of the best of these schools is kept by a blind man, who hears his scholars their lessons, and explains them with great simplicity; he is however liable to interruption in his academic labours, as his wife keeps a mangle, and he is obliged to turn it for her.

But this was Manchester, and as we have mentioned it was not entirely typical, despite its popularity among social historians. Consider a report from an industrial town. The Birmingham Statistical Society reported that:

The physical condition of the Dame Schools of Birmingham is much more satisfactory than could have been anticipated. None of them are kept in cellars, very few in garrets or bed-rooms, and they are generally more cleanly and better lighted than schools of the same description in Manchester and Liverpool.[12]

Forty-four per cent of the Birmingham Dame School scholars were under five years old. Clearly anxious to enquire about the moral and religious aspects of the teaching, the Statistical Society's investigators were often taken aback by the replies: "A mistress in one of this class of schools, on being asked whether she gave moral instruction to her schol-

10. Manchester Report, (p. 6).
11. *Ibid.*
12. Report for the year 1838, *J.L.S.S.*, April 1840.

ars, replied, 'No, I can't afford it for 3d. a-week.'" Another replied: "How is it likely, when they can hardly say their A, B, C?"

In only 21 out of 267 schools was "moral instruction" professed to be attended to. The investigators were similarly disappointed with their performance in religious instruction and with the fact that in 229 schools the Church Catechism was repeated only once a week.

The Birmingham Statistical Society also regretted inefficient moral and religious instruction in the common day schools for older children, typically from 5 years to 12 years.

> Taken as a whole, the utmost amount of benefit which accrues to the public from this class of schools will include facility in reading and writing, and some knowledge of arithmetic. . . .[13]

In the twentieth century it is tempting to look back smugly on many aspects of Victorian life—not just schooling—in the nineteenth century. We often forget that Britain was still an underdeveloped country. In any case it is salutary to remind ourselves that in the 1970s we are still far short of the ideal in education.

In this book we argue the need for *relative* judgements. This distinguishes us from those who regard all discrepancies between the real and the ideal (Utopian) as inefficiencies. Those who share our standpoint will keep a firm comparative grasp of such Dickensian descriptions as the following:

> We noted the grim approaches . . . rubbish dumps on waste land nearby; the absence of green playing spaces on or near the school sites; tiny play grounds; gaunt looking buildings; often poor decorative conditions inside; narrow passages; dark rooms . . . books kept unseen in cupboards for lack of space to lay them out . . . and sometimes all around, the ingrained grime of generations.

It is from a desire to illustrate as strikingly as possible the need for due perspective that we now explain that this last quotation comes, not from the 1830s, but from paragraph 133 of the English Plowden Report: *Children and their Primary Schools* (1967). One must say immediately that this passage refers only to the worst areas of English schooling and that

13. *Ibid.*, p. 35.

improvement plans are already afoot. It serves to show nevertheless the need for *comparative* judgement; the need to compare past imperfections with present ones; and the need to avoid contrasting nineteenth-century achievements with an ideal educational world that we have not yet reached ourselves. It also illustrates how selective quotations unbacked by statistical perspective can seriously mislead; it similarly suggests the need for appropriate care when interpreting the evidence of the past.

Teacher Qualifications in the Nineteenth Century

Several of the local and national reports on nineteenth-century schooling were particularly critical of the frequent lack of credentials among teachers. The only qualification for the employment of so many teachers, complained the Manchester Report and repeated by Dickens, was their unfitness for any other occupation. Such remarks were often inconsistent; for the same investigators later complained that many teachers were continuing the job of teaching with other occupations (for which they *were* clearly fitted). They now objected that such teachers were inefficient because they were dissipating their energies. Later in the century, in the Newcastle Commission Report of 1861, one observer protested that so many teachers had "picked up" their knowledge "promiscuously" or were continuing the trade of school-keeping with another:

> Of the private school masters in Devonport, one had been a blacksmith and afterwards an exciseman, another was a journey-man tanner, a third a clerk in a solicitor's office, a fourth (who was very successful in preparing lads for the competitive examination in the dockyards) keeps an evening school and works as a dockyard labourer, a fifth was a seaman, and others had been engaged in other callings.[14]

Another observer found among the teachers, grocers, linen-drapers, tailors, attorneys, painters, German, Polish and Italian refugees, bakers, widows or daughters of clergymen, barristers, surgeons, housekeepers and dressmakers.[15]

14. Newcastle Commission Report 1861, p. 93.
15. *Ibid.*, p. 94.

As observed elsewhere,[16] while the average small boy would today probably display wistful wonder at the prospect of having such a colourful variety of experienced adults to teach him, the nineteenth-century investigator and commentators such as Dickens saw them as a collection of uncolleged, and therefore untrained, individuals with little redeeming qualities of possible benefit in the schoolroom. But on the basis of *relative* judgement we should compare with the subsequent products of the Victorian teacher training colleges. These colleges have been described by one writer as "pedant factories, whose machinery efficiently removed whatever traces of interest in human culture the scholars had somehow picked up earlier in their careers."[17] Rote-learning frequently became the passage-way through to the teaching profession via these new "seminaries of learning" as they were often called.

Consider now Dickens' description of teachers in the 1820s who were without training and then compare his attitude to the new class of trained teachers that appeared in the 1850s. With the aid of his unique literary talent, Dickens made full display of the complaint about lack of teacher qualifications. In *Nicholas Nickleby:*

> Although any man who had proved his unfitness for any other occupation in life, was free, without examinations or qualifications, to open a school anywhere; although preparation for the functions he undertook, was required in the surgeon who assisted to bring a boy into the world, or might one day assist, perhaps, to send him out of it; in the chemist, the attorney, the butcher, the baker, the candlestick maker; the whole round of crafts and trades, the schoolmaster excepted; and although schoolmasters as a race were blockheads and imposters who might naturally be expected to spring from such a state of things, and to flourish in it; these Yorkshire schoolmasters were the lowest and most rotten round in the whole ladder.[18]

The implication of Dickens' complaint that typical teachers were "without examinations or qualification" or that his only qualification for the occupation was his unfitness for any other, was that teachers should be

16. E. G. West, *Education and the State,* 1970, p. 167.
17. R. D. Altick, *The English Common Reader,* 1959, p. 162.
18. Second Preface to *Nicholas Nickleby.*

properly instructed and examined in teacher training establishments. By the 1850s his type of agitation was at last resulting in the creation of an increasing number of such institutions. Their products, however, were now ridiculed by Dickens. He poured upon them the same vitriolic indignation as he had previously bestowed upon the untrained. In his *Hard Times* published in 1854 his first paragraph describes the instructor of teachers, Mr. Thomas Gradgrind:

> Now what I want is, Facts. Teach these boys and girls nothing but Facts. Facts alone are wanted in life. Plant nothing else and root out everything else . . . Stick to Facts, Sir!

Mr. McChoakumchild, the new teacher, proceeded to copy the master in his best manner.

> He and some one hundred and forty other schoolmasters, had been lately trained at the same time, in the same factory, on the same principles, like so many pianoforte pieces, and had answered volumes of head-breaking questions. Orthography, etymology, syntax, and prosody, biography, astronomy, geography, and general cosmography, the sciences of compound proportion, algebra, land-surveying and levelling, vocal music, and drawing from models, were all at the ends of his ten chilled fingers . . . Ah rather overdone, Mr. McChoakumchild. If he had only learnt a little less, how infinitely better he might have taught more!

Perhaps schools, schoolteaching and education generally will always be the victims of the literati. Dickens was no exception. One wonders with what choice words he would describe present day teachers and especially present day methods in the teacher training colleges of which so many are now critical. We can hazard a guess that Dickens would not present his views in a White Paper; it would be Black or Red.

Part 2 · The Evidence on Schools

7 · Scottish Elementary Schooling

The Scottish system of parochial schools was the outcome of Protestant enthusiasm for an education that would, in the words of John Knox, prepare children "for the business of life and the purpose of eternity." The most important piece of legislation was the Act of 1696. This laid down that a school should be erected in every parish and that teachers' salaries were to be met by a tax on local heritors and tenants. Notice however that education was not made compulsory by law; and neither was it made free. The money derived from the tax on heritors in the country districts and from the municipal funds in burghs was far from sufficient to cover the full costs of schooling. The public funds were devoted largely to one part of the costs—the capital costs. In addition they provided some limited fixed stipend for the teacher. The parental fees, which made up a big part of the rest of the teacher's salary, were paid by every social class; in aggregate they provided a significant part of the total school revenues. The fees for the very poorest of families were paid by the kirk-sessions. Public finance was thus enlisted only up to a point, and beyond this the efforts of the schoolmaster were related to the fees from the voluntary attendance of his clients. It was a system which was the subject of considerable approval and pride in the works of Scottish classical economists and one which was often incorporated in the developing common school systems in nineteenth-century America.

All the parish schools taught reading, writing and arithmetic. In their early days especially they also taught some Latin; and the more ambitious sometimes included land-surveying, geometry, algebra, bookkeeping, geography, Greek and French. The strongest emphasis however was upon moral and religious teaching. Children were examined in their catechism at periodic inspections made by the kirk-session and the heritors. In many schools in the eighteenth century the Bible was almost the only reading book. Many champions of the system claimed that such inculcation of Christian truths and discipline was conducive to social order. Corporal punishment was widely used, at least in the early period.

In seeking an economic assessment of the system in the early-nineteenth-century Industrial Revolution we first need especially careful statistical perspective. This is necessary because this is not often apparent in conventional histories. The latter have typically relied upon contemporary individual eye witnesses, upon biographical or impressionistic testimony, and upon descriptive local case studies.[1] Curiously enough the deficiency is not in this instance due to the scarcity of contemporary statistical data. This, in fact, is abundantly available. The more important sources will now be examined.

The educational impact of the Industrial Revolution upon the Scottish system of parochial schooling may first be detected directly or indirectly from evidence contained in the "Digest of the Parochial Returns made to the Select Committee, appointed to enquire into the Education of the Poor" in 1818. Elaborate information is also available in a report by a committee appointed by the General Assembly to investigate conditions in the 1820s.[2] From these reports we learn that from the commencement of the Scottish compulsory parochial school system in 1696 down to 1803, nothing much further had been done by law to alter the conditions that were laid down in the original statute. Further legislation in 1803 made some small increases in the salaries of teachers; and some new regulations were introduced for the government of schools and schoolmasters. If we assume that the statutory parochial schools ac-

1. One notable exception is T. C. Smout, *A History of the Scottish People 1560–1830* (Charles Scribner's Sons, 1969).
2. S. C. Education of the Poor, *Parl. Papers,* 1818, III (hereafter "1818 Digest"). An account of both the reports is to be found in *Edinburgh Review,* XCI (1827), 107–32. There is some brief reference to some of this information in G. Balfour, *The Educational Systems of Great Britain and Ireland* (Oxford, 1898).

counted for the bulk of Scottish educational provision in the middle of the eighteenth century a serious decline in their share of total pupils educated had taken place by 1818 (see Table 1).

Table 1. Schooling in Scotland, 1818

	Pupils	*Schools*
Parochial schools	54,161	942
Private (unendowed) schools	106,627	2,222

Source: 1818 Digest

These figures would seem to show that the population "explosion" of the late eighteenth century had proved far too much of a strain for the system to carry, since by 1818 "non-legislated" private schools were bearing the main burden. The figures exclude the Sunday schools, Dame schools, and the schools for the education of the rich. It is worth repeating that very little of this education was free; nearly all the parents paid fees whether they used the parochial schools or the more numerous private establishments. Thus to take randomly the first item from the 1818 Digest report on the county of Lanark, we find: "Avondale: The parochial school, containing from 120 to 140 children, of whom 12 are taught gratis . . . the (master's) salary is £22 4s. 5d. besides a school-room, house and garden, and emoluments and fees amounting to £91 per annum. . . ."

Similarly with the county of Fife the first parish recorded reads: "Abbotshall: The parochial school, consisting of 80 children; the master's salary is £22 4s. 5d. besides £5 per annum payable out of an estate . . . and his emoluments amount to £25 and fees to £45 making in the whole £97 4s. 5d. per annum." (1818 Digest, pp. 1345, 1385).

Whilst it is true that by 1760 a widespread network of parochial schools had been established, the law had clearly not anticipated the growth of demand. It had typically provided for one school in each parish. Schoolmasters in the 1760s were having to teach fifty or sixty children each. One way in which the system sometimes tried to adjust was in the reduction of pressure to keep boys at school for more than about four years (for girls the duration was smaller still). Regularity in attendance was also not insisted on.[3] But these adjustments were almost irrelevant to the huge pressures in the new industrial regions caused by population expansion. The aggregate population of Glasgow, Greenock and Paisley for instance rose from 42,000 in 1750, to 125,000 in 1801, and to 287,000 in 1831. In the absence of publicly provided establishments an extraordinary growth of private schools was therefore inevitable especially in these areas.

How did the public authorities view this new expansion of competitive schools or "adventure schools" as they were prone to call them?

"Inevitably, the kirk-session was suspicious, partly because too many private schools might undermine attendance at the parish school, partly because they feared the teacher might be incompetent or doctrinally unorthodox. They therefore claimed and often exercised the right to shut down any school of which they did not approve."[4]

This religious protectionism however was not so serious as it had been in England. Some Scottish parishes eventually found that the private schools could be used to fill important gaps where it was impossible for one school to take all the children. In some cases the kirk-session paid for the fees of poor children attending private schools.[5] By the middle of the eighteenth century it appears that the authorities were powerless to prevent the growth of private schools. Several of them turned out men of distinction such as Robert Burns who was taught to read and write at John Murdoch's adventure school in Alloway, opened in 1765.[6]

Among those who were beginning to look with clerical dismay upon the clear supersession of the parochial schools by secular private schools in the growing industrial towns of Scotland was Dr. Thomas Chalmers. In a tract published in 1819 and significantly entitled: *Considerations on the System of Parochial Schools in Scotland, and on the Advantage of establishing them in Large Towns,* he expressed his chief complaint about the "deficient quality" of the growing private schools in the rapidly developing industrial cities as follows:

> These stations, too, whither children repair for their education, are
> continually shifting; and the teachers being often unconnected by any

3. Smout, p. 454.   5. Smout, p. 454.
4. Smout, p. 454.   6. Smout, p. 456.

ties of residence or local vicinity with the parents, there is positively, in spite of the sacredness of their mutual trust, as little of the feeling of any moral relationship between them, as there is between an ordinary shopkeeper and his customers.

The shopkeeper-customer relationship in education, however, had considerably increasing support in Scotland. Adam Smith in *The Wealth of Nations* published in 1776, had acclaimed the Scottish practice of fee-paying in the parochial schools for the very reason that it insured some respect by the supplier for the consumer. Smith was in fact a notable champion of the parochial schools. This no doubt was in large part due to the circumstance that his own boyhood education benefitted greatly from the parochial school in his native Kirkcaldy. But he struck a particularly good patch in the fortunes of this establishment. His own education at the school coincided with a time when its reputation had been freshly restored after a period of decline. One wonders how Smith might have reacted to the behaviour of the parents in turning against the same school thirty years later. The rebellion of parents in Kirkcaldy was provoked partly from their growing conviction about the commercial value of the 3 Rs. They increasingly resisted traditional parochial school emphasis on classical languages and Religion ("the fourth R"). Parents complained that their children did not get their due in the school "by not having been teached writing."[7] In self-defence the school was forced to revise its syllabus and fees thus:

Table of Fees per Quarter

English by itself:	one shilling and sixpence
English writing and vulgar arithmetic with one hour's writing daily:	two shillings
Latin by itself:	three shillings
Latin with writing and arithmetic:	three shillings and sixpence
Decimal arithmetic, mensuration, trigonometry and algebra:	three shillings
Church music (on occasion):	gratis

7. C. R. Fay: *Adam Smith and the Scotland of His Day,* 1956, p. 51.

Such an "à la carte" nature of this educational "menu" reveals native shrewdness and discrimination among the Scottish clientele. (Note the intriguing price of the fourth item on the list. Observe also the almost apologetic mention of Church music.) Robert Lowe remarked (approvingly) in the following century: "In Scotland they sell education like a grocer sells figs."

Consider next the statistical information that is necessary to test the widespread belief among historians (see for instance the quotation from R. Altick above, p. 5) that the Industrial Revolution was accompanied by educational failure and decline. To be consistent with this view the statistics should show a marked contrast between the growing industrial towns and other areas. How, then, did the non-industrial areas compare? It seems necessary first to divide the latter into the Highlands and the rural Lowlands.

The Highlands

By all accounts the Highlands were unambiguously the worst of all areas. In 1822 a society at Inverness was instituted for the express purpose of "educating the poor in the Highlands" and proceeded to measure the educational needs in those areas.[8] The society found that about one-third of the whole population was more than two miles, "and many thousands more than five miles, distant from the nearest schools." Half the population was unable to read. In the Hebrides and other western parts of Inverness and Ross, 70 per cent could not read. The Highlands population was 416,000. Of this, the children of school age numbered 52,000. Only 8,550 scholars were found to be at school. Despite the parochial schools legislation, the society concluded, "we are not much better furnished with the means of education than our predecessors in the last century; and the results of their tuition have only proved its deplorable inadequacy." The failure of these non-industrial areas to do better for them-

8. The results were published in: *Moral Statistics of the Highlands and Islands of Scotland; compiled from Returns received by the Inverness Society for the Education of the Poor in the Highlands* (Inverness, 1826).

selves than the towns was in effect attributed by these reports to the latter's superior income.

According to a survey by the Gaelic Society of Inverness in 1826 there existed in the Highlands (including Orkney, Shetland, and the shores of the Moray Firth) 500 schools with 25,000 children. One third were parochial schools, one quarter schools run by the Scottish Society for the Propagation of Christian Knowledge and the remainder belonging to Gaelic societies. The Highlands had been the target of special endeavour by the charity school movement for over a century. Yet out of a population of 400,000 only one in sixteen was enrolled in a school. Only about one half of those over eight could read.[9]

The Rural Lowlands

These were the areas where the parochial system was at its best. According to the *Statistical Account* of the 1790s there was one school in every Lowland country parish. Even here however there were problems due to large sizes of parishes and to the growth in population. The average population of children between 5 and 12 years in the 22 parishes of Stirlingshire was about 250 and the average parish was three or four miles long by two or three miles wide.[10] The system obviously had to be considerably supplemented by private and charity schools. Indeed the private schools were so dominant in the 1820s and 30s that it would give better perspective to argue that *they* were being supplemented by the parish schools; at least if the term "supplementing" implies providing quantitative minority support.

The attainments of both types of schools in the Lowland rural areas in the early nineteenth century have received such high praise by historians as the following:

"Between them, the parochial schools and adventure schools of the Lowlands were able to maintain a rural society in which almost everyone seems to have been able to read and write from at least as early as the mid-

9. Smout, p. 466.
10. Smout, p. 453.

eighteenth century, despite all the subsequent social demographic and
economic changes before 1830." [11] It is not always realized that the credit
that is implied in such testimony must attach to the adventure schools *at
least as much* as to the parochial school. Because in Scotland as a whole
there were twice as many adventure school pupils as parochial pupils
(see Table 1) the above quotation certainly implies considerable praise
of the former. Considering that "almost everyone" could read and write
in the rural Lowlands, and since on the average there were two adventure school pupils for every parochial pupil in Scotland, the private (adventure) schools must have been remarkably efficient. What is even more
arresting is that they contained the children of the working class and that
these families were paying fees that typically covered the full cost of the
schooling.

The adventure schools are usually described in historical surveys as
containing less well-qualified teachers and having lower educational standards than the parish schools. Whatever the degree of validity in these
observations they must be received in the perspective of the previous
paragraph. Moreover by "better qualified" was often meant having more
ability to teach Latin and other classical languages. It also often meant
greater competence to teach religious doctrine. One's judgement as to
the relative qualifications must therefore be linked to a retrospective view
of the relevance or priority of these components of the curricula. It must
also be connected with an opinion of the contemporary wisdom of those
increasing numbers of families who were expressing preference for emphasis on the 3 Rs, a preference which could be more quickly satisfied in
the more flexible and competitive private system.

We must now return to the central question of testing the commonly
held view that the Industrial Revolution was accompanied by educational
setback. To do this we must compare conditions in the two non-industrial
areas, the Highlands and the rural Lowlands, with those in the Lowland
towns—especially in the new manufacturing, engineering and ship-
building areas.

11. Smout, p. 455.

The Lowland (Industrial) Towns

On one issue there seems to be a clear consensus: the parochial system did not or could not rise to the challenge of the massive population increases in the towns after 1760. Certainly if we judge it as an organization having the objective or aspiration of catering for universal provision of schooling in Scotland the parochial system was more clearly a failure in the industrial centres. It is this major fact, it seems, that underlies the historian's view that the Industrial Revolution towns in Scotland witnessed widespread educational failure. Before we can agree with this verdict, we must first check the experiences in the towns with the Scottish alternative that was such a fact of early nineteenth-century life—the adventure schools. On the average it seems from the previous description that these schools were by no means inefficient agencies in the rural Lowlands. What was the extent of their efficiency and provision in the towns?

From the 1818 Digest we discover that it was in the growing towns, especially where industrialism was establishing itself, that the growth and predominance of private (adventure) schools for the working-class was most striking. In the county of Lanark, including Glasgow, while there were in 1818 fifty-six parochial schools with 3,437 children, the private school figures were about six times bigger: 307 schools with 18,270 pupils.[12]

Pointing out that it was in the new industrial areas that the private schools were flourishing most, the *Edinburgh Review* of 1827 observed:

> It is there that education is the most necessary and *the most easy to be got;* and yet these are the very places which are most excluded from the benefit of the parochial system. This, indeed, is the necessary result of the growth of the people in places for which there is, by law, only one teacher appointed. Whenever we look either at the digest of 1818, or at the recent returns, for a view of the state of education in great towns, we almost invariably find a blank space where the parish schools ought to be mentioned. There are none or rather, the solitary

12. *The Edinburgh Review*, no. XCI, June 1827, p. 113.

one provided by law forms such an atom, as scarcely to be visible, or worth mentioning.[13] (our italics.)

This contemporary claim that education was not only most necessary but also "the most easy to be got" in the towns is the first serious challenge to the hypothesis of industrialism's educational failure that we are testing.

Whilst acknowledging the quantitative supremacy of the adventure schools in the towns, T. C. Smout argues that nevertheless the experience of the early nineteenth century shows a relative decline compared with the rural Lowlands. His evidence rests very strongly upon a work published by George Lewis in 1834 with the striking title: *Scotland, a half-educated nation.* Smout observes that with reference to Glasgow, which "had about two hundred educational establishments, almost all adventure schools or church schools," only a third of the *children of school age* attended them. The phrase in italics will be examined time and again in this book. It has already been scrutinized in Chapter 1 and will be the subject of further discussion in this chapter below. It will be remembered that the neglect of close attention to this phrase has caused considerable confusion in the literature. In the present case, Lewis (who is being quoted by Smout), took as a definition of "children of school age" those between five and fourteen. If we take this to mean five to fourteen inclusive this implies that 10 years of schooling was "necessary." The use of such a base, as we saw in Chapter 1, raises several questions. It is essential here to stress that whatever the base elected it should be applied consistently to all areas of comparison. Bearing this in mind it should be remembered that in his treatment of the rural Lowlands, Smout concluded that in the exigencies of the situation of rising population in the early nineteenth century "there was often little pressure brought by the local authority (in this case the Minister and the kirk-session) to keep children at school for more than about four years, there was little pressure to keep girls at school even for so long (or to send them at all, sometimes). . . ."[14] Thus the average figure for boys *and* girls could well have been less than four years. Suppose we say that the average duration was

13. *Ibid.*, p. 112.
14. Smout, p. 454.

three and one third years. If we now apply the same base of school age population, defined as five to fourteen (i.e. 10 years duration), then only one third of the "children of school age" were attending rural schools in the Lowlands. On this reasoning industrial Glasgow was no worse in school attendance than these areas—the best of the parochial school regions.

In his *The History of Scottish Education* (1969) James Scotland selects the evidence of the Argyll Commissioners for 1867 as being "more reliable" for the urban areas. In ten parishes in Glasgow the Commissioners found 48,391 children on school rolls and 40,933 in attendance, whereas the number of "children of school age," i.e. between 3 and 15, was 98,767. James Scotland concludes: "It appears then that just over two-fifths of the children between three and fifteen years went to any school." His uncritical acceptance of the school base of 3–15 years is surprising. There are a sizeable number of children between three and fifteen who were not at school in the 1970s. The same authority subsequently observes: "Few children could remain at school after the age of eleven. On the other hand, they might go very early for the Infant School Societies provided education for children as young as three. In the towns an average school life might be taken as five or six years, but many children had no more than one or two, *and at least half, as we have seen, did not go at all.*" (our italics). The Argyll Commission evidently used a school base (11 years) that was twice as large as the *de facto* school life (5–6 years). Applying the latter, and assuming that the typical school age group was 4 years to 8½ years, the statistic "Children of School Age" would have been very roughly about half the figure used by the Argyll Commission— i.e. about 50,000. Comparing this with 48,000 discovered to be on the roll, the number "without any schooling at all" is almost negligible. The remark at the end of the last quotation that at least half did not go at all is therefore erroneous. Interpreted consistently the figures indicate that the vast majority of children in the towns were schooled.

If, in the rural Lowlands, the average duration of schooling was between three and four years it would not be surprising to find many children leaving school round about eight years old. More typically, however, the problem was one of discontinuity. Attendance was bad especially in the harvest time. In the counties of Aberdeen, Banff and Moray, the average on the roll in winter was 50 per cent higher than in the summer.[15] Such observations should be kept in mind when assessing the temptations that existed for parents in the towns to allow their children to leave school early to work in factories.

A more direct test of the effect of the Industrial Revolution upon educational standards is provided in the measures of literacy obtained from surveys of Scottish factory workers. According to a report from the Factory Inquiry Commissioners in 1834,[16] 96 per cent out of a sample of 28,000 Scottish mill workers could read! This is all the more remarkable when it is remembered that today—over a century later—the ability to read in Britain is still not completely universal. Although the ability to write was not so impressive, over half of the mill-workers in 1834 (56 per cent) could do so. The Factory Commission Report of 1834 observed: "The returns from factories in the rural districts are quite as favourable as those from the towns, which is attributable to the parochial schools." Clearly there is no indication here that the rural areas had *better* facilities; only that they were being able to keep up with the industrial towns.

T. C. Smout's contention that "on the whole" the provision for elementary education deteriorated between 1780 and 1830 is based on the argument that this "was primarily due to the shift in the distribution of population away from a rural environment where knowledge of reading and writing was still universal and the parochial system still provided the major channel of education towards an urban environment where illiteracy or semi-literacy, was widespread and the public authorities chose to ignore the evil." [17]

This argument provokes four comments. First from our survey the parochial system did not always provide the major channel of education even in the rural areas. Second, there is a need to place the expression "widespread illiteracy or semi-literacy" into some perspective. From the evidence just quoted for instance the majority (i.e. over 50 per cent) of mill-workers *could* read and write. Third, the problem was not simply

15. Smout, p. 459.
16. *Parliamentary Papers* 1834, Vol. XX, p. 42.
17. Smout, p. 472.

that of a geographical redistribution of people; the more momentous event was the unprecedented growth of population. Full proof of Smout's argument requires the test of counterfactual conditions. Suppose the population had *not* been redistributed; suppose too that it had grown at the rates actually recorded. Smout's argument amounts to the proposition that under these conditions there would have been no deterioration of elementary education; that literacy would have been universal; and that the parochial system would have provided the major channel of education. One has only to couch the problem in these terms to throw considerable doubt on Smout's conclusions. The fact that the law allowed typically for one parochial school in each parish would have remained the main stumbling block for the development of the system even if the population had stayed in the rural areas. In the 1760s the parish schools were already over-crowded. Indeed some might argue that our way of putting the problem seems to reverse Smout's conclusion. Serious deterioration in education might well have been avoided by the growth of the towns where new opportunities for income earning enabled families to purchase education increasingly from the growing network of adventure schools which arose spontaneously to meet their demands.

The fourth comment relates to "foreign" immigration. Smout argues that in the towns: "Part of the trouble was the mass of Irish who came from a society that laid no premium on education. . . ."[18] This observation has implications for the "counterfactual conditional" problem just mentioned. If the Irish had moved to the rural areas instead of to the towns would there have been no deterioration in education at all? In any case, where the Irish were concerned we should strictly ask whether their migration to Scotland provided these particular individuals with somewhat better (albeit poor) educational conditions? If the answer is positive then, to this extent at least, the industrial revolution was not a negative influence for educational development.

We conclude that the belief that the Industrial Revolution was accompanied by educational decline is definitely not proven by the evidence that compares the industrial areas with the Scottish Highlands. Compari-

18. Smout, p. 470.

son with the Scottish Lowlands leaves more room for discussion. Whilst respecting in particular the recent interesting analysis of T. C. Smout, this chapter has explained some fairly substantial difference in the balance of interpretation. The verdict here is that the historical case is not proven even in this instance and that further investigation would be helpful.

What now of the general influence of legislation in Scotland and what was its differential effect in comparison with England? Did Scotland ever really have a national system of education before 1871? Certain historians seem to have been responsible for encouraging vague impressions of substantial progressive early development of a Scottish "public system."[19] Legislation, however, is a many-sided activity. Primarily it can do one or more of four things in education: first, make it compulsory; second, provide partial and discriminate subsidies; third, make it "free" (full subsidy); fourth, organize it into a "nationalized" system. Modern writers who place Scotland in favourable contrast to England are sometimes too hasty in their reporting of the former's statutory coverage. Lawrence Stone, for instance, arguing explicitly that "the major driving force for popular education has been the direct intervention of the state to provide tax-supported free schools and to enforce legislation compelling parents to send the children to them,"[20] continues with the statement that among the countries which initiated these moves before the nineteenth century was Scotland, "which acted in 1646 and 1696." In contrast, the English state "was peculiarly slow to move. . . . Compulsion was not introduced until 1881 and non-payment until 1891." The facts are, however, that Scotland did not introduce compulsion and non-payment (free schooling) until about the same time as England did. Compulsion in Scotland came in 1872 and "free" schooling in 1891.[21] The main achievement of Scottish legislation in the first half of the nineteenth century was

19. D. W. Roberts, *An Outline of the Economic History of England* (1962), p. 200, observes: "In contrast with this appalling state, conditions in Scotland were greatly superior, due principally to the fact that an act had been passed there as early as 1694 requiring schools to be established in every parish." See also Trevelyan, *op. cit.*, p. 355, for an assertion that England "lagged far behind Scotland"; Curtis, *op. cit.*, ch. XIV.
20. Stone, *op. cit.*, p. 96.
21. Balfour, *op. cit.*, pp. 138–143.

to supply educational subsidies to the benefit of about one-third of the total school population (i.e. to that minority which happened to use parochial schools). Even this favoured section still had to contribute a significant part of the educational costs through school fees.

The belief that legislation in Scotland had much more substantial results is nevertheless widely held and has a long history. In Victorian times the influential authority of the social statistician Sir Robert Giffen set its seal upon the idea. In his inaugural address as President of the Royal Statistical Society in 1883 he stated:

> The children of the masses are, in fact, now (with the 1870 Forster legislation) obtaining a good education all round, while fifty years ago the masses had either no education at all or a comparatively poor one.
> . . . If Scotland has gained so much, what must it have been in England, where there was no national system fifty years ago at all?[22]

It should be noticed that with continuous growth of per capita income any society will normally be able to observe at any point that fifty years previously education was, to use Giffen's words, "a comparatively poor one." This will be true of societies with public or private systems of education. More important, however, we should next test Giffen's type of view by comparing official figures of English and Scottish schooling in the immediate post-Napoleonic period. The proportion of the total population in Scotland that was receiving schooling in 1818 was about one in 12 while in England it was about one in 14.[23] Henry Brougham told the House of Lords in 1835 that by that year, according to figures produced by government investigation into education in England sponsored by Lord Kerry, there was little difference between the two countries.[24] In view of the subsequent exposure of error in the English figures (in the direction of significant underestimation), the existence of any substantial quantitative difference between Scotland and England in the 1830s or 1820s seems questionable (see below, p. 103). Meanwhile, one broad

22. Sir Robert Giffen, *Economic Enquiries and Studies* (1890), p. 231.
23. P. P. 1819, IX (c.), 1450; see also Curtis, *op. cit.*, pp. 220–1.
24. Hansard, *Parliamentary Debates*, House of Lords, 21 May 1835.

similarity is clear: the majority of the Scottish schools, as in England, were unendowed and unsubsidized private establishments at which fees were being paid by large sections of the poor.

Interpreted in one way, Giffen's statement just concedes the possibility that there could have been equality in the quantity of education between the two countries; but only with the proviso that the English education must have been "a comparatively poor one." Judgement of the quality of education, however, is a much more complex task. Though further discussion of this must be deferred it may nevertheless be worth noting here that the Argyll Final Report on Scottish education in 1867 came to much the same conclusion about quantity and quality as had the "Newcastle Report" on England and Wales published in 1861.[25] In the year of the English Education Act of 1870, when comparative literacy statistics were just beginning to be made available, the proportion of Scottish males recorded as literate by the Registrars General was 90 per cent; that of England and Wales was 80 per cent.[26] Literacy, of course, measures only one dimension of the quality of education. It is clear at the same time that Scotland enjoyed some advantage on this score; nevertheless the superiority in this respect was marginal and not as substantial as Giffen's statement intimated. Moreover, to attribute even this lead to the Scottish legislation we need further arguments; for we have seen that the predominant number of Scottish children, in the large towns at least, received their schooling not from parochial schools but from competitive private fee-paying establishments. The question therefore arises: How far should the main credit for the superior progress in literacy be attributed not to the parochial schools but to the more widespread and more rapidly growing private schools?

Further arguments for the parochial schools are of course possible, but it is obvious that they require much more careful presentation and careful research. There is certainly an economic presumption that there would be a higher per capita educational expenditure in an aided system,

25. Balfour, *op. cit.*, p. 136. It should be pointed out, however, that English education had the beginnings of a "system" after 1833 when government subsidies began.
26. Stone, *op. cit.*, p. 120.

such as Scotland's, which obtained its educational subsidies from taxes raised on property values, than in one which, as in England after 1833, provided them from a general and regressive tax system dependent especially upon taxes on food and tobacco. It is also permissible to argue that the parochial schools set the tone and the example. This in turn could have built up a common "national ethos" in which high value was placed upon popular instruction. At the same time, however, it might be arguable that such a lead stemmed from the influence of the church or from "national character" and not in the first place from the legislation. It is not likely, moreover, that the "legislated" schools were always the main pace-setters; competition from the more numerous private establishments could well have had salutary effects upon the parochial establishments themselves, and it would be interesting to have further detailed studies on this point.

We conclude that writers seem to have accepted too readily the view that Scotland enjoyed substantially superior investment and progress in education compared with England, and the opinion that legislation was the most important agent in the former country and the most crucial missing link in the latter. We must of course probe much deeper into the facts of English education in England and Wales in the early nineteenth century to obtain a more precise conclusion.

8 · Education and the Industrial Revolution in England and Wales

In this chapter we shall attempt first to discover whether or not, in quantitative terms, the Industrial Revolution brought with it educational growth (a) in England and Wales as a whole and (b) in the industrial towns; next, to examine the facts of educational finance and estimate roughly the share of education in the national output in 1833; and finally to consider the special reasons why contemporaries believed that there was very serious underexpenditure on education.

National Statistics

In 1818 the report of the Select Parliamentary Committee to enquire into the Education of the Lower Orders illustrated growth in the demand for education in these words: [1]

> There is the most unquestionable evidence that the anxiety of the poor for education continues not only unabated but daily increasing; that it extends to every part of the country, and is to be found equally prevalent in those smaller towns and country districts, where no means of gratifying it are provided by the charitable efforts of the richer classes.

1. Third Report from the Select Committee on the Education of the Lower Order, 1818 (426) iv, 56.

The growing thirst for knowledge among poor families and indeed the degree to which education was competing with food as a claim upon family income were noted in the *Edinburgh Review* of February 1813:[2]

> Even around London, in a circle of fifty miles, which is far from the most instructed and virtuous part of the kingdom, there is hardly a village that has not something of a school; and not many children of either sex who are not taught, more or less, reading and writing. We have met with families in which, for weeks together, not an article of sustenance but potatoes had been used; yet for every child the hard-earned sum was provided to send them to school.

Most pieces of statistical evidence on education between 1800 and 1840 point to significant growth. The first attempted comprehensive official statistics on schooling came with Henry Brougham's Select Committee report in 1820.[3] This revealed that in 1818 about one in 14 or 15 of the population was being schooled. This considerable improvement since the beginning of the century was attributable partly to the energy of ecclesiastical groups, but more importantly, as we shall see, to the willingness of parents to pay fees, which indeed in most cases at this time covered the whole of the cost. In 1828 Brougham in his private capacity followed up this initial estimate with a 5 per cent sample survey of his own, using the same sources (the parochial clergy) as before. His findings indicated that the number of children in schools had doubled in ten years.[4] The natural increase in population over this time would of course mean that the per capita growth-rate of schooling was less than the total rate. The total population increase over this period, however, was only about one-fifth. Moreover the age-structure did not vary significantly.[5] Another

2. *Edinburgh Review*, xxi (1813) 216.
3. *Parliamentary Papers* 1820 (151) xii 341–349.
4. Speech in the House of Lords, 21 May 1835.
5. The population grew between 1821 and 1831 from 12 to 14 million. The age-structure was as follows:

   Age group 0–19:   1821   48.9%   1831   48.2%   1841   47.1%

The percentages for 1821 and 1841 are derived from the census figures. The 1831 percentage is taken from an estimate in James P. Huzel's "Malthus, The Poor Law, and

possibility which would qualify Brougham's findings is that the accuracy of local enumeration of schools could have improved in 1828 compared with 1818. Such an improvement, however, would have had to have been considerable to have accounted for *all* this appreciable growth. Among other items that seem consistent with significant educational growth is the observation that there was a noticeable surge in literacy rates after 1780.[6]

The Government began its programme of subsidies to education in 1833. It was something of a blind start, however, because it had no official figures of the over-all extent of schooling. The results of the survey of the whole of England, which it authorized under a motion by Lord Kerry in the same year, were not available until 1835. When the Kerry statistics did at last appear[7] they went quite a way in supporting Brougham's private estimate of the rate of growth. The numbers in schools had increased from 748,000 in 1818 to 1,294,000 in 1833 "without any interposition of the Government or public authorities."[8] It is interesting to notice how such a picture of the great spread of unendowed, fee-paying, private schooling for working families seems to have matched the Scottish experience.

The 1835 Kerry statistics have been widely reported in educational histories as unreliable. While some such works do not refer to the source of the criticism, others disclose it to be the Manchester Statistical Society.[9] What is rarely mentioned is that the complaint of this society against the Kerry statistics was that the true educational provision was significantly *under*estimated. Concerning the township of Manchester, at least, this criticism was indeed serious. According to the Manchester Statisti-

---

Population in Early Nineteenth-Century England," *Economic History Review*, 2nd ser. xxii (1969).

6. Stone, *op. cit.*, p. 98.

7. H. C. Paper 62, 1835 XLI–XLIII.

8. Brougham, House of Lords, 21 May 1835.

9. Curtis, *op. cit.*, p. 232 simply observes "it was well known that the statistics given in the report were unreliable"; Birchenough, *op. cit.*, pp. 71–2, merely states that it was the Manchester Statistical Society which "proved the date of the Kerry Parliamentary Return to be untrustworthy." Similarly Frank Smith, *A History of English Elementary Education* (1931), p. 151.

cal Society, which was one of the first bodies to undertake intensive local investigations, the total error made by the Kerry Report in this one
town alone amounted to an underestimate of 8,646 scholars—mainly day
scholars. This was a 27 per cent error when compared with the total figure of 32,166 day, evening and Sunday scholars.[10] The understatement
was much more serious when related to the population of day scholars.
There were omitted in the Kerry Report about half the day schools and
one-sixth of the Sunday schools. The underestimate of day scholars must
have been at least 33 per cent.

Manchester was no exception compared with other manufacturing
towns in the matter of official understatement.[11] The more the Kerry
figures are adjusted upwards for error the more impressive would the
growth-rate seem to be. For this to be fully accurate, however, we need
evidence that errors in the 1818 investigation were not equally big. If the
latter is demonstrated the more we need to revise our opinions of educational conditions in the earlier part of the Industrial Revolution and
to consider the possibility that quantitative equality with Scotland came
much earlier. Meanwhile even ignoring the underestimates of the 1833
returns, the findings revealed striking development. In the 1851 Census
(Special Report on Education) it was acknowledged that, in retrospect, a
"vast extension of Education" had been accomplished between 1818 and
1833. "The population had increased by nearly 24 per cent, while during
the same interval the number of Day scholars had increased by 89 per
cent."[12] The Census report concluded thus without taking into account
the underestimate of the Kerry returns which it acknowledged to be
about 10 per cent for the country as a whole. In all this development
moreover Sunday schools should not be forgotten. These played a very
special part in English education especially in the teaching of reading.

10. *Report of a Committee of the Manchester Statistical Society on the State of Education in the Borough of Manchester in 1834* (2nd ed. 1837), pp. 2–4. Manchester Borough contained nine townships of which Manchester town was the largest with about
70 per cent of the borough population. The school figures for Manchester town appear
on p. 43 of the Manchester Statistical Society Report for 1834.
11. See below pp. 114–115.
12. Census of Great Britain, 1851, Education, England and Wales, Report and Tables
(1854), p. xvii.

Their growth even exceeded that of the day schools. Indeed between 1818 and 1833 they increased by 225 per cent or over double the growth-rate of the day schools.[13]

Substantial expansion continued well into the 1860s. Between 1832–61 the growth in the number of day scholars (68 per cent) exceeded that of population (40 per cent). The membership of the Mechanics Institute rose from 7,000 in 1831 to 200,000 in 1860. There was other indirect evidence of educational and literacy achievement. Newspapers increased in circulation by 273 per cent; the number of letters sent by post increased by 600 per cent, and in addition cheap literature of all kinds was being purchased by the working classes in substantially increased quantities.

Education in the Industrial Revolution Towns

We have seen that the rising manufacturing and commercial towns of the Industrial Revolution in Scotland enjoyed above average growth. Was this experience shared by England and Wales? Here we have to rely mainly on the reports of the newly emerging local statistical societies, of which the Manchester Statistical Society was the earliest and most influential. The establishment dates of the 549 day schools and 83 evening schools reported by this body in 1834 suggest indeed a veritable school "explosion" in Manchester in the first four years of the 1830s. (see Table 1).

On first reflection this picture is modified when it is realized that the figures in the table refer only to school "births"; school "deaths" (not disclosed) would result in a qualified net growth figure. Yet most of the local statistical societies reported similar tables and it is difficult to believe they would persist with the practice if the "deaths" (closures) were substantial. Consider the report on Bristol wherein out of 479 known entries in 1840, 316 schools had been established since 1830. The Bristol Statistical Society commented:

> The great increase within the last 10 years cannot fail to be remarked, and as no less than 285 out of the 316 schools opened in this period are schools supported wholly by the payments of the children, it is a proof

13. *Ibid.*, Report.

Table 1. Schools in Manchester in 1834

	Total	*In or before 1820*	*Established*		*Not ascertained*
			1821–30	*1830–4*	
Day (95% of which supported by parental fees)	549	95	163	284	7
Evening (supported by payments of the scholar)	83	12	25	45	1

(Manchester Statistical Society Report on Manchester 1834 Table I p. 31)

that the business of the schoolmaster has not been made worse by the agitation and inquiry which the subject of education has of late years undergone.

It would have been curious if such statisticians did not check that the new schools were not largely replacing old ones closing down.

The "explosion" hypothesis receives some support from the 1851 Census Report. Referring (on p. XVII) to "public schools" the author of this part of the Census, Horace Mann, observed that the information collected "seems to testify to the existence of much modern zeal, and proves that within the past ten years a very considerable number of *new* schools must have been established or that old ones must have been enlarged." The term "public school" was a technical one. It referred to all those private (voluntary) schools that received any philanthropic or government aid whatever—however small. This category contained the bulk (two thirds) of the total school population.

It is in the early 1830s, that legislation might have begun to have some effect. The Factory Act of 1833, which is usually acknowledged to be the first one that was effectively policed, controlled the hours of textile workers of between 9 and 18 years. Children of between 9 and 13 years had to provide evidence that they had attended school part time in the previous week. No child was allowed to be employed who was 8 years old or under. There are five observations, however, that weaken the argument that this legislation was a substantial factor in the growth of day schools at this time. First, the legislation applied only to textile workers. Second, there is no evidence to suggest that before 1833 the number of children employees of 8 years and under was large.[14] Third, the evidence of part-time teaching that the 9 to 13 year olds had to produce related only to a schooling of "at least two hours per day in the preceding week."[15] Fourth, the educational clauses did not come into full operation until well after 1833. One authority dates their virtual commencement from 1836.[16] Fifth, towns that were not so dependent on textiles experienced similar rapid growth of schools in the 1830s to those towns that were. In Bristol, for instance, it was found that of the day and evening schools, apart from 33 schools whose establishment dates were not ascertained, 65 were established in or before 1820; 98 from 1820 to 1830 inclusive; and 316 from 1830 to 1840.

Another indication of educational growth given in the local statistical reports was the testimony of inter-generation differences. A detailed house-to-house survey of the Lancashire cotton and mining township of Pendleton in 1838[17] showed that the current generation was receiving more education than its predecessors: "not more than 2 to 3 per cent . . . of the juvenile population are at present left entirely destitute of instruction, whilst of the surviving adult population 8 per cent represent their education to have been totally neglected."[18] Similarly at Hull a survey of

14. In the textile town of Pendleton in 1838 37 out of 2,466 children under ten years (i.e. 1½ per cent) were found at work.
15. Curtis, *op. cit.*, p. 229.
16. Alfred A. Fry "Report of the Inspectors of Factories on the effects of the Educational Provisions of the Factories' Act," *Journal of the Statistical Society of London,* II (1839), p. 176; Smith, *op. cit.*, p. 143 quotes a witness to a select committee in 1834 who stated that in Manchester the educational classes were "a dead letter."
17. Pendleton is a borough of Salford. It was surveyed by the Manchester Statistical Society. The Report appears in *Jnl. Stat. Soc. London,* II (1839), 65–83.
18. *Ibid.,* p. 74. These figures at first sight conflict with the Society's report that in Manchester in 1834 one-third of children between 5 and 15 were not at school. The Society found in its Pendleton Report that most children left school at around the age of 10. At this rate the proportion without any schooling would be very much less than one-third in Manchester and could well have been 2.3 per cent as in Pendleton. The 1833 government return was also seriously misleading in its estimate of children "without

1839[19] showed that whereas out of 14,526 ascertained cases of adults 417 had never been at a day school (i.e. 2.8 per cent) only 47 out of 3,039 ascertained cases of minors between the ages of 15 and 21 had never been at school, a proportion of 1.5 per cent (the number of cases not ascertained was 759).

Growth figures of this sort are certainly not as dramatic as those of school increases. However, they at least conflict with the impressions of writers such as Trevelyan, the Hammonds and Altick, who believed (see ch. 1 pp. 4–5) that during the Industrial Revolution educational retrogression, or at best stagnation, prevailed especially in the industrial towns.

So far as the rural areas are concerned the report on Employment of Women and Children in Agriculture: Special Assistant Poor Law Commissioners Report in 1834, provides a general assessment. "Boys," it was reported, "begin to be regularly employed in farm work as early as 7 in some few instances, but generally at 9 or 10."[20] There was much interruption of schooling because of the demands of the planting and harvest seasons. Sometimes, "where a labourer has a large family, a farmer will be induced to take a child at the earliest possible age to relieve the father, and prevent his being driven to the poor house."[21] Clearly such evidence does not suggest that in general the position was better than in the towns.

Some further and possibly relevant pieces of evidence on comparative achievements in different areas come from the Registrar General's reports on literacy. In his first Annual Report of 1839 he observed that 88 per cent of the grooms in London were able to sign their names on marriage compared with the national average of 67 per cent. The report for the year 1845 contains comparative literacy attainments in the counties. The northern counties of Westmorland, Cumberland, Northumberland, Durham and Yorkshire had the highest rates.[22] Professor

---

schooling" since it also used a base of 5 to 15 years. This serious sort of ambiguity in nineteenth-century education statistics is examined in E. G. West, *Education and the State*, pp. 145–6 and in the Report of the Statistical Society of Bristol in *Jnl. Stat. Soc. London*, IV (1841), 252–3.

19. *Jnl. Stat. Soc. London*, IV (1841).
20. *Parliamentary Papers* 1843 (510) XII 28.
21. *Ibid.*
22. Seventh Annual Report of the Registrar General, P.P. 1846 (727) XIX, 245.

M. Hartwell observes generally that rates in the towns were regularly above those of rural areas.[23]

The Factory Commissioners of 1834 gave important testimony to this. The returns they collected on social conditions in factories included a special return on the education of employees. They showed that 86 per cent of factory workers could read (96 per cent in Scotland). The Commissioners observed: "It will be gratifying to the friends of education to find, from authentic documents, that so large a proportion of the working population in the towns and populous districts is able to read, *although we are unable to venture to hope for so favourable an account from the small villages and rural districts in England.*" (our italics.)[24]

The towns of course offered a much bigger variety of educational opportunities beyond formal schooling. This point has been well expressed by Frank Smith:

> Education is never synonymous with schooling; and the farther back we go the more important does this distinction become. In consequence, we can never measure the educational provision of the past by merely recording the numbers of schools and scholars; many children who never went to school got a sound education in other ways.[25]

In addition to some enlightened educational projects in the nineteenth-century factories[26] there was much stimulus from the new voluntary educational establishments, such as evening schools for young workers. Dr. James Kay told the government Select Committee of 1838:

> I think it would be found on inquiry that in the manufacturing towns in the north the number of classes of mutual evening schools instruction existing, and the number of persons attending schools of mechanics institutions, above the age of 13, are very much greater than in towns in any other part of the country.[27]

23. M. Hartwell, *The Industrial Revolution*, p. 238.
24. *Parliamentary Papers*, 1834 vol. xx, p. 42.
25. Smith, *op. cit.*, p. 36.
26. See Michael Sanderson "Education and the Factory in Industrial Lancashire, 1780–1840" *Econ. Hist. Rev.* 2nd ser XX (1967).
27. *Report of the Select Committee on Education of the Poorer Classes* H. C. Paper 589 183708 VII (hereafter "The 1838 Select Committee Report").

The reliance upon Sunday schools was particularly heavy; in Manchester, Kay observed: "The Report of the Statistical Society shows that education provided for the poorer classes in Sunday schools is considerably more extensive than in the day schools."[28]

When we turn to particular local reports of the statistical societies we find one which, as it stands, does not particularly favour the towns. This is the report by the Manchester Statistical Society on the county of Rutland. The following table shows a bigger proportion of schooling compared with the Lancashire towns.[29]

Table 2.

	Rutland in 1838	Liverpool in 1835–6	Manchester and Salford in 1834–5	York in 1836	Hull in 1839
Proportion of the total population of day and evening scholars between 5 and 15 years of age	12.13%	10.67%	8.51%	14.22%	13.12%

First, it must be noted that the Rutland figures, published in 1839, were based on an estimated population in 1838 of 20,000. The Census of 1841 reported a population of 21,340 which compares with 19,385 in 1831. The 1838 figure therefore must have been nearer 21,000 and this reduces the Rutland percentage of scholars to about 11.5. Next, even at their face value these figures still do not suggest the very stark contrast between educational provision in the growing towns of the Industrial

28. *Ibid.*, para. 67. In the Manchester Statistical Society's investigations Manchester was found to be superior to York and Rutland in the number and efficiency of the Sunday schools.
29. Taken from the "Manchester Statistical Society's Report on Hull" reproduced in *Jnl. Stat. Soc. London*, IV (1841) 158, 159.

Revolution and that of other areas such as is suggested in the writings of Trevelyan, Altick and the Hammonds.

Rutland had many more endowed and charity schools. Comparing the proportion of the population educated in the different areas out of the charitable funds and endowments, it was found that it was 2.45 per cent of the population in Manchester and 8.26 per cent in Rutland. If we are studying the contribution of the new industry to the growth of education we should compare conditions in the same area over time. We have already seen evidence of inter-generation improvements in the towns, as well as evidence suggesting the very rapid growth of schools in Manchester and Bristol especially in the 1830s, growth that was not much aided by endowments or charity. Unfortunately we do not have comparative indications of the reduction of the numbers entirely destitute of schooling in Rutland. Figures showing the dates of establishment of schools in Rutland[30] do not suggest the same pace of growth as in Manchester or Bristol. Moreover, the statistical superiority of Rutland was in terms of day schools. Manchester was found to have substantially more and better Sunday schools than average.[31] Furthermore, we must remember that over one-sixth of the family heads in Manchester were Irish. In such cases, measures of net growth in education from 1800 should be considered in the context of the educational conditions in the country of origin.[32]

Among the intensive local case histories *Education and Society in Nineteenth-Century Nottingham* by David Wardle[33] gives the impression that education in that town was below average. Writing of conditions in the mid-nineteenth century he concludes (p. 61):

30. "Report of the Manchester Statistical Society on the State of Education in Rutland," reproduced in *Jnl. Stat. Soc. London,* II (1839) Table II, p. 307.

31. In 1834 as many as 22,000 minors were taught writing in the evenings in Manchester Sunday schools during the week. Manchester Statistical Society Report on Manchester 1834, Table VI, p. 39.

32. Dr. Kay told the 1838 Select Committee that it was not immediately practicable to impose on manufacturers the rule that there should be no employment without some education, "on account of the immigration of the Irish, which the constant development of the cotton manufacture has stimulated, and by which it has been fed." (para. 95).

33. D. Wardle, *Education and Society in Nineteenth-Century Nottingham,* C.U.P., 1971.

On the average, therefore, children attended public-elementary schools for a school life of between one and two years, which probably finished by the time they were nine years old. . . .

The Newcastle Report of 1861 found that on average the children of the working class in 1858–9 were given an education of 5.7 years. Were conditions in Nottingham really as bad as Wardle's conclusion suggests? If so was Nottingham typical or exceptional? It is easy to misinterpret. Wardle refers to one or two years at *public* elementary schools. As he himself explains in a later chapter (p. 166) the private dame and common schools in the first half of the nineteenth century "were much the most numerous form of educational agency." In 1851 there were about 75 of them in the town and surrounding poor law districts.

Wardle's mention of a school duration of one or two years is based on inspectors' reports in the *public* sector. It relates moreover to a given school. Obviously many children would have experienced more than one school—especially in view of the wide choice; nearly all of them, public and private, charged fees. In 1750 the Nottingham population was about 10,000; a hundred years later it was 58,000. The large amount of immigration involved must have meant that many children had received schooling outside Nottingham or from other schools within it. Furthermore the public elementary schools to which Wardle refers were the main centres of the monitorial system.[34] This system was increasingly disliked by parents. The low duration of attendance at this one school may have reflected this. It was, of course, in the self-interest of inspectors to claim that inspected schools were the most efficient. Wardle seems to have accepted their observations too uncritically. In his general text book *English Popular Education 1780–1970* (C.U.P., 1970) where he refers (p. 65) to general conditions in England (as distinct from the particular circumstances of Nottingham), he makes the broad statement that inspectors were agreed that working-class children attended school on the

34. Under the monitorial system, teachers selected the most competent senior students as "monitors." They were then made responsible for the teaching of small groups of pupils, the teacher meanwhile acting as supervisor, examiner, and disciplinarian (Wardle, 1970, p. 86).

Table 3. Previous Schooling of Students in a Class of a Liverpool School in 1859.[*]

No.	Age	Occupation of Parent	Years in This School	Different Schools Previously Attended
1	13	Teacher	2	3 months National School Ireland
2	8	Sailor	2	No School
3	15	Clerk	$\frac{1}{6}$	4 private Schools for 6 years.
4	6	Teacher	2	No School
5	15	Painter	$\frac{3}{4}$	Public school, 4 years; private 3 years.
6	14	Paper Agent	$\frac{5}{6}$	Public school 3 years private 2 years
7	8	Sailmaker	$\frac{1}{2}$	4 schools, private.
8	10	(Orphan)	$1\frac{3}{6}$	4 schools; 2 public 2 private
9	13	Paper Agent	$\frac{3}{4}$	3 private schools for $6\frac{1}{2}$ years
10	13	Coalheaver	2	1 private school for 4 years
11	12	Tailor	$1\frac{3}{4}$	4 schools; 1 public 3 private
12	11	Cabdriver	$1\frac{3}{4}$	6 schools; 3 public 3 private
13	12	Sailor	$\frac{1}{6}$	4 schools; 1 public 3 private
14	10	Paper Agent	1	2 private schools for $3\frac{1}{2}$ years
15	13	Keeper of Ale Vaults	$\frac{1}{3}$	2 public; 1 private; $3\frac{1}{4}$ years
16	13	Labourer	$\frac{3}{4}$	7 different; all private
17	12	Barber	$\frac{3}{4}$	4 years at 5 different private schools
18	12	Cabdriver	$1\frac{3}{4}$	4 years at 7 private schools
19	10	Timekeeper	1	$3\frac{1}{4}$ years at 4 private schools
20	13	Baker	$\frac{1}{2}$	7 different schools; 2 years private, $3\frac{1}{4}$ public
21	13	Sailor	$1\frac{1}{4}$	6 schools; 2 public—1 year 4 private—3 years
22	14	Coalheaver	$1\frac{1}{2}$	3 schools; public 1 year, 2 private 4 years.

[*] From Table IX of the Report of D. R. Fearon in the *Return confined to the Municipal Boroughs of Birmingham, Leeds, Liverpool and Manchester, of all schools for the Poorer Classes of Children.* H. C. No. 91, 1870, page 159.

average for between one and two years. This suggests that Nottingham was not exceptional. This general statement however again conflicts with the findings of a 5.7 year schooling average in the Newcastle Report and the belief of Horace Mann that 4 years was typical.[35] Wardle however gives no explanation of the conflict. The discussion above would seem to resolve the problem. Finally we should note that when the first Nottingham School Board was elected in 1870 to "fill the gaps" it found a deficiency of only just over 2 per cent (30 school places out of a necessary 13,112), "if certain slightly sub-standard schools were improved."[36]

The previous points are graphically illustrated in Table 3. It is based on Inspector Fearon's Report on Manchester and Liverpool in 1869. From the fourth column we calculate the average number of years' attendance in this class of students (average age 12 years) to be just over one. A glance at the fifth column, however, shows the big variety of schools experienced by the same students previous to attendance at this institution. After adding the time spent at these earlier schools we arrive at an average schooling of five years. Inspectors were inclined to emphasize the type of information in the 4th column exclusively. The main reason why the inspector included the extra information (of column 5) in this instance was to draw attention to the "excessive" number of school changes and to demonstrate the adverse effect of it on student performance.

The Share of Education in Nineteenth-Century National Income

The fact that growth in privately purchased education in general has been demonstrated to the above extent does not of course demonstrate that public finance was not seriously required. Educational assistance to families with below-average incomes may well be indicated even if average families do not need it. But we have not even established that typical family education expenditure was optimum. Indeed we cannot assess this until we have some notion as to the "correct" share of resources that "should

35. Horace Mann, "National Education," *Transactions of the National Association for the Promotion of Social Science,* British Meeting 1869.
36. David Wardle, *op. cit.,* p. 86.

have" been employed. Such a figure has never, so far as is known, been derived or suggested. For the moment the best we can do is to attempt a rough estimate of the share of school education in the national income of the 1830s. Aggregate expenditure for one year, 1833, will be calculated and then related to national income estimates for the period. Since some degree of error will apply to each of the three relevant variables— aggregate school population, average fee, and length of the school year— the most suitable approach is to provide a range of estimates based on a corresponding range of assumptions.

The aggregate school population (day and infant schools) according to the 1833 government (Kerry) return was 1,276,947.[37] The local statistical societies, however, reported serious underestimates when they made their own checks shortly afterwards. The Manchester Statistical Society reported between a third and a half underestimate of day scholars. For the borough of Salford in 1835[38] it found that the Kerry returns had under-reported by 82 day schools and 3,440 day scholars, which amounted roughly to an underestimate of 50 per cent. A report on the town of Bury[39] for the same year also found serious underestimate in the Kerry figures. In Hulme,[40] containing a population of 9,609, the government return under-reported about one-third of schools and scholars (14 schools and 864 scholars). In Liverpool the omissions amounted to as many as 15,500 scholars, "and though some few duplicate returns were made, there seems to be no doubt but that the omissions largely preponderated."[41] A Birmingham report in 1838 showed a 50 per cent deficiency in the 1833 returns.[42]

We must decide, therefore, what degree of error to apply to the aggregate national figure in Lord Kerry's parliamentary returns. The 1851

37. H. C. Paper 62, 1835, XLI–XLIII.
38. *Report of the Manchester Statistical Society on the State of Education in the Borough of Salford in 1835* (1836), p. 5.
39. *Report of the Manchester Statistical Society on the State of Education in Bury in 1835* (1836).
40. Manchester Statistical Society Report on Manchester 1834, p. 4.
41. Census of Gt. Britain 1851, England and Wales, Education Report (1854), p. xvii.
42. *Report on the State of Education in Birmingham by the Birmingham Statistical Society,* reproduced in *Jnl. Stat. Soc. London,* III (1840) 27. The population increase between 1833 and 1838 would account for a small part of the difference.

Census report on education stated (without explanation) that for the whole country these returns were probably deficient by about 10 per cent. This observation seems to relate to total schooling, that is to the combined figure of day schools and Sunday schools. The underestimate of day schools was found by the local statistical societies to be a much bigger proportion than that of Sunday schools. We conclude that the national underestimate for day schools was probably at least 20 per cent and could have been as much as 33⅓ per cent. On the 20 per cent adjustment the day school population figure for England and Wales in 1833 would have been 1,596,184; on the 33⅓ per cent adjustment it would have been 1,915,420.[43]

The biggest part of the cost of day schooling in this period was covered neither by the church nor by philanthropy, but from direct payments (fees) from working families. The Bristol Statistical Society in 1841 found that a very big majority of its schools and scholars received no support whatsoever except from the parents. To these 446 schools the parents were paying £32,000 annually. In the 42 schools "assisted by subscription" parents were annually paying £2,500. Only 24 schools were free and endowed. The Bristol Statistical Society reported: "in the city of Bristol alone, with a population not exceeding 12,000 persons, a much larger sum is annually paid (by parents) for the purposes of education, than is contributed by the State towards the instruction of the five or six millions

43. The facts and estimates in this paragraph were first presented in an article in the *Econ. History Review*, April 1970. In a subsequent comment upon them, Gillian Sutherland has argued that the margin of error would have been less than the one-third reported for Manchester because the likelihood of error would have been less for the country districts. This is an *a priori* argument, as she admits; it is difficult to accept it however without further explanation. Moreover the Manchester Statistical Society reported a deficiency of between a half and one-third for Manchester and a half for Birmingham and Salford. Gillian Sutherland indicates (in the same comment) a preference for the 1851 Census Report's view that the national underestimate was 10 per cent. She refers to this however as an underestimate of *day* schools whilst, as is pointed out here, the 10 per cent seems to relate to total schooling—including Sunday schooling. The Kerry underestimate of day schooling was much greater than that for Sunday schools according to the Statistical Societies. It is day schooling that we are interested in here. Finally, even if we accept the 10 per cent figure it would not seriously upset the subsequent argument of this chapter. See Gillian Sutherland, *Elementary Education in the Nineteenth Century*, The Historical Association, London, 1971, p. 11.

of children in the United Kingdom."[44] (Even as late as 1869 parental payments in such towns as Leeds totalled half as much again as government grants.)

According to the Manchester Statistical Society 80 per cent of the school-children's education in Manchester was paid for entirely by parental fees.

Table 4. Statement of the Mode in Which Schools
(in Manchester in 1834) Are Supported.

		No. of Schools	Total No. of Scholars
Free		13	2,170
Not Free	1 in which part of the expense is borne by the scholars	15	2,106
	2 in which the whole expense is borne by the scholars	607	15,843
	Totals	635	20,119

Manchester Statistical Society Report on Manchester 1834, Table II

The government return for 1833 showed that 73 per cent of the day scholars paid fees; in 58 per cent of cases the parental fees covered the entire cost.[45] (See Table 5.)

The best method of approach to our problem of computing aggregate expenditure is to multiply the fees by the number of scholar-attendances. To this figure we can add estimates for the "free" schooling. The school fees in the common day schools in Manchester varied from 3d to 1s 6d

44. "Statistics of Education in Bristol" by a Committee of the Statistical Society of Bristol, *Jnl. Stat. Soc. London,* IV (1841), 255. The government's annual subsidy to education in England and Wales in 1841 was £30,000.
45. There has been much erroneous reporting on this subject. Thus the 1851 Census (Education Report) observed: "Up to this period (1833) the whole of what had been accomplished in the work of popular education was the fruit of private liberality incited mainly by religious zeal" (p. xvii). Similarly Curtis *op. cit.,* p. 224 gives the impression that "philanthropy" was the chief educational support prior to 1833. Clearly private purchase by working-class families was the main agency.

Table 5. Statistics of School Population and
School Finance Government Return 1833

Maintenance of schools	Infant Schools Scholars	Percentage Share of Total	Daily Schools Scholars	Percentage Share of Total
Endowment (no fees-free)	1,450	2%	152,314	13%
Subscription (no fees-free)	13,081	12%	165,436	14%
Payments (entirely) from scholars (fees)	40,721	46%	691,728	58%
Subscription & payments from scholars (fees)	33,753	38%	178,464	15%
Totals	89,005		1,187,942	

Summary of Education Returns, England and Wales 1833, H. C. Paper 62 (1835), Percentage columns added.

per week. The average weekly fee at common schools for boys was 8½d and for girls 10¼d; the average at Dame schools was 4d.[46] In the "superior" private schools, which contained about 3,000 or 15 per cent of the pupils, the average weekly payment could have been about two shillings.[47] There are grounds for believing that these figures were reasonably representative of the whole country.[48] Assuming that entirely "free"

46. "Manchester Statistical Society Report on Manchester 1834," Table III, p. 33. Unweighted averages; weighted averages are similar, 8.2d, 10.3d and 4d respectively.
47. The report of the Manchester Statistical Society on education in Salford in 1835 reported that the terms of the superior private schools varied from 10s 6d to £5 5s per quarter.
48. In the Manchester Statistical Society's report on the county of Rutland in 1838 the fees were about 1d less. The Birmingham Statistical Society's report for 1838 showed the same level of charges as Manchester. Figures reported by the Statistical Society of London for 1837 (see *Jnl. Stat. Soc. London*, Dec. 1838) show higher charges for three Westminster Parishes.

	Dame	Common Day	Middling	
			Boys	Girls
Average weekly fee	6d	10¼d	1s 3d	1s 0d

Superior schools charged an average of £1 10s per quarter or 1s 6d per week.

(endowed and subscription) schools gave an education which was worth at least as much as the average fee-paying establishments, and remembering that of the fee-payers 21 per cent had a schooling that was privately subsidized from other sources, we shall suppose that the average weekly cost throughout the country was in the middle of the above fee quotations at 9d per week.[49]

The next variable to consider is the length of the school year. On our reading of the evidence it is most doubtful that the number of weeks in the year when schools were officially closed for holidays would have been bigger than today. In view of the need to keep up their earnings many proprietors had every incentive to keep open for as long as possible. Let us assume that the average working time was 42 weeks in the year. The next problem is to adjust for absences. Although the 1833 returns are not helpful in this respect the 1851 Census report found that the number of children attending on any particular day in private schools which were dependent entirely on fees was 91 per cent of the school roll and in public schools (i.e. schools receiving any subsidy from *any* source) the number in attendance was 79 per cent.[50] We shall assume 80 per cent attendance—roughly the lower of these estimates for 1851. Such a figure is reasonably consistent with the 1838 report on Pendleton which classified one-third of the students as "irregular." Defining the "irregular" group in Pendleton as attending on average for only one-half of the school weeks (i.e. 21 weeks or 105 days) the average attendance for the whole school population would be about 80 per cent.[51]

49. Several of the free schools of course gave an education of an economic value considerably in excess of 9d per week. The Manchester Free Grammar School, for instance, educated 200 boys and was supported by an income of £4,000 per annum. Chetham's Hospital, or Blue Coat school, with 80 boarders, and several other generously endowed schools, similarly provided an education worth much more than 9d.
50. 1851 Census (Education Report) pp. XXX–XXXXI. This does not support Gillian Sutherland's guess (*op. cit.*, p. 19) that attendance at uninspected schools was lower.
51. The Report for Hull in 1838 showed that only one-fifth of the scholars were irregular. Some idea about average attendance can be obtained from the Manchester Statistical Society's estimate that common school teachers earned between 16s and 17s a week and that on average they had 32 pupils on their books and the typical fee was 9d per week. Misleading impressions about attendance are given in some school reports which complained that they could not keep some scholars for more than six months or

At this rate out of the 42 weeks of available day schooling the average scholar would attend for 34 weeks. The average weekly cost of 9d can now be converted into an annual cost per pupil of £1 5s 6d.[52] Our lowest estimate of scholars in 1833 derived from the Kerry returns was 1,596,184, say 1,600,000. This would mean that resources devoted to day schooling would have been of the value of approximately £2,040,000. Using our higher estimate of 1,915,420 (say 1,900,000) scholars in 1833 the aggregate educational value for the year would have been £2,422,500.

Any serious estimate of total educational resources used in 1833 must take some account of important nineteenth-century institutions, other than day schools, for the education of children. Probably the most important was the Sunday school. There were roughly the same number of scholars in Sunday schools as in day schools (after correcting for errors in the 1833 return). Nearly all the Sunday schools taught reading and a large number taught writing. The Kerry return described these institutions as being financed primarily by voluntary subscriptions.[53] Assuming we can regard attendance at these schools on Sundays as the equivalent of one day's attendance at a day school, then our estimate of aggregate resources devoted to schooling should be increased by one-fifth.[54] This would increase our valuation of total resources devoted to schooling from £2.42 million to £2.9 million and our lowest estimate from £2.04 million to £2.45 million.

In addition, in some areas there seems to have been considerable educational provision for young workers between 10 and 15 years old in factories. Dr. M. Sanderson observes that down to 1833 there were signs of "considerable advance in the direct participation of the factory owner in education."[55] He gives examples of small "factory colonies" in "obscure

---

50. Many scholars could well have transferred to other establishments so that their yearly school attendance could have been compensated.

52. This estimate would seem to be rather on the low side in the light of the Bristol Statistical Society's conclusion (see above p. 115) that parents were contributing £34,000 for schooling in Bristol with a total population of not more than 120,000 and a school population which we estimate to have been between 15,000 and 18,000.

53. H.C. 62, 1835, XLI–XLIII.

54. The nineteenth-century Sunday School Movement has no substantial counterpart today.

55. Sanderson, *op. cit.*, p. 267.

fell districts" where "paternalistic" mill proprietors were establishing schools in or close to the factories.[56] Examples are given by Sanderson of education-minded firms in Preston, Rochdale, Horwich, Bolton, Oldham, Didsbury, Caton and Galgate. In Bury, for instance, a firm with 23 apprentices had a schoolmaster "whose sole occupation was to instruct the children in reading during working hours." The addition of such activity to our estimates of annual total educational resources in 1833 (which so far ranges from £2.45 million to £2.9 million) presents the most difficult problem since we have no means of measuring it accurately. It would not seem unreasonable to us, however, to reach a tentative conclusion that total resources were just above or just below £3 million.

The gross national income of Great Britain in 1831 has been estimated at £340 million.[57] By 1833 it was probably £362 million.[58] To obtain the figure for England and Wales we have to subtract the share of Scotland. If we do this on a pro rata population basis we arrive at £310 million. Comparing this with our estimate of around £3 million on lower education, it seems clear that the latter accounted for not much more or less than 1 per cent of net national income.[59]

Great caution is obviously needed in comparing such early national income estimates with those of the twentieth century. Nevertheless, it

56. The extent to which such activity was "philanthropic" is debatable. Dr. Sanderson argues that this pattern of education "was an ideal way of exerting the social control of the firm over its workers and of raising up young labourers in obedience if not in scientific skill." Such "paternalism," Prof. Gary Becker has shown (*Human Capital,* Chicago 1964) "may simply be a way of investing in the health and welfare of employees in underdeveloped countries." Prof. Becker demonstrates that there are bigger incentives for firms to make educational investments in their employees the more specific is their productivity to the particular firm and the bigger its monopoly power. Sanderson's one pioneering factory settlement in "an obscure fell district" could well illustrate this case. Where the employees also profited from such educational investment we have instances of what are called reciprocal externalities which the private market internalizes.
57. B. R. Mitchell and Phyllis Deane, *Abstract of British Historial Statistics* (Cambridge 1962), p. 366.
58. Mitchell's and Deane's national income estimate for 1841 is £452 million. We have derived the 1833 figure on the assumption of a straight line increase between 1831 and 1841.
59. We have no exact figure for net national income in 1833; but clearly it would have been less than the gross national income of £310 million.

is interesting to observe that between 1920 and 1945 the share of day schooling (primary and secondary) in the United Kingdom was also around 1 per cent of the UK net national income.[60] The share for 1965 had increased to 2 per cent. If we take the category of children below 11 years then the 1833 share of the national income was about 0.8 per cent.[61] This was a higher share than in most years of the twentieth century. The following table summarizes the main results.

Table 6. Percentage of Net National Income Spent
on Day Schooling 1833–1965

	1833	1920	1965
Children all ages	1.00% (approx)	0.70%	2.00%
Children below 11 years	0.80% ''	0.58%	0.86%

It is this type of evidence that has relevance for any attempted assessments of nineteenth-century educational "underinvestment." Such evidence is similarly significant with respect to questions about the probability that governments will, or can, redirect and expand resources in the direction of objectives postulated in welfare economics. By 1850 government subsidies to private schooling had increased considerably although on average they still contributed much less than a third of the total school costs. In 1870 Forster told Parliament that there was a three-way split into parental fees, voluntary contributions and government grant. Thus considerable self-help continued. The subsidies moreover came from a regressive tax revenue to which all the working classes contributed. It is a moot point what would have happened had these taxes been lowered and no public subsidy to education given. The *differential*

60. John Vaizey and John Sheenan, *Resources of Education* (1967), Tables IX and X. The figures we have extracted relate exclusively to primary and secondary education, i.e. they exclude such things as meals and milk and inspection. They indicate approximate rates of 0.7 per cent for 1920, 1 per cent for 1945 and up to 1.25 per cent in the intervening years.
61. We base this estimate on the report of the student ages in the Pendleton Report for 1838.

effect of the legislation strictly can only be determined if we knew the results of such "counterfactual conditional" circumstances. We must next attempt to resume the quantitative results of the mixed public/private, or subsidized school era down to 1870 to place in perspective the need for and the consequences of, the most famous of all the interventions, the Forster Act of 1870.

9 · Schooling in England and Wales, 1850–70

The 1851 Census [1]

A full census of schooling for England and Wales was made in 1851. It showed that there were 2,144,378 children attending day schools out of a total population of adults and children of about 18 million, a proportion of 1 in 8.36.

We saw in Chapter 3 that Mann believed the average duration of schooling was about 5 years. Suppose there are 100 individuals in each of the age groups 0–4 years; 5–9 years; and 10–14 years, and this population pattern of 300 individuals remains constant every year. Assume every person receives 5 years schooling by the time he is 15 years old but one half of the population receives it between 5 and 9 years and the other half between 10 and 14 years. Then a census for one year would report that 50 per cent of the 5–9 years old population were scholars and 50 per cent of the 10–14 years old. In his interesting study of the 1851 census published in 1972, B. I. Coleman reports that in London 56 per cent of the 5–9 year olds, 46.3 per cent of the 10–14 year olds, and 8.6 per cent of the 0–4 year olds were scholars.[2] Coleman analyses the 1851 census

1. W. P. McCann, "Elementary Education in England and Wales on the Eve of the 1870 Education Act," *Journal of Education Administration and History,* June 1971.
2. B. I. Coleman, "The Incidence of Education in Mid-Century," *Nineteenth Century Essays in the Use of Quantitative Methods for the Study of Social Data,* ed. E. A. Wrigley C.U.P., 1972.

which was the first in which scholars were listed in the occupational returns. Clearly they are potentially consistent with Mann's findings. Coleman, however, urges more information on the precise variance of schooling between social groups. To illustrate he compares the London figures (just quoted) with those relating to one of the very poorest parts of the city, Bethnal Green. He found that the scholars were here 4.7 per cent, 50.4 per cent, and 33.9 per cent for the three respective male age groups.

Suppose, in our model, it was not given that *everybody* had a schooling and that this was the unknown factor we had to solve for. Assume that the census reports 50 per cent of the 5–9 year, and 50 per cent of the 10–14 year groups, to be scholars. At one extreme this information is consistent with only one in two having a schooling; but it is 10 years', not 5 years', duration. Coleman's research would seem firmly to dispose of such a possibility. Out of a total of 262 males between 4–14 years in one of the poorest parts of London (Bethnal Green) 107 were scholars. Obviously neither of the extreme results of our model apply. Some had 4 years', some 5 years', and some 6 years' schooling; but typically it was around 5 years'. Coleman's findings also indicate a strong rate of growth. The 1861 census showed, for Coleman's selected county (Warwickshire), that the percentage of male groups 5–9 years and 10–14 years reported as scholars had increased to 69.1 per cent and 40.8 per cent respectively. These new figures seem to offer strong support for the findings of the Newcastle Commission—to which we turn next.

The Newcastle Commission Evidence

After the 1851 census information came the mammoth report of the Newcastle Commission on Popular Education. This body was set up in 1858 and included the economist Nassau Senior; it reported in 1861. Its investigation deserves serious consideration because it was the first to be directed entirely and purposefully to national education. Moreover it showed many improvements in statistical method; it combined an assessment of aggregated statistics with a cross-check of intensive sample examinations from selected areas. The first branch of the Commissioners' enquiry, which referred to the whole of England and Wales, was concerned with statistics obtained through the religious societies connected with education and through public departments. The second branch of their enquiry consisted of reports from specimen areas from the Assistant Commissioners. They included the following:

> The result of the two branches of the inquiry has been, first that statistical information respecting the public week-day schools throughout England and Wales has been collected which may be regarded as approximately correct and complete: and secondly, that statistical details have been obtained from schools of all kinds in the specimen districts, which are not only exhaustive, so far as the districts are concerned, but which furnish proportions and averages which may be considered as representative of the rest of the country in relation to many subjects on which the statistics obtained through the societies and departments afforded no information.[3]

The specimen districts contained one-eighth of the whole population. The Assistant Commissioners' intensive surveys elicited the details of the non-inspected (i.e. non-subsidized) schools and their proportion to the inspected (i.e. subsidized) schools. Assuming this proportion to hold good for the whole country, the Commissioners made the necessary addition to the total number of inspected schools in the country, figures for which were, of course, centrally available. The result at which they arrived, and which referred to 1858, was that in the country as a whole there were 2,535,462 scholars in day schools. This figure seems quite compatible with the 1851 census which showed that the two million mark had already been passed. The next question was how many children did not receive a schooling. The Commission found that such general evidence as existed indicated that the bulk of the children who attended elementary schools had their names on the books of some school from six to ten years of age though a considerable number went before six and many remained until twelve. In order to calculate the number of children who ought to have been at school at a given time, the Commissioners assumed that the average period of attendance did not exceed six years.

3. Education Commission, Report of the Commissioners appointed to enquire into The State of Popular Education in England, Vol. 1, 1861, p. 553.

With this assumption they maintained that one-half of the total number of children between 3 years and 15 years should have been at school. This figure, obtainable from the Registrar General, was 2,655,767. Since the number actually on the books of all schools was 2,535,462 the shortfall was only 120,305. Much of this deficiency was accounted for by children who had bodily and mental infirmities, and also by children educated at home. Moreover, the Commissioners' information from the specimen districts showed that the actual average duration at school was in fact 5.7 years.[4] If this had been assumed in their general calculations instead of 6 years, the deficiency would have been almost negligible. In other words the figures indicated that nearly all the children were having some schooling.

Before we examine Forster's separate estimates of school deficiency in 1870, a word of precaution about statistical sources is necessary. By the 1860s a vigorous government Department of Education was in existence and there was an increasing tendency for ministers to rely upon it for their facts. Usually the basic information came from the Department's own Inspectors. We should now note that the modern "economics of bureaucracy" gives many clear warnings about the potentially self-serving nature of such data.[5] A brief digression on this subject should be helpful.

The theory focuses upon the fact that promotion and security prospects of senior public officials are linked with the rate of their bureau's growth. Mature bureaus enjoy an "all or nothing" bargaining advantage over their sponsor—the Government and/or Treasury. The central proposition to be tested is that the *primary* aim of the senior officers in bureaus is to maximize not public welfare but simply the size of the bureau's budget. This is not to say that high officials are consciously or cynically indifferent to what they believe to be the widest public good. The theory acknowledges that these individuals will have or can have a variety of motives. These can include a desire for public reputation as well as for private pecuniary gain (in all its manifestations including job

4. *Parliamentary Papers* 1861 xxi I, p. 84.
5. See especially William A. Niskanen, *Bureaucracy and Representative Government*, New York, 1971.

security). The contention is however that all the behavioural or motivational variables, "selfish" and "unselfish" are a positive function of the total budget of the bureau. Administrators need cash to demonstrate "public spirited" schemes. Being seen to be instrumental in providing a public benefit is always proportional to the size of the public funds that supports this same "benefactor's" efforts.

The new theory also predicts (for technical reasons that we have no space to demonstrate here), that the bureau will supply an "output" of services bigger than a competitive industry but would produce and generate smaller net benefits. More relevant for our purpose is that the bureau will be interested in some kind of alliance with factor supplies since factors will enjoy increases in rewards resulting from the sale of their resources to the bureau. The bureau is expected to increase faster than a competitive industry. Most interesting of all in our context, it is predicted that the bureau will engage in promotional activities favouring its own services.[6] It will be increasingly jealous of rival bureaus or private competitors. It will also urge the need for "mergers" for "proper coordination" of "centralization" and ultimately for one exclusive monolithic body. The bureau will sponsor analysis and statistics concerning the services for which it is responsible, but it will ensure that this research and information is sufficiently self-serving to obscure or avoid any risk of threatening the growth of demand for its own activities.

> If, as sometimes happens, some study sponsored by bureaus turns out to be objective, thorough, penetrating and lucid, it will usually be classified or otherwise restricted; if the distribution of the few penetrating studies cannot be restricted, the bureau will usually sponsor other studies on the same subject as an excuse for delaying action or to dilute the effects of the former studies.[7]

Such analysis breaks new ground in modern economic analysis. There is no pretention here to present a set of formal tests necessary to refute or

6. In economic terms it is interested in shifting to the right the demand curve for its services. It is also interested in making the curve steeper (less elastic).
7. Niskanen, *op. cit.*, p. 210.

support all the associated hypotheses. Instead we shall confine ourselves to some casual inspection of the education bureau that advised W. E. Forster on the eve of the 1870 Education Act. We shall show that there is at least some *prima facie* case for support of the new analysis or at least for the need for further application of it.

We have referred (see the last quotation) to the action of a bureau when there are publicly available a few penetrating and objective studies. In these circumstances the theory predicts the bureau will sponsor other studies to dilute the effects of the prevailing ones. In 1869 when Forster was preparing his Bill two major "outside" studies *were* available to him. These were the 1851 Census Report and the Newcastle Commission Report discussed earlier. The numerical findings of these documents are summarized once more in Table 1.

Table 1.

	Year	Number of Day Scholars	Total Population (all ages)	Proportion of Scholars to Population: one to
Census	1851	2,144,378	17,927,609	8.36
Newcastle Commission	1858	2,535,462	19,523,103	7.7

The Newcastle Commission's results, to repeat, were quite consistent with those of the 1851 Census when we allow for growth of national income and population between 1851–58. Moreover the National Society's Annual Report in 1869 was similarly consistent. One could assume with reasonable assurance therefore a day school population not far off 2½ millions. Presumably on the advice of his officials, Forster did not refer to these figures when presenting his Bill on February 17th, 1870. The only *national* statistic that he mentioned was 1,450,000 scholars. This figure, however, related only to aided schools. It is consistent with the theory of bureaucracy that these schools would receive the primary attention. In the eyes of the bureaucracy the unaided schools would be regarded as a threat and as competitors. It would be in the bureau's interest (a) to keep obscure the numbers of students attending them, (b) to be strongly disparaging about their efficiency, and (c) to mix up questions of quantity with those of quality. Forster's speech reveals these three same features. He proceeded:

> Some hon. members will think, I daresay, that I leave out of consideration the unaided schools. I do not, however, leave them out of consideration; but it so happens—and we cannot blame them for it—that the schools which do not receive Government assistance are, generally speaking, the worst schools, and those least fitted to give a good education to the children of the working class . . . my assertion is borne out by the reports presented annually by our departments, and particularly the report of last session.[8]

Thus Forster neatly by-passed the need to give details of quantity.

The judgements of inferior quality were made in the context of the departmental Revised Code whereby efficiency was measured in strict relationship to a child's ability to pass particular examinations periodically set by officials.[9] Schools were invariably classified as inferior if they did not contain an officially certificated teacher.

Recall next that the theory of bureaucracy predicts that where potentially "embarrassing" research and information are available the bureaucracy will sponsor more research in order to dilute, obscure, or supersede it. The behaviour of Forster and his Department seems to have been consistent with this hypothesis. Completely ignoring the evidence of 1851 and 1861, Forster proceeded in his speech to refer to an *ad hoc* investigation of four industrial towns hurriedly sponsored by his Department in the previous year. So much indeed was the haste that, in presenting it, Forster announced he had not read it himself. He was confident about its contents however: "That report, I have reason to believe, will abundantly confirm my statement that we cannot depend upon the unaided and uninspired schools."[10]

8. Presentation of First Reading, House of Commons, 17 February 1870.
9. W. P. McCann (*op. cit.*) warns that in examining the "universal" condemnations of inferiority "one must bear in mind a certain amount of professional disdain on the part of men who were looking for order and regularity obtaining under the Revised Code."
10. First Reading, 17 February 1870.

Having corresponded with "the two gentlemen who conducted the inquiries," Forster was able to quote some figures from them:

> It is calculated that in Liverpool the number of children between five and thirteen who ought to receive an elementary education is 80,000; but, as far as we can ascertain, 20,000 of them attend no school whatever, while at least another 20,000 attend schools where they get an education not worth having.

He proceeded to indicate similarly discovered deficiencies for Manchester, Birmingham and Leeds. Having produced this Departmental bombshell Forster then promptly left the subject with the words: "I am not going to deal with facts at any length tonight."

The figures for the four towns have been widely reproduced by historians. It is never very clear why they are treated as more reliable than the 1851 and 1861 figures which told quite a different story. In the subsequent passage of the Bill, Forster did not return to any detailed reference to this general Departmental report. Nobody seems indeed to have examined it very closely since. It is as well therefore to devote some time to it here.

The first thing to notice is that Forster's figures involve the same fallacy of misplaced school-age base that featured the Manchester Statistical Society's Report on Manchester in 1834 (See the Gladstone/Kay exchange: Ch. 2). Only one participant in the Parliamentary Debate in 1870, Lord Robert Montagu, seems to have been uneasy on this subject. His comments are worth reproducing:

> The right hon. gentleman alluded to the case of Liverpool, where he said there were 80,000 children between the ages of five and thirteen. Of these he said that 20,000 were in no school; and 20,000 went to inferior schools. The (Newcastle) Commissioners thought that for the children of the working class, six years schooling would be sufficient. Now, as there are eight years between five and thirteen, if every one of those children were to attend school for six years, three-fourths of the number ought to be at school in each year; and according to the showing of the right hon. gentleman, there were three-fourths of the number at school.

The real conclusion of Forster's figures therefore was that

> ... every child which should be at school was at school, but one quar-
> ter were at bad schools, which perhaps might be improved.

Basically Montagu was right. He could, however, have strengthened his
argument had he not referred to the Newcastle six year school base as
one that the Commission "thought suitable." More important it found an
average of 5.7 years existed. This was the average school life in practice
regardless of its own views as to what was desirable. When this *de facto*
school age base is applied Forster's statement that in Liverpool "20,000
attended no school whatever" is quite misleading; for it suggests that this
20,000 *never had* an education. The same 20,000 however could have already experienced, or looked forward to experiencing, six years of schooling. In other words it is obvious that at the time of the investigation many
of the 11 and 12 year olds in the 20,000 could have already completed
their six years' schooling. At the younger end many could be on the point
of beginning theirs. Clearly these results are now much more compatible
with those of 1851, 1861, the 1869 National Society figures, and those of
Montagu who believed that the national deficiency was 300,000.[11]

The enquiries on the four towns were conducted for the Department by Messrs. J. G. Fitch and D. R. Fearon. The school-age fallacy appears in various forms throughout these reports. Fearon used a school
age of 5–13. Fitch, "to avoid dogmatic statement," used various ones: 3–
13, 3–15, or 5–13. Children were "neglected" who on a given day were
off the school books because of sickness or removals. We learn also from
these reports the detailed basis of the judgement that the education of
20,000 students in Liverpool was "not worth having." The number of
children "effectively taught" were represented by the numbers passing
the inspector. To qualify to be examined by the inspector however, the
child must have attended *that same* school for at least 200 times in the
course of the year. In practice very many who could have passed were
not able to for "physical" reasons. Many left school before the examina-
tion-day and could not be brought back for the inspection. Others were

11. Forster's Speech, 17 February 1870.

prevented on the day by sickness or accident. There were still others who had not been in *that particular school* for 200 times because they had migrated from another school or another part of the country. These could have scored well in class examinations had the system allowed them to be inspected. The main purpose of the inspection under the Revised Code was not primarily to measure the general condition of education but to ascertain how much public grant could be earned by each school. This fact incidentally reduced incentives to school managers to display the talents of the scholars. Every scholar was presented in as low a standard as possible so as to secure the maximum grant.

Mr. Fearon made much reference in his report to the failure to pass. In one place he states that "790 children who were more than 10 years old tried to pass in the four best standards and failed in the attempt." A reference to his Table VI however explains that they failed to pass *completely*. The figure of 790 included for instance children who had passed in dictation and reading but had made above a certain number of mistakes in their sums.

Both Fitch and Fearon seemed particularly anxious to show a big deficiency in school accommodation. In this we may have another example of the interests of a public bureau in suppressing or ignoring outside independent information. The reporters ignored the tables supplied by the Registrar General of accommodation in uninspected schools. Fearon estimated that in Manchester there was room for 35,783 children at the rate of eight square feet per child. Comparing this with 36,677 on the roll of all kinds of day schools he concluded that "the demand for day-schooling is greater than the supply of good schools of any kind to meet it." Based on the numbers who *ought* to have been at school 26,032 more places were needed on the larger estimate, and on the smaller estimate, for 17,488 more children than were provided for by the existing system.

This argument was defective. Fearon ignored all the space provided in uninspected schools despite the fact that elsewhere he classified several of these as "fit." His "lowest" and "highest" estimate of children requiring schooling again reflected Fearon's own value judgement about the proper school age. We have already seen that he used a base of 5–13 years; this was quite unrealistic in 1869. His "highest" estimate was at the rate of 1 in 4.9 of the population (in Prussia it was 1 in 5.9). This carried the remarkable implication that one in six of the population should not only be in schools but working-class schools. Fearon moreover estimated for the maximum—not the average attendance at schools.

The Department seems to have been keenly anticipating its own widening expansion. There was expectation of its involvement in a vast new school building programme and thereafter a bigger scale of inspection. The building programme in fact soon materialized in the school board construction "boom" after 1870. The emphasis by Fearon and Fitch on the need for new schools played its part. Had Forster received more independent guidance, or had he not been the creature of political circumstances that he was, it would have been possible for him to have steered a different course of government intervention.

It was possible for him for instance to have recognized that six years was the *de facto* school life on average and to have accepted the 1851 or 1861 findings that nearly all children were already receiving a schooling. He could have urged that 6 years was insufficient and that it should be raised to seven or eight. This being so however, his predominant policy campaign should have been to raise the school leaving age rather than to create new schools. As it transpired the authorities did not succeed in getting the school leaving age raised very much in the ten years after 1870. The only general effect of the Act of 1880, for instance, was to enforce complete attendance of children between 5 and 9 years inclusive. Children between 10 and 13 could be absent from school if they obtained a certificate (which thousands did) of having reached an educational standard fixed by the local by-law.

One result of the failure to raise the school leaving age significantly was that the extra schools (the new board schools) the Forster Act established created costly excess school capacity.[12] This problem was eventually resolved in many areas by the board school practice of lowering their fees[13] with the aid of local rate revenue. This aid was of course denied to

12. By 1875 school accommodation in the public sector had grown to 2,871,000 places but only 1,678,000 pupils were in attendance (Report for 1875).
13. See E. G. West, *Education and the State*, Chap. 10. In its Report for 1876 The National Society (p. 3) complained: "Voluntary Schools are labouring under great disad-

the voluntary schools—many of which were consequently compelled to close; a result that no doubt many participants in the debate implicitly desired. But Forster himself was not among them.

Our contention that Forster's figures exaggerated the number "that never had a schooling" has recently been taken up by W. P. McCann.[14] He points out that a statutory school life of 7 years (6–12) had been in operation since 1862 (10 years if infants are included). Forster, it is argued, used these figures in describing the national position "which West does not comment upon. Forster was therefore correct in assuming that children 'ought' to be at school for seven or ten year periods." A "statutory school life" however did not mean what it means today, a compulsory school life. Universal compulsion was not then enacted. The term "statutory school life" was in most cases a statement of administrative aspiration rather than of fact. The point is that if we want a measure of the numbers that *never* had a schooling it is the actual school life and not a particular administrative definition of it that is relevant. Moreover if Forster was correct in taking the administrator's statutory "school life" as showing "what ought to be" the question is why did he not express deficiency in these terms directly. For instance he could have claimed openly, as we argued above, that the actual school life of 6 years was one year short of the administratively desired statutory (target) school life of seven years. But in these terms the emphasis of policy would have shifted to the direct aim of raising the typical school leaving age.[15] This would have called primarily for marginal help to established institutions. It would

------

vantages. Board Schools have been erected in many districts which—however unintentionally on the part of the promoters—have injuriously affected Voluntary Schools. And while the ratepayers are compelled to furnish whatever sums the school board is disposed to spend, all deficiencies in the revenues of denominational schools must be supplied by voluntary contributions. As the Education Report increases, the ability to give on the part of subscribers is proportionally diminished." It went on to urge that laws were needed to "place the Denominational Schools in a position to compete with the Rate-aided Schools, which were called into existence solely to supplement them."
14. *Op. cit.*
15. We must remember however that the proportion of the national income devoted to education was already big by nineteenth-century standards (see Ch. 7). The same twentieth-century reason that has been offered for the delay in raising the British school leaving age to sixteen (lack of resources) could be applied a century ago to the raising of it to twelve.

typically have allowed marginal expansions of staff and accommodation in existing schools; it would have required entirely new schools only exceptionally. Parliament could then have openly debated the appropriateness of the administratively used, but practically unattained, "statutory life." It could have focused upon the central issue of whether it wanted to compel all families to "rise to" this level.

We have shown that, in his speech, Forster mentioned some national figures, but that these referred to aided and inspected schools only. Like James Kay in 1838, he evaded the question of the quantity of non-aided schools by switching to considerations of quality. The only guide to the overall national position in his speech was the report of the four towns. This report was produced in haste as some sort of urgent up-to-the-moment "key sample." McCann, however, does not comment upon it. Instead he concentrates on eliciting the national numbers in unaided schools—the numbers that were missing from Forster's speech. An Education Department formulation of 1868 stated that the number attending unaided schools was estimated to be seven-tenths of the aided ones.[16] Forster stated that 1½ million were being aided; the actual figure in 1869 was 1,420,020. On the basis of the seven-tenths calculation given above McCann correctly argues this would mean 994,000 on the books of unaided schools. The total figure of national attendance is thus 1,420,020 plus 994,000 = 2,414,020. McCann argues that the only detailed figures available were those supplied by the education bureau—the Committee of Council Office. This is not so. Detailed figures were produced in the 1851 Census, the 1861 Newcastle Report, and the 1869 Annual Report of the National Society. But notice that McCann's estimate using the bureau's own formulation now comes to nearly 2½ million which is consistent with the 1851 census figure of 2⅐ million and within reach of the Newcastle Commission's figure for 1858 of just over 2½ million. Having got this far, however, McCann makes the same type of misleading final statement that was made by James Kay (see pp. 16–17 above) and by Forster's advisors Fearon and Fitch. The 2½ million students were from the age range 3–12 years. The total in this age group was 3,937,000. Sub-

16. This same calculation is made in the Department's Report for 1869. The ratio of seven-tenths is derived from the Newcastle Commission's Report.

tract the numbers actually found at school from this figure and, McCann argues, "we are left with 1,523,000 children *unknown to any school*"[17] (our italics). We disagree. McCann himself argues that the *de facto* school life was not more than about five years. If every child had a schooling of this duration and there were about 4 million children between 3 and 12 years old only about 2 million would be expected to be found at school at any one time. McCann found nearly 2½ millions. He cannot conclude therefore that the 1½ million children were "unknown to any school" because many of them would have completed their 5 year schooling and would still be known by the schools they had left.

McCann makes the same type of claim about school accommodation shortage that was made by Fearon. His "target" for school places rests upon the total 3–12 school age group, i.e. a ten year schooling. This was quite unrealistic in 1869. A ten year schooling was not achieved in fact until the twentieth century. Again McCann is erroneous when he claims that because one million places were physically absent on the above (3–12 year) target reckoning the figure of one million represents "the number of children for whom no places were available and *for whom no schooling was possible*"[18] (our italics). Schooling in fact was possible and was actually attained by most children.

The Newcastle Commission and the Historians

One of the most singular aspects of the history of education is the charge of "unreliability" that is invariably placed by historians on the Newcastle Commission's Report.[19] This report as we have shown was the most exhaustive document on education in the nineteenth century and was conducted with impressive mid-Victorian thoroughness. There seem to be two reasons for subsequent reaction against it. First, some writers have

17. *Ibid.*, p. 24.
18. *Ibid.*, p. 24.
19. In his *The Elementary School Contest*, 1882, Francis Adams (p. 179) asserts that the Commission's figures have often been disputed, ". . . and it has been made abundantly clear, that from some cause they greatly underrated the deficiency of education in the country." The boot could be on the other foot. Adams was a partisan of the Birmingham League. Its figures also were often disputed.

argued that its terms of reference resulted in prejudicial findings; second, others have discounted them as only "estimates." On the first point the Commission's terms of reference directed it to "inquire into the present state of popular education in England and to consider and report what measures, if any, are required for the extension of *sound and cheap elementary instruction* to all classes of the people" (our italics). Many historians emphasize that having spent heavily on the Crimean War the Government of 1858 (which set up the Commission) was looking with apprehension at its expenditure programmes and not least the increasing cost of its annual education grant. The implication is that this atmosphere constrained the Commission's findings. Such danger of bias however is applicable to all statistics. We have given reasons to suggest that a danger was also attached to the statistics coming out of the expanding education bureau in the subsequent decade, statistics that historians have accepted with hardly any question.

Some have chided the Newcastle Commission's terms of reference relating to the need for "cheap" elementary education. There are no doubt several connotations of this adjective and several critics have seized on all of them. There can be no question however that the word was used to mean "non-extravagant." Resources are always limited in any age and this fact is exposed more dramatically in some years than in others. (Witness the drive for economy in British universities.) If scarce resources are used more effectively the greater will be the quantity of education.

Laaden Fletcher has recently argued that the drive for "cheap" education was simply to produce a competitive low fee to price poor families into the market for more sustained education. If successful the subsidies would have *increased* public expenditure; indeed the government was prepared for this. The Commission did not favour reducing the fees to zero because of the general feeling that recipients would not appreciate its value. (This is confirmed on page 73 of the Newcastle Report.) Parents would therefore expect education to be sound if a positive price were paid. Hence "sound and cheap" was a phrase that related to the promotion of education among parents.[20]

20. Laaden Fletcher, "Payment for Means or Payment for Results: Administrative Dilemma of the 1860s," *Jnl. of Educational Adm. & History*, June 1972.

On the second criticism, that the Commission's figures were only "estimates," the same can be said of most other statistics that we have examined. For example we have seen that all the official reasons for school deficiency have been based on estimates of difference between student numbers and "target" school-age populations of all sorts. The Committee on Council's view as to the number of students in unaided schools were again based on an estimate of seven-tenths (see above). The Newcastle Commission in fact contained much *census-type* material from the selected sample districts and these contained one-eighth of the whole population. Indeed these statistics were more intensive than those obtained in the 1851 Census. In other words, the charge of being only "estimates" cannot be made against these substantial sections of the Commission's Report. The estimating part of its enquiry used the specimen district information as a cross check with the assessment of aggregate statistics obtained through the public department and the religious societies. Finally the Newcastle findings are quite consistent with those of the 1851 Census Report to which the charge of being only "estimates" cannot possibly apply.[21]

We shall close this subject with reference to a person who was probably the most respected of Victorian educational statisticians—Horace Mann. Mann was employed not by the Education Department but by the Registrar General. His findings are therefore free from the presump-

---

21. Gillian Sutherland (*op. cit.,* p. 19) has described the Newcastle Commission's conclusion that the average school life was 5.7 years as "optimistic." This figure relates to the findings of the specimen districts that the Commission investigated intensively. Sutherland quotes McCann's objection that evidence is available suggesting that 5.7 years is "much too high." McCann (*op. cit.,* p. 25) quotes from selected inspectors' reports on children attending Church schools in some areas in the late 1860s. He observes, for instance, that in Lincolnshire, Nottinghamshire and Yorkshire in 1867 only 6.5 per cent had put in 5 years attendance. The first point to note is that the Newcastle Commission's suggestion of a five year schooling was a typical or modal experience. Since there is always some deviation around the average in any distribution of schooling it is always possible to pick on individual examples that show lower school durations (and others that are higher) than the average. The second point is that the inspectors' figures usually related to attendance at one particular school only. Since there was frequent migration (as McCann observes) the total school life will comprise attendances at more than one school which will not normally appear on the Inspector's report.

tions of prejudice about information that was supplied by education bureaus. Writing in 1869 on the eve of Forster's Bill he observed.

> . . . it is well to recollect that the number of children under tuition at the present time is equal to one in seven and a half of the population in England and Wales. . . . The estimate sanctioned by the Royal Commissioners of 1858 (The Newcastle Commission) makes the proportion one to every 7.7 which is not far short of the highest proportion practicable in a highly industrial community. Mr. Matthew Arnold, indeed, objects to this estimate on the ground that it *is* an estimate and not the result of a census. He is probably not aware that an exhaustive census of the number of schools and scholars in England and Wales was taken in 1851 and that *the estimate of 1859 [Newcastle Commission] is supported by the results of the previous and more extensive inquiry.* Of schools and teachers in the aggregate therefore, there is no great lack, and the deficiency as to scholars is less a deficiency in general than in certain crowded centres, *and less of numbers than of the time passed in school.* New schools are wanted in some populous places, and better schools and a better distribution of schools in other parts of the country; but the statements which are frequently made by eminent persons as to the enormous number of children (sometimes put at from 1,000,000 to 2,000,000) growing up wholly without education, rest upon an obvious arithmetical fallacy. That a certain number of children is always found absent from school is no more a proof that so many never go there, than the fact that a certain number of members of Parliament is always absent from the House of Commons is a proof that so many never attend to their duties [22] (our italics).

22. Horace Mann, "National Education," *Transactions of the National Association for the Promotion of Social Science,* Bristol Meeting 1869. London, Longmans Green Reader and Dyer, 1870, pp. 364–72.

Part 3 · Nineteenth-Century Visions of National Systems

10 · Tom Paine's National System

The classical economists, as is commonly known, were in favour of appreciable government intervention in English schooling.[1] Their arguments were based on the conviction that large numbers of families, if unaided, would seriously underinvest in education. This conviction was based on two simple observations: first, that many parents were too poor to buy education; second, that many others did not sufficiently value it. Such reasoning led some of these writers to advocate compulsory laws. It is especially interesting to notice also that it led them to propose government subsidies to the *schools* rather than directly to the *scholars* (or their parents). This chapter will show how Tom Paine, a contemporary of the classical economists, advocated quite different means. Believing that the majority of poor people were much more aware of the benefits of education than was commonly supposed, and contending that it was heavy taxation of the masses that was the chief cause of their poverty, Paine made particularly interesting and original fiscal suggestions to promote education which seem to have hitherto been neglected by historians of economic thought.

The widespread incidence of poverty at the end of the eighteenth and

---

1. For further details see: E. G. West, "Private versus Public Education: A Classical Economic Dispute," *Journal of Political Economy,* October 1964; West, *Education and the State* (London: Institute of Economic Affairs, 1965), Chapter 8; William L. Miller, "The Economics of Education in English Classical Economics," *The Southern Economic Journal,* January 1966, pp. 294–309.

the first half of the nineteenth century was a powerful factor which influenced nearly all the classical economists in their advocacy of state aided education. But it is at first sight, surprising that in the context of education, they did not so readily associate parental poverty with the prevailing heavy burden of taxation. It is often forgotten that the bulk of the central revenue in those days came from indirect taxes, most of which were strongly regressive. Taxes on food and tobacco for instance typically accounted for about 60 per cent of all central revenue in the first half of the nineteenth century. In addition, the independent poor were obliged to pay increasingly burdensome poor rate levies, particularly after 1800. Lack of clarity or sophistication concerning the true incidence of taxation, together with a certain moral asceticism in favour of taxing some "unnecessaries," provide two explanations of the attitude of several of the early economists. Adam Smith's view was that taxes on the necessities of the poor were all passed on to the employers in the form of higher wages. J. R. McCulloch objected to income tax, proposals for which were being increasingly pressed after 1820, on the grounds of the difficulty of making individual assessments. He was even more critical of the principle of graduation because he thought it would have uncontrollable redistributional consequences.[2]

In practice, contemporary governments had become habitually accustomed to enormous revenues from taxes on necessaries and looked upon them "as of right." Once the revenues from the indirect taxes had been collected, it was certainly difficult to claim that the poor deserved to be refunded. For, as many economists emphasized, there were certain benefits which the government supplied, such as defence, which were indivisible and enjoyed by all and so were regarded as deserving of a contribution from all. Propositions for a *new* universal government service in aid of the poor to be provided *ex ante* from *new* levies specifically for that purpose would have been open to clearer debate. If, for instance, the new levies could have been shown to be expected to fall mainly on the poor themselves then the policy would have been more clearly seen as one of paternalism rather than one of redistribution. The appropriate-

2. See J. R. McCulloch, *Treatise on the Principles and Practical Influence of Taxation* (1845), pp. 7, 42, 119–26.

ness of such a policy could then have been discussed more directly in the light of evidence on the responsibility of the average poor in spending their own money.

However, as so often when decisions were proposed or actually made through the political process, demand choices became arbitrarily separated from supply choices. Thus in educational policy, as in many other fields, the tendency was for schemes to be pushed in advance of the determination of the requisite finance. In the nineteenth century, when incomes were rising, governments were typically enabled to find the finance for particular measures *after* the event of legislation. Their path was made easier by virtue of what Gladstone called the "buoyancy of the revenue." Because of this constant syphoning process upon gradually rising incomes, poor families were prevented from having as much disposable income as they would have otherwise enjoyed. It is not at all clear that, had taxation been restrained and disposable incomes increased, *average* families would not have used the difference to buy much more education directly. As our Chapter 6 has shown, an educational threshold was reached by very large numbers of ordinary people in the early nineteenth century.

Considering the number of adherents to the "ability to pay principle," in public finance, adherents such as J. S. Mill and his followers, it is surprising that the movement for more equity in nineteenth-century taxation was not more vociferous than it was.[3] It has often been observed, however, that in the early nineteenth century there were formidable administrative obstacles hindering such reform. The common view is that the principle of equity is effected much more easily and accurately through a system of income tax allowances. Furthermore, and especially in view of the argument that, in education, there is a strong case for financial contributions from non-parents, some modern writers would point to the necessity of a negative income tax over some range of income. Income

---

3. J. S. Mill recognized the principle thus: "The principle, therefore, of equality of taxation, interpreted in its only just sense, equality of sacrifice, requires that a person who has no means of providing for old age, *or for those in whom he is interested*, except by saving from income, should have the tax remitted on all that part of his income which is really and *bona fide* applied to that purpose." *Principles of Political Economy*, Ashley edition (London: Longmans, 1915), p. 813 (italics supplied).

tax, however, had hardly begun in the nineteenth century. Nevertheless, Tom Paine did attempt to show the feasibility of such sophistication and discrimination even within the framework of an indirect tax system. His work as an economist has suffered neglect due partly no doubt to the extent with which his political views embarrassed other economists and indeed the country at large.[4]

At the end of his, *The Rights of Man,* Paine made a review of the current taxation situation. He first examined the contention that there was an inexorable law that taxes increased with the passage of time. This he condemned as fatalistic. Quoting Sir John Sinclair's *History of the Revenue,* he showed that the English people had succeeded in getting their taxes continually *reduced* for the four hundred years starting from 1066. At the expiration of this time they were reduced by three fourths, viz., from £400,000 to £100,000 in 1466. Since that time, however, the taxes had risen so much that Paine thought the national character of the English had weakened. For in 1791 taxation amounted to £17,000,000. The main increases, said Paine, were associated with war years which gave rise to an enlargement of the national debt.[5] The composition of the taxes in 1788 were as follows:

Land tax	£1,950,000
Customs	3,789,274
Excise (including old and new malt)	6,751,727
Stamps	1,278,214
Miscellaneous taxes and incidents	1,803,755
	£15,572,970

Between 1788 and 1791, therefore, taxes had risen by one and a half million pounds. The land tax, paid by the Aristocrats, was the only one which was falling, having dropped by half a million pounds over the previous century.[6]

---

4. Smith and Malthus openly denounced his political writings.
5. A thesis since developed by A. Peacock and J. Wiseman, *The Growth of Public Expenditure in the United Kingdom* (Oxford University Press, 1961).
6. The aristocrats also avoided the beer tax because home-brewed ale did not pay duty, and they alone brewed it in large enough quantities to make it economic. The proceeds of the beer tax exceeded that of the land tax.

Nine millions of the total revenue were applied to servicing the national debt, the remaining eight millions went on current expenses. It was the latter which Paine thought to be extravagant.[7] Independently of all this, the cost of administering poor relief, which amounted to two millions, was largely escaped by the rich.

Paine gave several reasons why the ordinary current expenses of eight millions could be reduced to one and a half millions. But the question then arose of how to dispose of the surplus of over six millions. Reducing the excise would be a step in the right direction but there was need for a nicer discrimination within the group that paid it. He looked next to the reduction of other taxes: "where the relief will be direct and visible, and capable of immediate operation."[8] The poor rates, he said, were a direct tax: "which every housekeeper feels, and who knows also, to a farthing, the sum which he pays."[9] Furthermore the poor rate, together with other taxation, was the main cause of the poverty itself. Money taken in taxation from average families was much more than enough to finance a basic education of their children. A labouring man with a wife and two or three children paid between seven and eight pounds a year in taxes. "He is not sensible of this, because it is disguised to him in the articles which he buys, and he thinks only of their dearness; but as the taxes take from him, at least, *a fourth of his yearly earnings*, he is consequently disabled from providing for a family, especially if himself or any of them are afflicted with sickness"[10] (italics supplied).

Paine, the son of a weaver, had a great respect for the good sense of average parents, and of all institutions that of the family was in his mind the most noble. His own experience led him to value the moral instruction by his own father.[11] He objected to the impartial effects of the taxes: "Speaking for myself, my parents were not able to give me a shilling be-

---

7. With regard to the interest on the national debt, he thought it was heavy: "yet as it serves to keep alive a capital useful to commerce, it balances by its effects a considerable part of its own weight. . . ."
8. Tom Paine, *The Rights of Man,* Everyman Edition (London, 1961), Ch. V, p. 245.
9. *Ibid.,* p. 245.
10. *Ibid.,* p. 246.
11. In retrospect he preferred the instruction of his father to that of his schoolmaster who had filled him with "false heroism."

yond what they gave me in education; and to do this they distressed themselves."[12] Paine argued that small householders were more injured by
the taxes than others just because they consumed more of the taxable
articles, in proportion to their property, than those of large estates and
their residences were chiefly in towns where the poor rates were more
severe.

It was easily seen, said Paine, that the bulk of the really poor, consisted
of two groups: first, large families of children, secondly, old people. Equity demanded therefore that the surplus should be distributed to these
two classes. He proposed in lieu of the poor rates: "to make a remission of
taxes to the poor of double the amount of the present poor rates, viz., four
millions annually, out of the surplus taxes. By this measure the poor will
be benefited two millions, and the housekeeper two millions."[13] Moreover, and this is where Paine was even more in advance of his time, the
distribution of the surplus four millions was to be according to the size
and age of the family. Thus he would pay *as a remission of taxes:* ". . . to
every poor family, out of the surplus taxes, and in room of poor rates four
pounds a year for every child under fourteen years of age; enjoining the
parents of such children to send them to school, to learn reading, writing, and common arithmetic; *the ministers of every parish, of every denomination to certify jointly to an office, for that purpose, that this duty
is performed*"[14] (italics supplied).

By simple statistical estimate, Paine calculated that this education
grant would cost approximately two and a half million pounds. This
whole operation would, he thought, relieve the poverty of the parents:
"because it is from the expense of bringing up children that their poverty
arises."[15] It would also abolish ignorance and help to set young people on
their feet.

Paine was also concerned with the difficulty of inaccessible schooling

12. *Ibid.*, p. 234. His father was a Quaker.
13. *Ibid.*, p. 247.
14. *Ibid.*, p. 248. This suggestion which seems to share the same basic philosophy as the
voucher principle first put forward by Milton Friedman in 1955, published in R. A. Solo,
Economics and the Public Interest (Rutgers).
15. *Ibid.*

in sparsely populated areas. To meet this problem, he proposed a special allowance for each child living in these areas. The allowance would amount to ten shillings a year: ". . . for the expense of schooling for six years each, which will give them six months' schooling each year, and half-a-crown a year for paper and spelling books." [16] He estimated that this would have cost one quarter million. He was confident that persons could be found in every village capable and willing to teach, such as distressed clergymen's widows. "Whatever is given on this account to children answers two purposes; to them it is education—to those who educate them it is a livelihood." [17] So comprehensively had Paine worked out his scheme, that he had not forgotten to consider that ever-important final test of any fiscal scheme—its administrative feasibility. He claimed that his plan was easy in practice; "It does not embarrass trade by a sudden interruption in the order of taxes, but effects the relief by changing the application of them; and the money necessary for the purpose can be drawn from the excise collections, which are made eight times a year in every market town in England." [18]

Thus, Paine offered a series of fiscal innovations to meet the desire for increased popular education, a desire which the classical economists shared. Paine's scheme distinguished itself from the means proposed by the latter mainly in that it directed the finance *not at the school but at the scholar (via his parent or guardian)*. It will be remembered that Adam Smith argued for a wide dispersal of educational expenditure and decision making in order to prevent the teacher's rewards from being made independent of his efforts. To this end Smith always wanted some part of education expenses to be paid in the form of fees; the public subsidies which he proposed to be confined mainly to the construction and maintenance of school buildings. But Paine's proposal, judged by the criterion of decentralized decision making, went much further than that of Smith. For it ensured the possibility of the exercise of a still wider choice on behalf of the child. Accordingly, still greater competition would emerge

16. *Ibid.*, p. 252.
17. *Ibid.*
18. *Ibid.*, p. 256.

since a much bigger proportion of educational expenditure would go through parental hands.[19]

Again, Paine's scheme was more consistent with J. S. Mill's taxation principle of "ability to pay." It also answered the latter's fear that many parents could not be trusted; for parental freedom was joined with the corroborative evidence of a wide selection of local inspectors.[20] Furthermore, the dispersion of decision making was one answer to J. S. Mill's fear that central government control of education would lead to government "despotism over the minds" of people. According to Paine, decentralized education would counter the prevailing desire of the aristocrats to maintain their power by depending on ignorance. "A Nation under a well-regulated Government should permit none to remain uninstructed. It is monarchical and aristocratical Government only that requires ignorance for its support."[21] Finally, Paine's proposals contained the independent aim of abolishing the pernicious effects of the poor law. This in turn was intended to achieve that reduction of crime which most of the classical economists wanted to remove by education alone. For it was Tom Paine's belief that the real source of the growth of crime was the demoralizing influence of the system of parish relief.

> By the operation of this plan, the poor laws, those instruments of civil torture, will be superseded, and the wasteful expense of litigation prevented. The hearts of the humane will not be shocked by ragged and hungry children, and persons of seventy or eighty years of age, begging for bread. The dying poor will not be dragged from place to place to breathe their last, as a reprisal of parish upon parish. Widows will have a maintenance for their children, and not be carted away, on the

---

19. Paine upheld the principles of commerce with no less vigor than Adam Smith. Thus: "In all my publications, where the matter would admit, I have been an advocate for commerce, because I am a friend to its effects. It is a pacific system, operating to cordialise mankind, by rendering Nations, as well as individuals, useful to each other. As to the mere theoretical reformation, I have never preached it up. The most effectual process is that of improving the condition of man by means of his interest; and it is on this ground that I take my stand."

20. I.e., in the shape of the ministers of the parish of every denomination. (See page 148 above).

21. *Ibid.*, p. 252.

death of their husbands, like culprits and criminals; and children will no longer be considered as increasingly the distresses of their parents. The haunts of the wretched will be known, because it will be to their advantage, and the number of petty crimes, the offspring of distress and poverty, will be lessened. The poor, as well as the rich, will then be interested in the support of Government, and the cause and apprehension of riots and tumults will cease.[22]

22. *Ibid.*, p. 256.

11 · The National System to Promote Order: The Benthamite Prescription

There was a striking consensus among the middle classes in the nineteenth century that education was the best means of reducing crime and achieving political stability. The classical economists subscribed to this belief with special conviction. Adam Smith for instance, argued the case for intervention in education on grounds which today's economists would call "external economies" or "neighbourhood effects."

> The third and last duty of the sovereign or commonwealth is that of erecting and maintaining those public institutions and those public works, which though they may be in the highest degree advantageous to a great society, are, however, of such a nature, that the profit could never repay the expense to any individual or small number of individuals, and which it therefore cannot be expected that any individual or small number of individuals should erect or maintain.[1]

Although it was thus necessary for the state to act only if such institutions had obvious advantages to all its members, Adam Smith thought that ignorance was so pitiful that it should intervene to remove it if only on charitable grounds. But:

> The state, however, derives no inconsiderable advantage from their instruction. The more they are instructed, the less liable they are to the delusions of enthusiasm and superstition, which, among ignorant nations, frequently occasions the most dreadful disorders. An instructed

1. Adam Smith, *Wealth of Nations,* Book V.

and intelligent people besides, are always more decent and orderly than an ignorant and stupid one. They feel themselves, each individually more respectable, and more likely to obtain the respect of their lawful superiors, and they are therefore more disposed to respect those superiors.[2]

Smith was here undoubtedly influenced by the Physiocrats. There is a marked change of emphasis in his references to education before and after his continental tour on which he met the French economists. The *Wealth of Nations*, which was written after this tour, partly reflects the supreme optimism of the Physiocrats in the ability of education to achieve political harmony. It was Quesnay's opinion, for instance, that: "when a nation is fully educated, tyranny is automatically ruled out."[3] Turgot in a memorandum addressed to his King claimed:

> I venture to affirm that if this programme (universal state education) be adopted, your subjects will have changed out of all recognition within a mere decade, and their intelligence, good behaviour, and enlightened zeal in your service and their country's will place them far above all other modern nations. For by that time children now ten years old will have grown into young men trained to do their duty by the State; patriotic and law-abiding, not from fear but on rational grounds, understanding and respecting justice, and prompt to help their fellow citizens in time of need.[4]

The nineteenth-century English middle class was similarly convinced that education was the best means of reducing crime and bringing political stability. It is not entirely clear however what different people meant by the term "education." Some advocates at least conceived it primarily as a means of conveying and spreading their own particular religions, philosophies or nostrums. James Mill exclaimed:

> So obvious, and unspeakable are the advantages of a good education to the body of the people, and so miserable, and undesirable are the

---

2. *Ibid.*
3. Quoted in Alexis de Tocqueville: *The Old Regime and the French Revolution*, Part III, Ch. III.
4. *Ibid.*

disadvantages which necessarily attend a bad one, that we really know no reasons which can be urged in favour of a good education but what must appear perfectly trite. This is one of those extraordinary cases in which all men are equally wise. . . .[5]

Everybody wants a "good" education. The claim that a "good" education has advantages is usually a tautology. Everybody can support such a proposition when they all have exclusive conceptions of the adjective "good."

The French Physiocrats wanted a national system of education because they could use it to propagate their new found knowledge of the "secrets" of the workings of the economy. "Abolishing ignorance" to them meant primarily the removal of the ignorance of their scientific system. Adam Smith wanted governments to support education because he believed that the spread of scientific knowledge to the ordinary people would make them become absorbed with the wonder of intellectual problems arising from their everyday work. This, he thought, would lead to aesthetic and noble sentiments which in turn would result in a tranquil and reflective society.

As he put it: "Science is the great antidote to enthusiasm."[6] From Book IV, Chapter IX of *The Wealth of Nations* we know that Smith opposed the "science" of the Physiocrats. It is not surprising that his science which he also wished to spread through education, was of a different nature and purpose from theirs.

For the nineteenth-century cleric, the "ignorance" which led to crime was primarily the ignorance of the teaching of his particular church. For the utilitarian the crucial issue was ignorance of the laws of the state or in other words the want of knowledge and effective warning of the pain that would inevitably follow from certain actions. For Malthus it was the ignorance of his population principle which mattered most. Public education for him was needed to suppress the "sophistries" of persons such as Condorcet. The latter happened to be the successful instigator of French state education, and undoubtedly intended it to instruct according to *his* conception of truth.

5. *Literary Journal,* 1806, 2nd series, Art. XII, Vol. II.
6. *Wealth of Nations,* Book V, Article III.

In his speech to the Commons in 1847 Macaulay pressed for the further intervention of the state on nearly every ground so far mentioned starting with Adam Smith's argument:

> On that subject I cannot refer to higher authority, or use more strong terms, than have been employed by Adam Smith; and I take his authority the more readily, because he is not very friendly to State interference. . . .
>
> The education of the poor he pronounces to be a matter in which Government is most deeply concerned; and he compares ignorance, spread through the lower classes, neglected by the State, to a leprosy, or some other fearful disease, and says that where this duty is neglected, the State is in danger of falling into the most terrible disorder.

Macaulay went on to commend the vision of Smith whose words were published only four years before the riots of 1780. These disturbances, Macaulay agreed, were clearly attributable to ignorance.

> . . . would it have been supposed that all this could have taken place in a community were even the common labourer to have his mind opened by education; and be taught to find his pleasure in the exercise of the intellect, taught to revere his Maker, taught to regard his fellow creatures with kindliness, and taught likewise to feel respect for legal authority, taught how to pursue redress of real wrongs by constitutional methods?

Anxious as Adam Smith was for the education of people in the three Rs and some science, it is very doubtful if he would have shared the legislative enthusiasm of the Benthamites and their supreme confidence that a Government could successfully organize it. The government of Adam Smith's day was corrupt and inefficient. The utilitarians, especially the younger ones, based their programmes on the assumption of a "reformed" Parliament, which to them meant a Parliament which was strengthened by themselves and their ideas. Bentham wanted an education with more specific content and purpose than that of Smith. In particular he wanted schooling that acquainted ordinary people with the laws, so that what society (or the utilitarians) regarded as offences, could be readily recognized by legal labels and signposts. The last few words of the above quotation of Macaulay show that he was influenced as much by Bentham as by Smith. Chapter XX of Part III of Bentham's *Principles of Penal Law* is the source of the relevant utilitarian doctrine:

"Education is only government acting by means of the domestic magistrate."[7] If government funds to be spent on education amounted to less than would otherwise have to be spent in keeping criminals in prison and maintaining an adequate police force, then it should intervene. The state:

> . . . ought not only to watch over orphans left in indigence, but also over the children whose parents no longer deserve the confidence of the law with regard to this important charge—over those who have already committed crimes, or who, destitute of protection and resources, are given up to all the seduction of misery. These classes, absolutely neglected in most states, become the hotbeds of crime.[8]

Whitbread used the same "reduction of crime" argument for education in his speech of 1807; a speech that received the full support of Robert Malthus.[9] In 1846 William Thornton thought that the expense of education

> . . . no doubt would be considerable, but it would scarcely be so great as that already incurred for prisons, hulks, and convict ships; and it is certainly better economy to spend money in training up people to conduct themselves properly, than in punishing them for their misdeeds.[10]

Senior and Chadwick vigorously pressed the same point in their advice to Government Commissions and professional associations in the 1850s and 60s.

But it was the striking speech of Roebuck to the "reformed" Parliament of 1833 which had given the utilitarians their chance of putting the idea into legislative practice. This was the address that initiated the first effective intervention by the State in education. It was a mirror of Bentham's ideas.

---

7. *The Works of Jeremy Bentham*, 1843, Vol. I, pp. 569, 570.
8. *Ibid.*
9. McCulloch's opinion is to be found in his *Principles*, 1825: "It is no exaggeration to affirm that nine-tenths of the misery and crime which afflict and disgrace society have their source in ignorance. . . ."
10. W. T. Thornton: *Over Population and Its Remedy*, 1846.

We all of us seem to feel the necessity of supervising our Criminal Code—our Code of Prison Discipline—our Poor-laws; but all these are only off-shoots of, or adjuncts to, a system of Education. That is the great touchstone the mainspring of the whole. We allow crime and misery to spring up, and then attempt, by a vast and cumbrous machinery, to obviate the mischief. We punish, we do not prevent—we try to put down effects, without caring for the cause. Like ignorant physicians, our minds are absorbed by a consideration of symptoms, while the disease is making head, to the utter destruction of life. And why are we thus remiss? Shall it be said, that because simply the benefit of the whole community was concerned in the matter, and no selfish interest could be promoted by it, we were careless regarding it? Shall it be said, that the Government of England only abstained from interference in that case where its assistance might have been afforded with the most pure and unalloyed benefit; and that though boasting of our acts and our learning and proudly claiming to be placed at the head of the civilized world, we were content to suffer the mass of our population to be educated as chance might direct, and to form what habits and desires the merest hazard might determine; that while we minutely inspected, and jealously guarded the interior of a beer-house, the school that was next door, where the minds of all the parish—and not a few— might be framed to good or evil, was passed by with utter—ay, and scornful—indifference.[11]

As a final example we can cite Miss Martineau, the well known popularizer of the political economists. She seems to have faithfully represented her classical peers when she wrote:

Nor can I see that political economy objects to the general rating for educational purposes. As a mere police-tax this rating would be a very cheap affair. It would cost us much less than we now pay for juvenile depravity.[12]

From the vantage point of a subsequent century of experience and much more systematic evidence, the early writers and advocates now appear as

11. Hansard, Vol. X, 30 July 1833.
12. Quoted in H. Spencer, *Social Statics*. Spencer also quotes Macaulay as having stamped upon the subject the full seal of his oratory with the exclamation: "We hold that whoever has the right to hang has the right to educate."

"false optimists." Even when we give due regard to a proper historical perspective there remains a surprising measure of dogma. Adam Smith's opinion, for instance, that "intelligent and instructed" people are more "decent" than others seems to have been a curious and somewhat "professorial" generalization. Even as an *a priori* judgement, it neglects the possibility that the more intelligent and instructed among the criminally disposed, are more likely to effect more "efficient" crimes. Herbert Spencer exclaimed in 1850, by which time the idea was at the height of fashion:

> It is, indeed, strange that with the facts of daily life before them in the street, in the counting-house, and in the family, thinking men should still expect education to cure crime. If armies of teachers, regarded with a certain superstitious reverence, have been unable to purify society in all these eighteen centuries, it is hardly likely that other armies of teachers, not so regarded, will be able to do it. . . . The expectation that crime may presently be cured, whether by State education, or the silent system, or the separate system, or any other system, is one of those Utopianisms fallen into by people who pride themselves on being practical.[13]

Benthamism, however, was all pervasive. It was too an integral part of Continental European thought. Conversely many of Bentham's intellectual antecedents were to be found in the French Enlightenment; there was much affinity especially with Helvetius. All Bentham's writings were immediately published in French and received prompt admiration everywhere in Europe.

Bentham's basic proposition was that all human beings want the greatest amount of happiness. A corollary of this was that *good* conduct of life would lead to this. Good conduct in turn meant *intelligent* conduct. The social problem was to design efficient institutions so that the course of action most beneficial to an individual would be always beneficial to others. At the same time, actions which harmed others were to be discouraged by penalties which brought obvious personal injury to the individual concerned. Ethics were reduced to a science. An action which was "good" was simply one that was "desired." The fact that in real life people

13. *Social Statistics*, 1892 edition. Williams and Norgate, p. 171.

did "evil" actions (i.e. actions which are undesired) arose simply from ignorance of the true results of their actions—from faulty anticipation. It
can be seen why education played such an important role in Bentham's
scheme. He did not believe in a pre-established or providential harmony,
but in a harmony that could be engineered by "rational" planning and by
science. His belief in the ability of legislation to achieve this end was more
confident and ambitious than that of Adam Smith. Bentham wanted to
use the powers of Government widely and purposefully to make people
see for themselves that what was happening through legislation was in
their own interest. It is significant that he wanted to extend Smith's curriculum to include such subjects, for instance, as elementary political
economy.[14]

In the hands of his leading disciple, James Mill, Bentham's "pleasure-
pain" system of education was united with the French "associationist"
psychology of Helvetius. This kind of thinking was represented in England by David Hartley to whom James Mill also paid acknowledgement.
If, as these writers maintained, the whole of our mental life is made up
of responses or reflexes conditional upon physical or mental stimuli, then
it was scientifically possible for a system of education to design model
citizens. For although men still remained pleasure seekers, those pleasures could be encouraged which also gave pleasures (or avoided harm)
to others. Such was the reasoning of James Mill's celebrated article on
education in the *Encyclopaedia Britannica* in 1818.

Of the circumstances which affected an individual's happiness Mill
gave greatest attention to the physical. In this article Mill correctly included Adam Smith among those thinkers who shared this kind of physical determinism. Smith had condemned in particular the "stultifying"
effects of the division of labour, as manifest in the workers' restricted op-
erations in his famous example of a Scottish pin factory. James Mill, in
addition, stressed that bad health also influenced the state of a person's
mind and one of the most important duties of schools was to make scientific observations and recordings on such influences. Good food and
the right air and temperature were also emphasized, and this foreshadowed the thoroughgoing specification for school architecture to be made

14. Malthus was the first to suggest it in his *Essay on Population.*

by Chadwick later in the century. Mill's treatment of this subject was more elaborate than these examples convey, but they are sufficient to illustrate the detailed enthusiasm of his science of education which he thought could deliberately transform and perfect human society in the same way as the Greeks had attempted, although with more universal application.

Formidable difficulties always present themselves when ardent believers in new systems try to apply them. Let us suppose that their world is ruled by science; they will still be troubled by conflicting opinions of scientists themselves. The new social science of psychology which has conspicuously affected all types of education since Mill wrote has certainly not been characterized by that unanimity of opinion which he seems to have expected. But if society is led also by philosophy, sentiment, emotion and religion, then conflicts become still deeper.[15] If also that society professes to be a liberal democracy, then it is obliged to allow minorities the daily opportunity of expressing and influencing others with their own opinion. Morality cannot be legislated for as a thing of science when many people persist in alternative opinion about its nature and origins.

James Mill's proposals did not at first imply, however, that it was *the Government* which had to form for itself the pre-conception of a model citizen. He pronounced against "excessive" Government intervention along the lines of the classical economists, and repeated their conclusion that each individual knows his own interests best. He had unbounded confidence in the influence of reason over the minds of mankind. Given representative government, complete freedom of discussion would, he believed, lead to the general acceptance of his ideas of education. He was convinced in any case that private groups could perform the bulk of the educational function. Yet he was impatient with those schools sponsored by the Church.

Mill and Bentham both favoured a secular education. But since the radical education movement comprised many Dissenters, it was not

15. William Petty and Thomas Chalmers are examples of economists who advocated specifically an education in religious doctrine to meet crime. Chalmers explicitly rejected the notion that the secular education of Malthus could be effective.

expedient for them openly to oppose religious instruction in schools. They therefore compromised with a demand for undenominational teaching only. Bentham was by far the most hostile to the Established Church, which he condemned as a downright enemy to educational progress. The most severe attack appeared in his "Church of England-ism" in 1818 in which he accused the church of being jealous of the Quaker, Lancaster, for his success with his new schools in which the Bible only was used: ". . . the Bible might prevail over the Catechism and the Church of England might thus be brought to an end."[16]

The younger utilitarians displayed less patience. Referring to his father's ideas, John Stuart Mill declared:

> These various opinions were seized on with youthful fanaticism by the little knot of young men of whom I was one: and we put into them a sectarian spirit, from which, in intention at least, my father was wholly free. . . . The French *philosophes* of the eighteenth century were the example we sought to imitate, and we hoped to accomplish no less results.[17]

Encouraged by the success of the 1832 Reform Act and by their representation in the new House of Commons, the spokesman of the utilitarians, Roebuck, attempted to show the house (and apparently with success) not only "the more prominent benefits to be obtained by a general education of the people," but also "why the Government should *itself supply* this education . . ." (italics supplied). The mainground upon which Roebuck rested this important proposal was none other than the utilitarian "reduction of crime" argument again.

> If, then, we seek no higher ground, we may here safely rest, and say, that, as mere matter of police, the education of the people ought to be considered as a part of the duties of the Government.[18]

16. See also his remarks on the Church's despotism in the Bentham Mss (University College), VII, ff. 142–49. In "The Book of Fallacies," 1824, Bentham resumed the attack and referred to those who "loved darkness better than light."
17. *Autobiography,* J. S. Mill, Columbia University Press, Ch. VI.
18. Hansard, Vol. X, Cols. 139–166. 30 July 1833. In his Autobiography J. S. Mill referring to Roebuck wrote ". . . it is his title to permanent remembrance, that in the very first year during which he sat in Parliament, he originated (or re-originated after the unsuccessful attempt of Mr. Brougham) the parliamentary movement for National

Roebuck thought the Government should not leave such a duty "to chance." The extent of the cleavage between Roebuck's young followers and the earlier generation can be seen by comparing the attitude of William Godwin, a member of the earlier group of radicals. Godwin wrote in 1796:

> It is not easy to say whether the remark, "that government cannot fully punish offenders, unless it have previously informed them what is virtue and what is offence," be entitled to a separate answer. It is to be hoped that mankind will never have to learn so important a lesson through so corrupt a channel. Government may reasonably and equitably presume that men who live in society, know that enormous crimes are injurious to the public weal, without its being necessary to announce them as such, by laws to be proclaimed by heralds, or expounded by curates. . . . All real crimes are capable of being discerned without the teaching of law. All supposed crimes, not capable of being so discerned, are truly and unalterably innocent.[19]

Roebuck regarded the "police" argument as only the lowest ground for state provision of education. The "higher ground" rested upon the duty of government "directly to promote good." He maintained that once the Government took upon itself the business of administering justice and the regulation of money, this was proof that it could take part in an active way to promote the well-being of the people and that it should extend its functions to education.

The "Roebuck utilitarians" in a sense challenged the basic starting assumption of the classical liberal economists that beyond the provision of a basic legal framework to give protection there should be maximum freedom on the grounds that the individual was the best judge of his own interests and chooser of the best ends. Roebuck argued that adult individuals were too "ignorant" to know their own interests.[20] If pressed, sev-

---

Education; . . ." p. 136. Yet J. S. Mill himself fervently opposed Government *supplied* instruction—at least by the time he came to write the *Principles of Political Economy* in 1848.

19. *Enquiry concerning Political Justice and its influence on Morals and Happiness*, W. Godwin, London 1796, p. 299.

20. "The people at present are far too ignorant to render themselves happy even though they should possess supreme power tomorrow." Hansard, *op. cit.*

eral of his followers would no doubt have protested that they were speaking only of infants who were a special case needing the protection of the State. But protection against what or against whom? For them to have answered that it was necessary to legislate against parental neglect, would have only posed the question in different terms, since the word "neglect" needed definition. Roebuck defined such neglect as the avoidance of the obligation of the parent ". . . to educate the child in such a way that he be a *virtuous* citizen" (italics supplied). The word "virtuous" however was one for which there was no one tribunal (unless it was a government of Benthamites in a unanimous Benthamite world).

To the twentieth-century observer the typical statistical evidence which was used in its support of the "reduction of crime" argument was astonishingly superficial and impressionistic. One observation which was frequently made was that the Scots were more law-abiding than others and that this must be due to their superior education. Adam Smith having made the suggestion, Malthus and James Mill were quick to pursue it. It was the opinion of Malthus that:

> The quiet and peaceful habits of the instructed Scotch peasant, compared with the turbulent disposition of the ignorant Irishman, ought not to be without effect upon every impartial reasoner.[21]

Addressing the opponents of education James Mill stated:

> It is not necessary that they should compare a Turkish and a British population. Let them only reflect upon the state of the Irish as compared with the English population; then compare the population of Scotland with that of England.[22]

Whitbread, who was avowedly influenced by Malthus, was one of the first to quote crude statistics in support of such arguments in Parliament. In the debate on his "Bill for establishing a Plan for the Education of the Poor" in 1807, he said:

> Search the Newgate calendar. The great majority of the executed in London every year were Irish; the next in order were English, and the

21. *Essay on Population*, 7th Edition, Ch. IX.
22. *Westminster Review*, 1813, Art. IX.

last Scots. This was in exact proportion with their respective systems of education among the lower orders.[23]

Such triumphant reference to figures like these continued for half a century.[24]

James Mill pursued the case of his native Scotland still further: he quoted statistics to show that there were eleven times as many criminals in England compared with Scotland in proportion to their respective populations:

> We desire our opponents to tell us in what respect the circumstances of the English population have not been more favourable than those of the Scottish except in the article of schooling alone?[25]

One answer to Mill was that Scotland did not have the English Poor Law.[26] All the classical economists, and not the least James Mill, were persuaded of the demoralizing effect of this legislation and, therefore, they could not neglect it in this particular case. Indeed Mill made the same observations in his article and thereby answered his own question to some extent. Earlier he had advised that the reform of the Poor Law was far more urgent in England than provision for education.

Mill also partly answered himself later in the article when he declared that schooling was rapidly growing in England. By 1826 he was convinced that literacy was typical among "the lowest people."[27] England had almost caught up with Scotland in school provision by 1835 without any compulsory provision.[28] William Cobbett, indeed, opposed Roebuck's Bill on the ground that crime in England was increasing at the same time as education was spreading.

23. Hansard, Vol. IX, Cols. 539–550.
24. See for instance the more elaborate tables in *The Social Condition and Education of the People in England and Europe*, 1850 (Longman Brown) by Dr. J. Kay.
25. *Westminster Review*, 1813, Art. IX.
26. The Scottish poor-relief system was based on the Acts of 1503 and 1579. Its outstanding feature was that no legal recognition was given to the right of able-bodied poor to support. Vagrancy and mendicity were therefore more prominent in Scotland.
27. *Westminster Review*, Vol. VI. Oct. 1826.
28. See Brougham's speech in the Lords. 21 May 1835.

"If so, what reason was there to tax the people for the increase of education?"[29]

In 1835 Brougham claimed to be able to prove without doubt the connection between vice and ignorance.

One or two examples may suffice: 700 persons were put on their trials, in the winters of 1830 and 1831, charged with rioting and arson, and of those 700 how many could write and read? Only 150; all the rest were marksmen. Of the number of boys committed to Newgate, during three years, two-thirds could neither read nor write.[30]

Brougham presented the 550 as being unable to read *and* write. Since people in those days were taught to read *before* writing there were a considerable number who had left school with the ability to read only. Many of the persons in this example left school at the end of the Napoleonic wars. His own select committee concluded that less than 1 in 15 of the whole population was receiving a schooling at this time. On these estimates it does not seem that the convicts were so much different from most people in their educational attainments. Again, the statement concerning the boys committed to Newgate was not very helpful since he failed to give details of the ages of the boys—many of whom were presumably still receiving instruction. Nothing was said about the selection of the special date for these figures so we do not know if any special circumstances were operative.[31]

Rioting of course occurred at other times besides 1830–1, the years selected by Brougham. The causes of civil unrest were complex and it

29. Hansard, 1833. Vol. XX. Cobbett continued, "It was nothing but an attempt to force education—it was French—it was a Doctrinaire plan, and we should always be opposed to it."

30. Speech to the Lords. 21 May 1835.

31. The Report of the Poor Law Commissioners in 1834 concluded that one of the most important causes of the disturbances in the depressed years 1830/31 was the bad administration of the poor laws. Thus in answer to their question on the causes of the rioting at this time the 15 parishes of Bedfordshire responded as follows: 3 gave no answer, 3 attributed the riots and fires to distress and want of regular employment, 2 to private enmity or political feeling and 7 accused directly the Poor Law administration. Cambridgeshire gave a similar picture. In Sussex it was conspicuously the main cause.

was as naïve to think then that more education would remove the root cause as it would be now to believe that it would dissolve the grievances of trade unionists or university students, many of whom come close to rioting behaviour. Nineteenth-century riots, rick-burning and so on were, in pre-franchise times, a contemporary form of social protest. Rioters were often in fact men of the "higher" working class or even middle class and riots were frequently instigated by radicals, dissenting ministers and farmers. Speaking of rioters who were convicted to be transported to Australia in the early nineteenth century, a modern observer writes:

> . . . evidence suggests that most were settled family men, that their standard of literacy was relatively high, and that comparatively few from certain counties—for example, Buckinghamshire and Wiltshire— appear to have left their wives and families on the parish. Above all they were for the most part men of high moral character. . . .[32]

In 1849 Joseph Fletcher Esq., a barrister, and one of Her Majesty's Inspectors of Schools, published some research which pointed in a different direction. He summed up his investigations as follows:

1. In comparing the gross commitments for criminal offences with the proportion of instruction in each district, there is found to be a small balance *in favour* of the most instructed districts in the years of most industrial depression (1842–3–4), but a greater one *against* them in the years of less industrial depression (1845–6–7); while in comparing the more with the less instructed portions of each district, the final result is against the former at both periods, though fourfold at the latter what it is at the former.

2. No correction for the ages of the population in different districts, to meet the excess of criminals at certain younger periods of life, will change the character of this superficial evidence against instruction; every legitimate allowance of the kind having already been made in arriving at these results;

3. Down to this period, the comparison of the criminal and educational returns of this, any more than of any other country of Europe, has

32. George Rudé, *The Crowd in History, 1730–1848*, John Wiley & Sons, 1964.

afforded no sound statistical evidence in favour, and as little against, the moral effects associated with instruction, as actually disseminated among the people.[33]

We end this chapter with two or three general and rather obvious comments. Statistics of convictions are never likely to be accurate measures of criminality. The authorities in different areas and at different times will show fluctuating efficiency in pursuing offenders. Criminals will show varying ability in escaping detection (one would expect the more intelligent to have the best chance). Again the judgements of magistrates are not likely to be reliably standardized. Even if the statistics of conviction were accurate the dangers of incorrect inference were even more serious. If one attempts to show that a lack of schooling is the main differentia between the offenders and other people, it must be shown that the two groups are the same *in all other respects* such as the stability of home background, health, degree of poverty and so on. Otherwise ignorance and crime may not be cause and effect but concomitant results of the same cause.

From these elementary considerations we must conclude, that the nineteenth-century case for state-aided education on the grounds of the reduced cost of crime was in retrospect far from satisfactorily presented. Among the several weaknesses, the most outstanding was the utilitarian habit of defining criminal action in a dogmatic, confined and rationalistic way, so that the solution of more schooling was implied in the definition itself. Beyond this, the empirical evidence presented was incomplete, ingenuous, and of the general quality that typified the pre-statistical era. But present beliefs are often rooted in evidence supplied by "reformers" and polemicists of bygone ages. Periodic rehearsals of their forgotten and outmoded debates are obviously worthwhile.

33. *Summary of the Moral Statistics of England and Wales, 1849.* A similar verdict is contained in a report of the head chaplain of Pentonville Prison in the *Morning Chronicle* of 25 April 1850. This evidence should be set side by side with that of Dr. J. Kay: *The Social Condition and Education of the People in England and Europe,* 1850.

12 · A System to Complement Poor Law Legislation: Senior and Chadwick

Proposals for education in the early nineteenth century were embodied in much of the voluminous discussion about Poor Law Reform. Before 1834 poor relief was based on the 43rd Elizabeth which enacted that the overseers of the poor "shall take order from time to time, by and with the consent of two or more justices, for setting to work the children of all such, whose parents shall not by the said persons be thought able to keep and maintain their children: and also such persons, married or un-married, as having no means to maintain them, use no ordinary and daily trade of life to get their living by; and also to raise weekly, or otherwise, by taxation of every inhabitant, and every occupier of lands in the said parish, (in such competent sums as they shall think fit,) a convenient stock of flax, hemp, wool, thread, iron and other necessary ware and stuff, to set the poor to work."

This provision was condemned by several of the classical economists as a piece of *legislative delusion* on the grounds that it spread the belief that the funds for the maintenance of labour could be increased at will, and without limit by a *fiat* of government. "Strictly speaking," Malthus protested, "this clause is as arrogant and as absurd as if it had enacted that two ears of wheat should in future grow where one only had grown before."[1] According to Malthus, the primary error was that the law sought to share the existing output more equally rather than to create ad-ditional produce.

1. *Essay on Population,* Ch. VI, Book II.

Furthermore, economists such as Malthus, James Mill and McCulloch, argued that there were profound secondary effects and ramifications of this law. Several were illustrated in the 1834 Poor Law Commissioners' Report, which was written by Senior and Chadwick.[2] The most important detriment of the poor law legislation, they argued, was the tendency of the burden of support to fall upon the class of workers immediately above the poor. It was contended, also, that the attempt in times of scarcity to raise revenue from the landlord would result in the latter reducing the wages of his employees. This process would continue, so the argument went, until the economic condition of more and more workers would be depressed to the stage of seeking parish relief themselves. The deleterious effects involved not only the economic condition of the workers, but also their moral characters:

> The poor-laws may therefore be said to diminish both the power and the will to save among the common people; and thus to weaken one of the strongest incentives to sobriety and industry, and consequently to happiness.[3]

The Report of the Poor Law Commissioners fully supported this reasoning of Malthus in the following words:

> We have seen that in many places the income derived from the parish for easy or nominal work, or, as it is most significantly termed, "in lieu of labour," actually exceeds that of the independent labourer; and even in those cases in which the relief-money only equals, or nearly approaches, the average rate of wages, it is often better worth having, as the pauper requires less expensive diet and clothing than the hardworking man. In such places a man who does not possess either some property, or an amount of skill which will ensure to him more than the average rate of wages, is of course a loser by preserving his independence. Even if he have some property, he is a loser, unless the aggregate of the income which it affords and of his wages equals what he would receive as a pauper. It appears accordingly, that when a parish has become pauperized, the labourers are not only prodigal of their earnings, not only avoid accumulation, but even dispose of, and waste in

2. See below.
3. Malthus, *Essay on Population*, Ch. VI, Book II.

debauchery, as soon as their families entitle them to allowance, any small properties which may have devolved on them, or which they may have saved in happier times.[4]

Another alleged effect of the system was that landholders were inclined to pull down rather than build cottages in the belief that this would discourage early marriages and *therefore would keep in check the numbers of new candidates for relief in the form of an increasing local population.* In turn this led to overcrowding, disease and great mortality. Inflation with all its damaging effects was also shown to be a possible consequence of the operation of poor law relief in times of scarcity. Again the system resulted in arbitrary power being given to administrators. Malthus referred to: "the capricious and insulting manner in which it is sometimes distributed by the overseers."[5]

The evidence collected by the Commissioners stressed in addition many other indirect effects of the poor law. It was alleged that in bad years, such as 1830, parish allowances were extorted by violence and incendiarism. Theft often went unpunished for no one would prosecute for fear of bringing a family upon the parish rates. Magistrates often supported persons "of vicious habits" in opposition to the parochial authorities. The system was alleged to have induced early and improvident marriages and to have destroyed in many cases the reciprocal feeling between parents and children. Children often lost respect for the father because they were soon aware that they were not dependent upon him. Men were induced to desert wives and children in order that they could be supported by the parish.

This sort of evidence from eye witnesses was just becoming widely circulated when Roebuck introduced his Education Bill in July 1833.[6] Roebuck argued the case for state intervention to protect children from parental neglect at a time when the evidence just published argued that the poor law system was often a serious contributing cause of such neglect. Among other things Roebuck also wanted state provided education to

4. Report of the Poor Law Commissioners in 1834, p. 77.
5. Malthus, Ch. VI, Book II.
6. See the copious references in *Extracts from Information Received By The Poor Law Commissioners.* 19 March 1833.

combat growing crime and according to the Poor Law Commissioners' evidence much crime was attributed to the old system of poor relief.[7]

The Poor Law Report, as written by the Utilitarians, Senior and Chadwick, condemning these defects in the Elizabethan legislation, argued for new and more positive state legislation to rectify the situation. State education emerged in the Report as one part of the proposed new poor law legislation which was designed to root out the evil influences of the old. Poor Law Reform and State Education were in fact among the very first subjects to which Parliament turned its attention immediately after the 1832 Reform Act. Roebuck was successful in initiating state education in 1833 when the first subsidies started. The Royal Commission on the Poor Law was set up in 1832. One of the Assistant Commissioners, later promoted to Commissioner, was Edwin Chadwick who, like Roebuck, was an enthusiastic disciple of Bentham.[8] It is thought that Chadwick, a prodigious worker, probably drew up the first draft of the Report of the Poor Law Commission which appeared in 1834, before it was refined by Nassau Senior. The same negative and positive aspects of utilitarian planning, which appeared in Roebuck's speech introducing his Education Bill in the previous year, were clearly evident. Reforming the Poor Law, according to the concluding page of the Commissioners' Report, was not enough:

> It will be observed, that the measures which we have suggested are intended to produce rather negative than positive effects; rather to remove the debasing influences to which a large portion of the Labouring Population is now subject, than to afford new means of prosperity

7. "Whichever impels any class into courses of sustained industry must necessarily diminish crime; and we find that one characteristic of the dispauperized parishes is the comparative absence of crime. In Birmingham, before the change of system took place, scarcely a night passed without mischief; and during the two years preceding 1818, seven men of the parish were transported for felonies; now there is scarcely any disorder in the place. In Uley and Southwell parishes crime has similarly ceased." Poor Law Commissioners' Report of 1834. (page 241).

8. Chadwick told the National Association for the Promotion of Social Science—15 November 1869: "Bentham did not fill up the details of the functions of the several ministers. Some early writings of mine, led him (Bentham) to do me the honour of charging me with the duty of filling up for him the detailed functions of the Minister of Health."

and virtue. We are perfectly aware, that for the general diffusion of right principles and habits we are to look, not so much to any economic arrangements and regulations as to the influence of a moral and religious education; and important evidence on the subject will be found throughout our Appendix. But one great advantage of any measure which shall remove or diminish the evils of the present system, is, that it will in the same degree remove the obstacles which now impede the progress of instruction, and intercept its results; and will afford a freer scope to the operation of every instrument which may be employed for elevating the intellectual and moral condition of the poorer classes.[9]

The last sentence seemed to indicate at first sight that the state, having corrected the impediment of its own legislation, could leave the provision of education to the existing private resources. However, it is immediately followed by two more sentences showing the belief of the authors that much more economical disposition of educational resources could be achieved from central direction. The chief economy they had in mind was almost certainly the encouragement of large scale enterprises such as the new monitorial schools under the systems of Bell and Lancaster.

We believe, that if the funds now destined to the purposes of education, many of which are applied in a manner unsuited to the present wants of society, were wisely and economically employed, they would be sufficient to give all the assistance which can be prudently afforded by the State. As the subject is not within our Commission, we will not dwell on it further, and we have ventured on these few remarks only for the purpose of recording our conviction that as soon as a good administration of the Poor Laws shall have rendered further improvement possible, the most important duty of the Legislature is to take measures to promote the religious and moral education of the labouring classes.[10]

Benthamism inside the reformed Parliament had to be represented by Utilitarians who were also men of the world and practical politicians. Such were the law reformers Mackintosh, Brougham, Romilly, Joseph Hume and Grote. They were accustomed to the parliamentary necessity

9. Report of the Poor Law Commissioners: page 362 (1834).
10. *Ibid.*

of making practical compromises. The requests of those who just wanted an abolition of a poor law could not be met. In the outcome the poor law was not abolished, but reformed and amended. Malthus, Mill and Mc-Culloch had all advocated the policy of gradualism.[11] Further, they upheld the support of those people who were by accident or natural infirmity obviously unable to keep themselves.[12]

Bentham's contribution to the debate was the idea of solution through scientific legislation based on the principle of utility. According to Dicey this "invention" was welcomed in all sorts of unexpected places since it seemed to pacify both the individualist Whig elements and the aristocrats who were worried about the possibility of revolution in the continental style. Bentham's slogan "Sound Legislation" was a relatively harmless one compared with the demands for "National Rights." Dicey also contended that the omnipotence of Parliament, which Bentham learned from Blackstone, when turned into reality by bold and enthusiastic reformers, could easily grow so large as to be difficult to restrain.

> The formation of an effective police force for London (1829)—the rigorous and scientific administration of the Poor Law (1834) under the control of the central government—the creation of authorities for the enforcement of laws to promote the public health and the increasing application of a new system of centralisation, the invention of Bentham himself—were favoured by Benthamites and promoted utilitarian reforms; but they were measures which in fact limited the area of individual freedom.[13]

From the point of view of such enthusiasts as Roebuck and Chadwick it was not *legislation* that was bad per se; what was wrong was *unscientific* legislation. By substituting one *good* law (including the education provi-

11. Thus McCulloch wrote: "All changes in the public economy of a great nation and especially those which deeply affect the interests of the poor should be brought about gradually and slowly." *Principles of Political Economy,* Part III, Ch. 3. *Poor Laws* (1825).
12. As McCulloch argued: "With respect to the important poor, there does not seem to be much room for doubt as to the policy, as well as humanity, of giving them a legal claim to relief." (*ibid.*).
13. See Dicey: "Law and Opinion in England." Lecture VI. Herbert Spencer criticised the utilitarians on the grounds that their pursuit of the greatest happiness for the greatest number, often sacrificed the freedom of individuals to the real or supposed benefit of the State. See "Man v The State" and "Social Statics."

sion) for the *bad* (Elizabethan) law, *things would be better.* Such provision would not only help to restore the self-respect of the workers and so reduce pauperism (negative utilitarianism), but it would go further and open the gateway to new found happiness (positive utilitarianism).

There were some differences as to the correct priorities. In the *Literary Journal* of 1806, James Mill reviewed Colquhoun's system of education for the labouring poor. Colquhoun was alarmed by the fact that 537,139 healthy adults under 60, out of a total population of 8,872,980, had been chiefly supported in and out of workhouses at the expense of the public in the year 1802. Mill rejected Colquhoun's major solution — a national education system — on the grounds that it was giving additional charity to the poor. Colquhoun thought that education would be such a good investment that the extra money to be provided for it would be more than offset by the diminution of the amount extracted from the parish. Mill thought that education alone would not provide the requisite shock-treatment:

> The disposition to indolence and pleasure which prevails over so many persons of the best education will always prevail over a great proportion of the lower orders, in spite of the best education which their condition permits them to receive, when all the most powerful motives to industry and frugality are withdrawn. . . . *Thinking, in this unhappy situation that to set on foot a plan for the education of the poor is to begin at the wrong end; . . .*"[14] (our italics).

James Mill was nevertheless one of the leading Utilitarian spokesmen on the philosophy of education and saw it as one of the important keys to social harmony

> the question whether people should be educated, is the same as the question, whether the people should be happy or miserable. The question, whether they should have more or less of intelligence, is merely the question, whether they should have more or less of misery, when happiness might be given in its stead.[15]

14. James Mill, *Literary Journal,* 1806, 2nd Series, Vol. II.
15. Article *Education* in the Encyclopedia Britannica and republished in *Essays of Government,* 1882. The article is now available in W. H. Burston, *James Mill on Education,* 1969 (see p. 105).

Presumably Mill's objection to Colquhoun's proposal for "national education" implied not an opposition to education but only to the way Colquhoun was proposing to finance and organize it.

The proposals of the Commissioners in their Poor Law Report of 1834, emphasized the need to amend the law to improve the administration of poor relief, as indeed the Act of that year attempted. Chadwick, who was appointed secretary to the Commissioners set up by the 1834 Act, attributed the main hindrance to the proper implementation of statutory poor relief in the past to the "imbecility or to the sinister interests of ignorant local administrators."[16]

The confidence of most of Bentham's followers in a solution to the problem of indigence by scientific administration in which education had its due role, can be traced to a project which Bentham had published in 1797 entitled: "Outline of a Work to be called Pauper Management Improved."[17] Workhouses were to be run by a board of directors similar to that of the India Company. Administration was to be centralized in one London office and the board was to be elected by the members of a society which would provide initial finance on the ordinary shareholding principle. The board would obtain revenue by finding a market for large contracts, so making use of the labour of the assisted poor. The administrators were to work in the full public eye (the "transparent management principle"). This same publicity was to be given to the assisted inmates. Assistance was only to be granted in strict proportion to work done (the "self-liberation" principle). Such *discriminate* relief would sort out the industrious from the idle so that nobody would suffer unduly on account of something which was his *misfortune* rather than his *"fault."* The *natural* identity of interests which was normally brought about by the free market, would here be *artificially*, but nevertheless effectively, reconstructed in the "industry-house."

The most important alleged collateral benefit from this system was the education of the children in the workhouses. Bentham was impressed with the power of environment upon the building of character. This followed from his attachment (like Mill's) to the psychological Principle of

16. Address to the National Association for the Promotion of Social Science. Oct. 1863.
17. Published in Arthur Young's "Annals of Agriculture."

Association, and it accounted for the strategic position in which, he believed, even the most ordinary schools, and certainly the teacher-training colleges, were placed. If the utilitarians could achieve some success by setting up their teachers or, at least, establishing *some* of their principles in fee-paying day schools, what attainments could they not reach in schools within the workhouse walls where the *whole* environment was under their jurisdiction? As Bentham put it:

> The influence of the schoolmaster on the conduct of the pupil in ordinary life, is as nothing compared with the influence exercised by the Company over those its wards.

Clearly, as far as their pedagogic ideas were concerned, the control of the workhouses in 1834 provided the Utilitarians with a main chance.

The Poor Law Commissioners were appointed in 1834 with extensive powers, vaguely defined and with no representative in Parliament. One of their duties was to see that relief was severely checked and the total number of paupers reduced. By 1839, however, there were still 98,000 paupers in workhouses compared with 560,000 still receiving relief outside. These provided Chadwick with material for extended study which carried him especially far in the fields of sanitation and town planning, as well as education. He and his colleague, Dr. J. Kay (the treasurer and founder member of the Manchester Statistical Society), found themselves compelled to state that it was impossible to administer the deterrent Poor Law successfully before *preventive* measures against dirt, disease and ignorance were taken. Kay moved from the Poor Law Commission to become in 1839 the first secretary to the Committee of Privy Council on Education, an office which was the forebear of the present Minister of Education.

The Benthamite authors of the English Poor Law Amendment Act of 1834 provided detailed plans for education in their new workhouses. The new Poor Law Board was directed to regulate the education of children in workhouses three hours at least every day in the 3 Rs and Christian religious principles. In 1837 a House of Commons Committee on the working of the new Poor Law stated that it was both the duty and interest of the community to take all means to see that pauper children were educated to prepare them for an independent adult life. Children were to be separated from the evil adult influences in the workhouses. The Poor Law Commissioners were empowered to combine parishes or unions for setting up huge schools into which could be drawn all the pauper children of the districts. The organization was another example of the application of the Benthamite principle of centralized administration.

The freedom of initiative allowed to the Poor Law Commissioners enabled them to make many *ad hoc* experiments in methods of schooling. This experience prompted them to make suggestions in the sphere of education as a whole. In 1841 the Poor Law Commission published a report to the Secretary of State on the Training of Pauper Children. The first chapter was written by Chadwick and much of the rest by Kay. Kay pleaded that the "protection of minors" principle applied with especial force in the case of pauper children because their dependence was "unavoidable and absolute." Even apart from this duty the state had an interest in "eradicating the germs of pauperism from the rising generation, and of securing in the minds and in the morals of the people the best protection for the institutions of society."[18] Whilst the physical condition of the children should be no better than that of the household of the self-supported labourer the state should not take as a standard the type of secular and moral education of the labouring classes since this was "meagre and inadequate."

> England is the most pauperised country in Europe, and that in which the Government has effected little or nothing for the education of the poorer classes, while every other Protestant kingdom has, during the present century, employed its best resources wisely and vigorously for the elementary education of the people.[19]

The Report to which Kay contributed was instigated because the education provision of the 1834 Act had not really got under way.[20] Kay, who

18. Report to the Secretary of State from the Poor Law Commissioners. 1841, p. 19.
19. *Ibid.*, p. 21.
20. He presented statistics of children in the 35 Unions of Norfolk and Suffolk to show what he thought was excessive ignorance. Yet his figures revealed that of 483 boys from 9 years to 16 years, 421 (or 87%) could read. Of 547 boys from 2 years to 9 years, 280 (more than a half) could read, but Kay did not specify which age above 2 years a typical boy could be expected to read. As would be expected, ability to write was not so high, yet 56% of the boys between 9 years and 16 years could do so. Kay promised the

was by this time the new secretary to the Council Committee on Education was obviously keen to succeed in experiments with pauper schools so that his ideas would be more readily acceptable elsewhere. He advised against the apprenticeship system for children leaving workhouses at 14 because he thought it had pernicious tendencies and the cost of apprenticeship premiums were formidable. Instead he urged that children should be given a good preparation for their future industrial duties by the tutors in the workhouse schools. Kay argued that there were substantial economies of scale which could be reaped from the amalgamated union schools. Specialist teachers and pupil teachers could be appointed and a useful "monitorial" type division of labour could take place.

> The schoolmaster should be provided with some simple elementary works on gardening, husbandry, seamanship, and handicraft trades, from which some of the oldest boys should read extracts daily to the school.[21]

The girls could learn household duties such as needlework, cookery, etc. He favoured a scheme whereby all the children *could do paid labour* for a portion of the day, say three hours, and this, partly for the workhouse and partly for themselves in their own gardens. This was the famous "Half-Time" system which Chadwick elaborated and strongly advocated for all types of school in subsequent years. The idea was supported by the reports of the Factory Inspectors who showed that the progress of "Half-Timers" who went to school 15 hours and to the factory for the rest of the week was often equal and sometimes superior to the progress of those children who in the same schools attended for the full 30 hours.

This educational experience which emerged from the administration of the poor law was used by Nassau Senior in his capacity as a member of the 1861 Newcastle Commission on Popular Education. Senior gave Chadwick the task of collecting evidence for him on the "Half-Time" system and used it to advocate a shortening of hours in ordinary schools. This proposal was most relevant at a time when the practitioners of Gladstonian public finance were looking for economies in the 1860s. In his rec-

---

Secretary for State, "Every week will, I trust, remove a portion of this reproach, so that it may soon cease to exist."
21. *Ibid.*, p. 34.

ommendation to this Commission, Senior repeated Kay's argument for special protection for pauper children. He cited the results of Chadwick's research to show the superiority of big (Benthamite) schools over little schools. Twentieth-century arguments for large comprehensive schools were foreshadowed in Senior's quotation of Mr. Tufnell's evidence:

> In the large school there is the subdivision of labour of teachers. In the Central London District School, for example, there is the headmaster with a large salary, and two under masters, and eight pupil-teachers. These masters have not all the same talents or capacities, but are often appointed for their specialities.[22]

Senior did not entirely share the cautious satisfaction shown by some of his colleagues on the 1861 Commission on the accumulating evidence provided by their officials of the growth of unassisted and assisted (subsidized and inspected) private schooling. He was disturbed that too many families were choosing the wrong type of schools and was impressed that typical private schools, especially the uninspected ones, were much inferior to those large scale establishments that he, Chadwick, and Kay had outlined. He quoted the complaints of assistant commissioners that the teachers that many families were choosing were often people who were not properly trained and frequently consisted of inferiors who had failed in other trades. He thought that many parents were still not to be trusted because they were not choosing the type of school which he thought best. Senior complained that many parents were of the opinion that the state subsidized and inspected school was vulgar:

> . . . or their boy had been punished there, or he is required to be clean, or to be regular, or the private school is half a street nearer, or is kept by a friend, or by some one who will submit his teaching to their dictation.[23]

He complained that his fellow Commissioner Dr. Temple, who wanted to give parents more control over the schools, would place the education

---

22. *Suggestions on Popular Education.* Mr. Crampton, headmaster at Brentford demonstrated that because of the necessity of grading arithmetic classes the chances of success were 10 times in favour of a school of 500 compared with one of 50. Building costs per head were lower too.
23. *Ibid.*

of the country: "under the control of the lowest, morally and intellectu-
ally, of its inhabitants."[24] Dr. Temple had argued that:

> . . . the people's misgovernment of their own affairs is government in
> the learning. . . . That if the labouring classes are ever to learn any kind
> of self-government, the management of their children's education is
> the most within their reach—That it is a business in which mistakes
> rapidly show their fruits; and that though the parents would make
> many mistakes, they would not long persist in mistakes whose conse-
> quences became speedily visible.[25]

Senior dismissed this reasoning. He believed that in order to profit by
experience men needed to start with much more education. This he
thought was proved because:

> For fifty years they have been managing their own trades unions. There
> is not one which is not based on folly, tyranny and injustice which
> would disgrace the rudest savages. They sacrifice their wives', their
> children's and their own health and strength to the lowest sensuality.
> The higher the wages the worse seems, in general, to be the condition
> of the families.[26]

The Commission was advised by Senior that individual family choice was
for the future. Intervention was necessary now—but it would be regarded as of the self-liquidating sort over the next century. Although the
Commission ought not to be diverted from the policy which was appropriate then by their wishes or hopes as to what may occur after a hundred years—that is in the 1960s:

> So far as we are influenced by those wishes or hopes, we ought to try
> to prepare the way for their regulation, by giving to the present gen-
> eration an education which will fit them to educate still better another
> generation, which in time, may further improve a third, until England
> becomes, what no country has ever yet become, an Utopia inhabited
> by a self-educated and well-educated labouring population.[27]

24. *Ibid.*
25. Oxford Essays, 1856, p. 258.
26. *Suggestions on Popular Education.* Senior's remarks could not embrace all parents
since trades unions represented only a minority of the working population.
27. *Ibid.*, p. 5.

13 · John Stuart Mill's National System and the Problem of Liberty

The term "liberty" invokes such universal respect that most modern political economists and moralists endeavour to find a conspicuous place for it somewhere in their systems or prescriptions. But in view of the innumerable senses of this term an insistence on some kind of definition prior to any discussion seems to be justified. For our present purposes attention to two particularly conflicting interpretations will be sufficient. These are sometimes called the "negative" and the "positive" notions of Liberty.[1] According to the "negative" notion, my own liberty implies the reduction to a minimum of the deliberate interference of other human beings within the area in which I wish to act. Conversely the absence of liberty, or coercion, is regarded as undesirable because it amounts to the prevention by other persons of my doing what I want. On the other hand, the "positive" sense of the word "liberty" consists in the attainment of self-mastery, or, in other words, the release from the domination of "adverse" influences. This "slavery" from which men "liberate" themselves is variously described to include slavery to "nature," to "unbridled passions," to "irrational impulses," or simply slavery to one's "lower nature." "Positive" liberty is then identified with "self-realization" or an awakening into a conscious state of rationality. The fact that it is contended that such a state can often be attained only by the interference of other "rational" persons who "liberate" their fellow beings from the "irrational-

---

1. Cf. Isaiah Berlin: *The Two Concepts of Liberty* (Oxford 1958), to which this analysis is much indebted.

ity," brings this interpretation of liberty into open and striking conflict with liberty in the "negative" sense.

This conflict will be illustrated with reference to the historical struggle for improvement in the provision of education in the eighteenth and nineteenth centuries. It must be observed first, however, that the already ambiguous notions of liberty became further complicated in this field by their unavoidable connection with another chameleonic term: "educational reform." In turn both concepts were found to be inextricably involved in policy proposals which raised questions of the desirability or otherwise of parliamentary legislation. The kind of liberty which was usually in most men's minds in the context of eighteenth-century education was that which we have described as "negative" liberty. Accordingly, "educational reform" usually meant agitation to negate previous legislation which had given the predominant control to the Church and state, rather than to make fresh legislation to supplement or replace private initiative. On the other hand, in the nineteenth century, it was liberty in the "positive" sense which began to dominate the educational scene. "Educational reform" now called for positive legislation as part of the conscious and deliberate architecture of a new society. Such legislation was designed to set up new and "necessary" institutions which, allegedly, a more individualistic world had so far failed to produce. Utilitarianism was the main inspiration of this outlook, and by its novel apparatus of "social engineering" *via* "scientific legislation" a prominent place was reserved for the "liberation" of the masses through specially designed state educational institutions. It was characteristic of these revolutionary blueprints for the new school systems that they typically revealed Bentham's penchant for centralized administration and the economies of large-scale buildings. But the main point to notice is that the "liberty" of the Benthamites in this sphere was quite different from and indeed opposed to the "liberty" of the educational radicals such as J. Priestley and W. Godwin in the late eighteenth century.

Before analysing John Stuart Mill's attempt to synthesize these different concepts it will be helpful to examine representative opinions in the works of two of his acquaintances. William Godwin, who was a member of the circle of friends of J. S. Mill's father, James Mill, and frequent visitor to his home, was perhaps the most vehement upholder of the concept of "negative" liberty in education which was typical of the late eighteenth century. On the other hand, J. A. Roebuck, who was a member of the younger generation of Utilitarians, and personal friend of J. S. Mill, seems to have made the first striking claim for the "positive" concept of educational liberty to be found among the parliamentary speeches in the early nineteenth century.

William Godwin and the Case for Negative Liberty in Education

According to Godwin the only true education was self-education. He maintained that men would only begin to fulfil themselves when they saw that there were no obstacles which they could not break down by their own efforts. Education was needed not to instruct mankind, as one of his opponents, T. R. Malthus, wanted to do, but to "unfold his stores." But since men had to discover their potentialities by themselves it was a grave hindrance to their development to make the Government responsible for their education. Furthermore, Godwin believed that governments were corrupt anyway and provided only too easy a channel for thinkers who were arrogant enough to believe that they had the monopoly of the truth and that their doctrines alone were worthy of forced consumption through the agency of the state. Godwin accused the Benthamites of such arrogance, for instance, in their claim that they could reduce crime by educating the people in the recognition of legal rules, an education which was to be given in special Benthamite schools. Such rules, argued Godwin, should not be manufactured by one section of society such as the Utilitarians and then "heralded" to the world. The laws were meaningless if they were not equally discoverable by the whole of the people. As another example Godwin would have contended that the population theory of Malthus was not such a profound revelation as to require, as Malthus advocated, a state initiated education to make universal announcement of it: "There is no proposition, at present apprehended to be true, so valuable as to justify the introduction of an establishment for the purpose of inculcating it on mankind."[2] Indeed, Godwin would prob-

2. *Enquiry concerning Political Justice,* 1796, Ch. VIII, "Of National Education," p. 296.

ably have accused all the contemporary classical economists of hypocrisy in their insistence for the minimum amount of government interference with the freedom of individuals on the ground that each individual knew his own interests best. For, like the physiocrats who preceded them, each classical economist seemed to have in reserve his own private plan of manufacturing the characters of the same individuals in the first place, through the exceptional provision of a state educational system, in which his own ideas were to mould individuals to his liking from the start.[3] Godwin would have imposed this indictment more severely upon the Malthusians and Utilitarians than upon Adam Smith, who displayed more hesitation in this whole matter because of his much greater distrust of government. Adam Smith, despite his own predilection for some exceptional measures in education, would have gone a long way with the following three general criticisms of governmental power in the sphere of instruction.

First, objected Godwin: "All public establishments include in them the idea of permanence. They endeavour, it may be, to secure and diffuse whatever of advantage to society is already known, but forget that more remains to be known." In time this inertia meant that even obsolete knowledge would continue to be purveyed. But then the public establishments do something far worse: "They actively restrain the flights of the mind, and fix it in the belief of exploded errors."[4] Only some "violent concussion" would oblige the authorities to substitute a new system of philosophy for an old one: ". . . and then they are as pertinaciously attached to this second doctrine as they were to the first."[5] Public education always supported prejudice: ". . . it teaches its pupils not the fortitude that shall bring every proposition to the test of examination, but the art of vindicating such levels as may chance to be previously established."[6]

Godwin's second criticism stemmed from his conviction that man's activity in doing things for himself was of supreme value in giving him the

3. "This just transfers the problem of limiting governmental or social interference from one plane to another." Jack Lively: *The Social and Political Thought of De Toqueville*, 1962.
4. *Op. cit.*, p. 293.
5. *Op. cit.*, p. 294.
6. *Op. cit.*, p. 295.

only sure springs of progress. Whatever others did for him was not done so well: "It is in our wisdom to incite men to act for themselves, not to retain them in a state of perpetual pupillage. . . . This whole proposition of a national education is founded upon a supposition which has been repeatedly refuted in this work, but which has recurred upon us in a thousand forms, that unpatronified truth is inadequate to the purpose of enlightening mankind."[7]

Godwin's third objection was based on what he thought would be education's "obvious alliance" with the prevailing national government: "Before we put so powerful a machine under the direction of so unambiguous an agent, it behoves us to consider well what it is that we do. Government will not fail to employ it to strengthen its hands and perpetuate its institutions."[8] It was not true, he argued, that youth should be instructed to venerate the virtues of the British Constitution. If anything, they should be taught to venerate *truth*. Godwin was here posing the problem of indoctrination which had its contemporary example in Napoleonic France and which has been demonstrated in several totalitarian states since then. It was a problem which deeply concerned John Stuart Mill, as we shall see. Godwin contended that if schemes of national education were established at the height of a despotic power, whilst it could not perhaps stifle truth for ever, yet it would be: ". . . the most formidable and profound contrivance for that purpose that imagination can suggest."[9] Furthermore it was no use arguing that in countries in which more liberty prevailed this sort of injury would not take place. At any one time even under the best government it was reasonable to assume that there were important errors: ". . . and a national education has the most direct tendency to perpetuate those errors, and to form all minds upon one model."[10]

J. A. Roebuck and the Case for Positive Liberty in Education

Among John Stuart Mill's personal friends who represented Benthamism in the new House of Commons immediately after the Reform Act of

7. *Op. cit.*, p. 296.
8. *Op. cit.*, p. 297.
9. *Op. cit.*, p. 298.
10. *Op. cit.*, p. 298.

1832, one of the most active was J. A. Roebuck. In his *Autobiography,* J. S. Mill wrote of him: "it is his title to permanent remembrance, that in the very first year during which he sat in Parliament, he originated (or re-originated after the unsuccessful attempt of Mr. Brougham) the parliamentary movement for National Education."[11] Roebuck devoted his crucial speech to Parliament in 1833 to the three following subjects: "I would first solicit the attention of the House to the more prominent benefits to be obtained by a general education of the people. Secondly, I would endeavour to show why the Government should itself supply this education; and lastly, I shall attempt to trace a rude outline of a plan by which every inhabitant of this empire might receive the instruction requisite for the well-being of society."[12] With regard to the first of these subjects, Roebuck argued that the most prominent benefit from state education would be that it would teach people how to be happy and therefore would reduce violence, mischief and political unrest. This, of course, was the orthodox Utilitarian doctrine. Unhappiness existed because people were ignorant of the proper understanding of the circumstances on which their happiness depended: "let them once understand thoroughly their social condition, and we shall have no more unmeaning discontents—no wild and futile schemes of Reform; we shall not have a stack-burning peasantry—a sturdy pauper population—a monopoly-seeking manufacturing class."[13]

With regard to his second subject, the reasons why the Government should itself supply the education, Roebuck first argued from the authority of the "most enlightened" countries in Europe, i.e. France and Prussia, which had already accepted the principle. But his main argument was simply based on precedent. Because it was generally accepted, he argued, that the Government did some things, it should therefore do others. To maintain the peace of society the Government administered justice, for the furtherence of intercourse it superintended the roads and indeed to regulate public morality it passed laws thus involving itself with

11. J. S. Mill, *Autobiography* (New York, 1944), p. 136.
12. Hansard, 1833, Vol. XX, Cols. 139–66.
13. *Ibid.*

the business of training the "public mind." Roebuck therefore concluded: "Inasmuch, then, as this training is among the chief means of regulating public morality—as it is one of the chief means of furthering generally the well-being, the happiness of society—insomuch, we may say, without fear of refutation, that the business of education ought to be deemed one of its chief concerns."[14]

It is at this point that the contrast with Godwin is the most striking. For the latter, happiness could only be the product of self-discovery. The Utilitarians on the other hand genuinely believed that they alone could instruct people how to be happy. It is not surprising that the clash between the two freedoms became fully exposed later in Roebuck's speech. Answering the charge that the state was robbing people of their freedom Roebuck protested: "I ask, Sir, in the first place, if it rob the people of *rational* freedom? We every day coerce the people by laws, and rob them of freedom. . . . Freedom in itself is not a good thing—it is only good when it leads to good—if it leads to evil, it must be, it is every day, restrained by the most stringent and coercing bonds."[15] (Italics supplied.)

Freedom for Roebuck was thus indissolubly linked with goodness and the arbiter of goodness should be the Government. If the Government were a bad one, asserted Roebuck, then this was an argument for replacing it with a good one. Now in Roebuck's mind there can be no doubt that a good or "reformed" government was one that consisted largely of Utilitarian philosophers like himself. The charge of intellectual despotism was side-stepped by the persuasiveness of the word "good." In this way, therefore, Roebuck demonstrated his version of liberty in education. His was a "positive" notion of liberty, one which had to be translated and authorized by "a good Government," that "*deus ex machina*" of the whole Utilitarian programme. The liberty of W. Godwin, in contrast, preferred full reference to the individual's own choice because there was usually no better criterion and it was certainly preferable to reliance on "good government" which was to him no more than a disembodied abstraction.

14. *Ibid.*
15. *Ibid.*

So much for the representatives of the two opposing notions of liberty in the first half of nineteenth-century England. It remains now to examine John Stuart Mill's attempted reconciliation and his own particular version of a "national system."

J. S. Mill's Special Treatment of Education

After much serious thought J. S. Mill argued for very special treatment for education and accordingly made the following proposals: first, education was to be made compulsory by law; secondly, the State was to see that this law was respected not by providing state schools (except in exceptional circumstances) but by instituting a system of examinations. Should a child fail to attain a certain minimum standard then his parents were to be taxed and the proceeds devoted to his continued education. Cases of exceptional poverty were to be met by special financial dispensations from the state earmarked for the payment of subsidies or fees. In the light of our discussion of liberty, it will be interesting to trace the course of Mill's reasoning which led to these conclusions. It will be argued that his deliberations point to an uneasy compromise between the two notions of liberty as represented in Godwin and Roebuck, a compromise which, on the whole, leaned in favour of the Utilitarian doctrine of the latter.

John Stuart Mill is probably the most celebrated champion of what is known as the English nineteenth-century liberal point of view. This view carries with it in the popular mind the fullest expression of "negative" liberty as we have defined it above. Deeply embedded in this concept, as we have seen, is the belief that coercion is bad as such, even though it may have to be chosen sometimes as the lesser of evils. The conviction is that there are certain parts of an individual's life where he is entitled to freedom from interference since it is no business of government at all.[16]

16. Mill's championship of this view has been recently demonstrated by I. Berlin, *op. cit.* See also H. L. A. Hart, "Immorality and Treason," *Listener,* Vol. 62, No. 1583, pp. 162–3. This is a contribution to the debate which was provoked by the report of the Wolfenden Committee on Homosexual Offences and Prostitution.

This is the view which is commonly associated with Mill's essay *On Liberty* (1859). The following is a key quotation:

> The object of this Essay is to assert one very simple principle, as entitled to govern absolutely the dealings of society with the individual in the way of compulsion and control, whether the means used be physical force in the form of legal penalties, or the moral coercion of public opinion. That principle is, that the sole end for which mankind are warranted, individually or collectively, in interfering with the liberty of action of any of their number, is self-protection. That the only purpose for which power can be rightfully exercised over any member of a civilised community, against his will, is to prevent harm to others. His own good, either physical or moral, is not a sufficient warrant. He cannot rightfully be compelled to do or forbear because it will be better for him to do so, because it will make him happier, because, in the opinions of others, to do so would be wise, or even right.[17]

Once stated, however, this belief in freedom as a value in itself is not repeated by Mill as much as one would expect. One explanation of this is that he had a second, but quite independent notion of liberty and one which increasingly occupied him. Liberty was desirable, he thought, because it had a special utility. This took the shape of certain presumed consequences of which Mill approved, such as variety of effort and experiment and the pursuit of self-perfection. Such "desirable" development, thought Mill, could only arise from dispersed free choice and healthy spontaneity. Again, Mill buttressed his case for liberty with another subordinate argument, the contention that "each is the best judge and guardian of his own interests." This proposition, which was widely supported by his fellow classical economists, is again an argument which is independent of the idea of liberty for its own sake for it is conceivable that if people were not good judges, then liberty could be dispensed with.

However, when we examine Mill's basic case for intervention, that is "to prevent harm to others," we discover that he moved away considerably from the purely "negative" concept of liberty. For to be strictly

17. *On Liberty*. 1962 edition (Fontana), p. 135. This edition will be implied henceforth.

consistent with this notion, the only kind of "harm to others" which would be relevant is the harm of impeding another's freedom. The only acceptable formula in other words would be "coercion to prevent coercion." [18] In fact Mill's idea of "harm to others" is so wide that he fails to conceal his profound and complementary theory of the state with regard to which liberty has only a subordinate role to play. Thus by "harming" others, Mill sometimes implied physical injury but at others, as with his opinion on offences against decency, he included injury to good manners. Again, harmful treatment to animals was yet another extension of the idea. Apart from this, "harm" consisted of failing to perform what Mill considered to be "assignable duties." One of the most important of these was the "correct" treatment of dependants and accordingly the proper education of children was the appropriate duty "assigned" to the parent.

Mill took it to be the main duty of the state to protect all individuals regardless of age. He agreed with Roebuck that the power of the parent over his child was delegated by the state. The state could intervene the moment it was established that the parent was abusing this power, i.e. on the grounds of doing harm to others. Such propositions, however, become less clear when subjected to precise definition. Even charges of deliberate physical cruelty are not always easy to establish. But Mill extended the ideas of harm and cruelty to include the act of *neglecting to develop the child's mental faculties*. This implied the belief that each child had a right to a minimum of education: "Education also, the best which circumstances admit of their receiving, is not a thing which parents or relatives, from indifference, jealousy or avarice, should have it in their power to withhold." [19] Now even if "the best education which circumstances allowed" is capable of easy definition, some upholders of "negative" liberty would still question whether it is relevant to a legitimate case of doing harm to others. They may concede that the state's duty of protection is clearly called on when any of its members is physically ob-

18. The analysis at this point owes much to H. J. McCloskey: *Mill's Liberalism* in *The Philosophical Quarterly*, April 1963.
19. *Principles of Political Economy*, Ashley edition 1915, p. 958. All subsequent references will be to this edition.

structed or injured so that his faculties are in some way impaired. But if a parent neglects the education of a child it is not clear that its faculties have been impaired or injured in the same way. Accumulating modern psychological and educational research does suggest that the early years are the most crucial in the learning process. The debatable area however is the degree of significant help that "active" or "conscious" parental help can generate, bearing in mind (a) that the poor parent himself has to struggle against his environment and (b) that his child has already inherited genetic features that are beyond the parent's control.

Certainly, a "minimum education" appropriate to circumstances cannot be rigorously defined in any way that would satisfy all opinion. Education, for instance, is a wider term than formal schooling. J. S. Mill himself expressed the point thus: "Even if the government could comprehend within itself, in each department, all the most eminent intellectual capacity and active talent of the nation, it would not be the less desirable that the conduct of a large portion of the affairs of the society should be left in the hands of the persons immediately interested in them. The business of life is an essential part of the practical education of a people; without which, book and school instruction, though most necessary and salutary, does not suffice to qualify them for conduct, and for the adaptation of means to ends. Instruction is only one of the desiderata of mental improvement; another almost as indispensable, is a vigorous exercise of the active energies; labour, contrivance, judgement, self-control: and the natural stimulus to these is the difficulties of life."[20]

It seems to follow from this that the person most in contact with the "difficulties of life" in a child's family environment would be the parent and that he would at least be an appropriate person to consult. To take one example, if in mid-nineteenth-century England (when that country was relatively underdeveloped) a parent had decided that his child leaving school at the age of twelve would have contributed best to his own and to his family's interest, whereas a state official had contended that thirteen years was a more suitable leaving age, it seems that there would

20. *Principles of Political Economy*, p. 948.

have been a case here of honest difference in opinion. Now the plea for the proper ventilation of honest opinion was another important feature in the *Essay on Liberty*. Mill maintained that we should indulge "false" opinions because of the possibility that they were right. In the case of education, however, Mill himself in several parts of his writings reveals a predilection for overruling parental opinion by state decree in order that his own view, or that of a group of educated, "rational" or cultivated superiors should predominate. It certainly seems that strong elements of the positive concept of liberty appeared in Mill's work in the context of state protection of infants. For here he does give the impression of having found a formula whereby in many cases the child would be "liberated" from the "uncultivated" influences of his parents.

We are given this impression most forcefully when we discover that in the context of education he throws away completely his subordinate argument for liberty, the argument that "each is best judge of his own interests." Ultimately it seems that his main anxiety was not so much that infants could not judge for themselves. His more serious assertion was that most adults could not judge properly either and that therefore freedom must after all be taken away from them at least in this sphere. For this indeed is the first of Mill's major exceptions to the laissez-faire principle which he discussed in *The Principles of Political Economy:*

> The uncultivated cannot be competent judges of cultivation. Those who most need to be made wiser and better, usually desire it least, and if they desired it, would be incapable of finding the way to it by their own lights. It will continually happen, on the voluntary system, that, the ends not being desired, the means will not be provided at all, or that, the persons requiring improvement having an imperfect or altogether erroneous conception of what they want, the supply called forth by the demand of the market will be anything but what is really required. Now any well-intentioned and tolerably civilized government may think, without presumption, that it does or ought to possess a degree of cultivation above the average of the community which it rules, and that it should therefore be capable of offering better education and better instruction to the people, than the greater number of them would spontaneously demand. Education, therefore, is one of those

things which it is admissible in principle that a government should provide for the people.[21]

These seem to be the words of a philosopher wishing to "liberate" his fellows into his state of rationality. One certainly does not associate such views with "negative" liberty. It is a position in which many "wise men" find themselves. They are persuaded that this is not really a case of coercion, or if it is, excusable because in the words of Fichte "you will later recognize the reasons for what I am doing now."

In spite of all this, however, J. S. Mill, the popular champion of liberty shows, in this field, anguished mental struggle over the whole question of state education. The scepticism inculcated by Godwin emerges now and then with so much compulsion as to amount to apparent contradiction with the statements so far examined. The upholder of negative liberty usually protests against coercion and the word despotism is one of the strongest terms in the language which is used to convey his dislike of it. Similarly in his moments of doubt Mill feared that even the educational powers of government could lead to despotism and that they needed the same cautious vigilance, if not more, as other powers. Consider this striking "Godwinian" passage in Mill's essay *On Liberty:*

> A general State education is a mere contrivance for moulding people to be exactly like one another: and as the mould in which it casts them is that which pleases the predominant power in the government, whether this be a monarch, a priesthood, an aristocracy, or the majority of the existing generation; in proportion as it is efficient and successful, it establishes a despotism over the mind, leading by natural tendency to one over the body.[22]

21. *Principles of Political Economy*, p. 953. Notice that Mill's complaint concerns the quality, not the quantity, of education. From the evidence of the 1861 Commission on Popular Education, England, which was about the only remaining European country without a national system of education, was still abreast of its neighbours in quantity. The average working class parent was paying fees for his children's education and this covered one-third of the cost. The question was whether the state should subsidize this vast voluntary system, in which the parent's voice was respected, or supersede it with state schools.
22. *On Liberty*, p. 239.

Such statements seem to obscure the assertion of the previous quotation that a "well intentioned" government should be capable "of offering better education and better instruction to the people" than they would themselves demand. For if governments in reality turn out to be a current predominant power such as a majority or a priesthood then the "well intentioned" government either does not exist or becomes suspect if it claims to be benevolent.

To construct practical proposals out of such a dilemma was no easy task for Mill. His final prescriptions show much greater reflection and caution than those of his friend, Roebuck, with whose reasoning nevertheless Mill seems to have gone a considerable way. In his parliamentary speech Roebuck had openly faced the problem with these words: "It is dangerous, they say, to put such an instrument as education into the hands of Government; lest thereby the public mind be debauched, and slavish ideas and habits alone be propagated."[23] Like Mill, Roebuck took the point seriously. But he thought his particular plan avoided this danger:

> . . . because, though I propose to make the education of the people a matter of national and not merely individual concern, I should propose that the persons to determine, in the last resort, on the subject matter of instruction, and on whom the actual task of instruction shall fall, should be the people themselves; the people acting, however, in a public, and not in a private capacity.[24]

This solution was not very satisfactory. The danger of despotism is magically spirited away if the people after all are to exercise the power. But this scheme, in effect, was the device of shifting the activity of education from the market and the voluntary system to political organization. Only such a newly enfranchised audience of his day could, however, have accepted the abstract assertion that a political system, even a democratic one, could be interpreted as the rule of the people. A study of Roebuck's subsequent "machinery" for education shows clearly that his attempt to answer the charge of possible despotism was only superficial. For the supervision of the national schools in the kingdom was to be the

23. Hansard, 1833, Vol. XX, Cols. 139–66.
24. *Ibid.*

duty of a minister of public instruction with cabinet rank. "He would apportion the sum of money to be given to each district, for masters, for books, and repairs and a hundred other things. Besides this, the Normal Schools [i.e. the Teacher Training Schools] would be wholly under his control, and he would select for himself, and on his own responsibility, the masters and governors of each . . . also, it would be a very important part of his duty to watch over the composition of books of instruction." [25] Indeed the general public, even though it paid the requisite taxes, was subsequently told that its guidance was not really important:

"The great object, however, in any plan of general education would be to make '*the most instructed classes*' the guides. . . . Do what you will, say what we will, this class must guide and govern." [26] (Italics supplied.)

It is clear therefore that in wanting to give the power to "the people" Roebuck really meant only one section of them and a section that constituted the "proper" governing class.

J. S. Mill was much more apprehensive: "Though a government, therefore, may, and in many cases ought to, establish schools and colleges, it must neither compel nor bribe any person to come to them." [27] He advocated that a state school should exist: "if it exist at all, as one among many competing experiments, carried on for the purpose of example and stimulus, to keep the others up to a certain standard of excellence." [28] But even here it is interesting that Mill still could not conceal the presumption that the state schools would always be the superior pace-makers. Mill however recognized what Roebuck was not so willing to acknowledge, that if the country contained a sufficient number of qualified persons to provide "government" instruction, as Roebuck's proposed national system implied, then the same resources would be available under the market or voluntary principle "under the assurance of remuneration afforded by the law rendering education compulsory, combined with State aid to those unable to defray the expense."

Mill agreed with Roebuck that education should be made compulsory.

25. *Ibid.*
26. *Ibid.*
27. *Principles of Political Economy*, p. 956.
28. *On Liberty*, p. 240.

Beyond that, however, he was not so enthusiastic for the type of direct Benthamite apparatus of centralized control which Roebuck had outlined. Mill preferred to support the compulsion of education with the system of enforcement of public examinations to which children from an early age were to be submitted:

> Once in every year the examination should be renewed, with a gradually extending range of subjects, so as to make the universal acquisition and what is more, retention, of a certain minimum of general knowledge virtually compulsory. Beyond that minimum there should be voluntary examinations on all subjects, at which all who came up to a certain standard of proficiency might claim a certificate.

Bentham's system of examinations as the price to be paid for the right to vote had been included by Brougham in his educational proposals to Parliament in 1837. J. S. Mill also advocated this idea.

Strictly speaking this solution did not remove the power of the state over education, it only narrowed it down to the power of those officials who were to be appointed on behalf of the state to set the examinations. Mill thought that this would not matter so long as the examinations were confined to the "instrumental parts of knowledge" and to the examination of objective facts only. Where higher classes of examinations were concerned:

> The examinations on religion, politics, or other disputed topics, should not turn on the truth or falsehood of opinions, but on the matter of fact that such and such an opinion is held, on such grounds, by such authors, or schools, or churches.

But the fact that Mill did not enter into further details as to what was to constitute "a certain minimum of general knowledge," leaving his proposal in the form of a few generalizations, enabled him to escape many of the serious difficulties which lay beneath the surface of his plan. For instance, who was to determine the subjects to be taught? How would one choose between, say, elementary political economy and geography? Could powers of censorship be easily exercised? Suppose that certain individuals had aversions to certain subjects, who would be the arbiter? J. S. Mill himself, for instance, had a particularly strong objection to the teaching of theology and was insistent that national education should be purely secular.[29] Once again we have here the overtones of the intellectual paternalist. Certainly such treatment of other people's opinions seemed to contradict the spirit of *On Liberty* as it is popularly conceived.

Altogether, therefore, in the hands of J. S. Mill, the relationship between education and liberty was a complicated and unsettled one largely because of his difficulty in determining how far education was a means towards liberty and how far it was one of the ends for which liberty existed. Whilst he shared a substantial part of Godwin's reasoning and the latter's dislike of "patronified truth" yet there was an inner conflict arising partly no doubt from Mill's Platonic and almost religious reverence towards knowledge and learning that his father had struggled so hard, in his supreme pedagogic experiment, to build into the person of J. S. Mill himself.[30]

The emergence from this conflict of such pronouncements by J. S. Mill as: "Those who must need to be made wiser and better usually desire it least . . ."[31] obscures his eloquent plea for the freedom of the individual in the *Essay on Liberty.* Such inconsistency is not to be found in Godwin nor in Kant who observed: "Nobody may compel me to be happy in his own way." Kant really did treat the individual as an end in himself, as the ultimate author of values who needed no prior conditioning by "superior" people. J. S. Mill's individual in the end therefore is not perfectly free but to some extent manipulated by the Victorian intellectual paternalism of J. S. Mill himself and his own educated middle class. In the end, the "negative" liberty which Mill strived to establish becomes difficult to distinguish from an intellectual's special brand of "positive" liberty, i.e. the idea that what truly liberates is knowledge, rationality or culture.

---

29. Mill would make no compromise on this point. If the education was to include religion then he would have opposed any Bill for national education. Letter to C. Dilke, 1870. See also his Letter to T. H. Huxley, 1865, in: *The Letters of John Stuart Mill* edited by H. S. R. Elliott, 1910.
30. J. S. Mill was educated entirely by his father, who thus shared Godwin's ardour for private initiative instruction. See I. Cummins: *A Manufactured Man,* 1960.
31. *Principles of Political Economy,* p. 953.

14 · A Homogeneous National System: Horace Mann

Chapter 9 ended with the belief of Horace Mann that there was no great lack of schools and teachers in the aggregate in England and Wales in 1869. The fact that he was one of the strongest advocates of a national system of education may therefore come as a surprise. A close examination of Mann's case for a national system will give us an insight into the new strand of philosophy which was developing in the late nineteenth century.

Mann ended his address to the British Association in 1869[1] with the following words:

> the case for a national system is strong enough on various grounds, and is only discredited by wild exaggerations from numerical deficiency.

In the same vein at the beginning of his address he had argued that "... the future of England may be influenced much less by the quantity of education provided than by the nature of the system which provides it." He was of the opinion that the public was prepared for extensive changes and desired to have the existing "composite contrivance" superseded by a "national system." In our terminology there was a choice between two universal systems: the heterogeneous system, called by Mann the existing "composite contrivance," and an *homogeneous* system that was one of centrally planned uniformity. Mann complained that whilst

1. Transactions of the National Association for the Promotion of Social Science, Bristol Meeting, 1869.

everybody spoke of the need for a national system no one had a very definite notion of what a national system was. One common view, he explained, was that it was a plan for supporting schools for the children of the labouring classes out of local rates. This notion, however, Mann held to be objectionable. It was not consistent with the self-respect of low income groups for them to be left a separate race dependent upon upper or higher income groups. "The amount of strength, material and moral, which a nation loses by the presence in her midst of a pauperized, in addition to a pauper class, can hardly be exaggerated." He estimated that nearly three-quarters of the population of England and Wales were receiving assistance from the other fourth. Working-class parents could not be deluded that by paying a fee of one penny or twopence per child per week they were defraying the cost of their children's education. "They have on the contrary, a clear conviction that they are getting aid in discharging this part of their obligation from benevolent persons or a benevolent State; and the pity is they are quite content to have it so."

In regular English fashion, Mann argued, the country had *drifted* into such a position. Yet there had been no deliberate intention of relieving the majority of parents from their duties. Only to a minority, he thought, was there virtue in a system which was developing a lower order that was dependent on a higher one, and was deferential in its bearing towards its rulers in the church and State. To the majority of observers however the existing patchwork system had grown haphazardly out of a sense of benevolence and Christian duty. School aid had always been intended for the indigent classes only. Some had believed that even this was only a temporary intervention. After initial assistance had been given it could be withdrawn and families could stand on their own feet. This theory, however, had now been given up. "Even the pure voluntary party, which most fondly cherished this lofty, if impossible, ideal, has at length abandoned the position which the rush of circumstances, more perhaps from the force of argument, has made untenable. Gradually the circle which defined the assisted and assumed-to-be-needy classes had expanded, until now, as we have seen, it includes well-nigh three-quarters of the population and there is no longer any pretence for believing that the aided schools, are schools for the poor alone."

He was convinced of the danger that the country was going to continue to drift in this same direction since all sorts of fashionable arguments were there to rationalize it. One of these arguments was that we
should "educate our masters." Whilst Mann agreed with this he insisted
that it was ". . . tenfold more essential that we should train our masters
to be men, or at least not train them to be children." The question was
how to create a system that would not demoralize the people by relieving them from their natural obligations ". . . obligations which multitudes,
at least, of them could easily discharge at the cost of sundry pipes of tobacco and pints of beer." In fact "pipes of tobacco" and "pints of beer"
were already contributing significantly to the state revenues, revenues
from which aid to education was being dispensed. Mann was exceptional
in drawing attention to it.[2]

The solution, Mann argued in effect, was to go in for a full policy of
"universality"; the old policy of "selectivity," designed exclusively for the
poor, should be dropped. There was no stopping short of this point because already about three-fourths of the people were more or less helped
in the performance of their duty to education. Inevitably the question
arose: "Why should they, or the greater part of them, be helped any more
than the other fourth?" The correct answer was that neither the three-
fourths nor the one-fourth should be *helped.* The benefit of a common
provision should be received by *all;* and everybody should contribute to
the cost. This being done the depressing notion of charitable assistance
would be substituted by the inspiring notion of united effort. The best
policy was to make it clear that all the schools were maintained from public taxes to which all contributed ". . . i.e. with the money of the people
themselves." Possibly it might not be entirely true that the workers would
pay their precise share of the common cost. They should be encouraged
to believe it however.

Such belief would have a better chance if the cost of education was
defrayed out of general taxation rather than local rates. Local rating was
"tainted by an overpowering odour of pauperism." Rates were levied on

2. The economist Nassau Senior was another who acknowledged the point in his *Suggestions on Popular Education,* 1861.

a portion of the population only and could not be made to reach the whole. With local rates the workers would be convinced that the cost of education was being provided by one section of the community, the property owners. Workers would have a different view, Mann insisted, if the cost were defrayed from the Consolidated Fund. "The workman could tell himself, or be told by others, that in the price of every pint of beer, or pipe of tobacco . . . he was paying his contribution to the general education fund. So, when the principle of 'compulsion' is advocated, it should be remembered that the only sensible form of compulsion upon a man who can afford to pay for his children's education is to compel him to pay for it, not to compel him to receive it for nothing, at other people's expense; and that this preferable form of compulsion could be applied if national, but not if local, taxation were resorted to."

Predominantly then Mann was anxious that the spirit of independence should be fostered among parents. This could be done, by persuading them that it was they in the last resort who were paying for the subsidies. Certainly the taxation that fed the education subsidies was mainly indirect. It could not be shown that working people were not in fact themselves the source of their State-aided education.

After the 1867 Reform Act which brought the biggest extension of the franchise there was, at least in theory, little remaining case to treat the "State" as an elitist body. Governments were now, according to the new democratic model, agents of individual-voter-taxpayer-beneficiaries. This indeed seems to have been the drift of Mann's recognition that a "universal" State aid system, would be financed largely by the beneficiaries. Even if critics objected that non-parents also financed it Mann could have persisted with his "self-help" theme. Individual members of low income groups require education only over certain periods of their life. Taxes upon them could be regarded as supplying a common pool from which each member would draw at the period of his life when his children were going to school. At other periods of adult life—before marriage and in middle age—the individual (non-parent) could be regarded as paying taxes in anticipation of "free" educational services or for services that they had received in the past.

Such pooling arrangements however need not be confined to the public sector. The Wesleyans had practised it for years. Their weekly church collection was contributed to by all persons whether married or single and was used to finance the schooling of Wesleyan children. In 1852 Matthew Arnold cited an example of an Iron company that deducted every week from the wages of every person employed in the works to form a fund for the expenses of a school, a library, and a medical service. "Those who have families pay no more than those who have none, and any number of his children may be sent to the school by the head of the family without his having to pay any additional subscription. The school is regarded as existing for the common benefit of all, directly or indirectly, now or at a future time."[3]

Sixteen years later this voluntary welfare system had spread throughout the industrial area of Wales and by all accounts was meeting with much success. In his annual Report for 1868 Mr. Bowstead, Inspector of Schools for Glamorgan and Monmouth, observed that it was then a "common practice" in South Wales. Masters of works provided schooling out of a school fund accumulated from a small poundage deduction from everybody's wages whether the workmen had children or not. Individual choice was respected and there was no feeling of "pauperization."

> It is much to the credit of the great majority of the employers that they consult the wishes of their working population in the class of schools which they establish.[4]

He reported "large well organized schools" in Ebbw Vale, Dowlais, Mountain Ash, Maesteg, Rhonda, Morgan Copper Works, The Kilvey Copper Works (Swansea) and many other places.

> . . . all the schools give entire satisfaction to the workmen, whilst most of them are in admirable condition; and if a general system of compulsory education were introduced forthwith these works would be prepared to meet the demand.[5]

Where efficient capital markets exist parents can always borrow to finance the schooling of their children; the loans can then be repaid over their

3. Matthew Arnold, *Reports on Elementary Schools, 1852–1882*, London 1908, p. 9. The Iron Company mentioned was in Maesteg, S. Wales.
4. *Annual Report for 1868, Parl. Papers*, XX, p. 280.
5. *Ibid.*, p. 281.

lifetime. In the absence of such markets the pooling arrangements described above obviously provided an alternative. On Mann's reasoning, as explained so far, he would have applauded these local welfare schemes, but only up to a point. The company schools were partially subsidized. They were drawing annual grants from government funds destined exclusively for low income groups. As such they were still encouraging a sense of dependence.

Mann did not recommend a policy of reducing the taxes so that families have more disposable income from which to spend directly. This would however have been compatible with his arguments that one should encourage independence and that the poor paid for their subsidies through regressive taxes. So far as we know, the only person during the Industrial Revolution period who suggested this alternative was Tom Paine.[6] He recommended repayments of indirect taxes in the interests of education. These were however conditional upon evidence that parents were spending the proceeds on education.

Horace Mann certainly recognized this kind of thinking and indeed seems to have had much sympathy with it. However, he argued that the climate of opinion was against it in 1869.

> There was much to be said, in years gone by, for the theory of individual action; and a dream, in which some of us indulged, of a State, in which every parent should be paying, fully and directly and consciously, for his children's education, presented as fair and lofty an ideal as any rival theory can boast. But that dream has vanished; even the arch prophets of the faith have now abandoned the shrine; and the only present question is, what faith to substitute—whether to adopt a policy of "thorough" or a policy of compromise; to form on the theory of co-operation, a perfect system, covering the whole of the community and consistent with the self-respect of all, or to try and satisfy ourselves with half a system, touching only a portion of the people, and touching them with the icy, numbing hand of charity. . . . If we cannot now hope to create a self-educated people by one method, let us hope to do it by another—if not by separate effort, then by combined exertion. But let us not rest satisfied with anything short of this; and

6. E. G. West, "Tom Paine's Voucher Scheme for Education," *Southern Economic Journal,* 1966.

especially let us not, by another kind of Poor Law, doom the mass of our future population to be a sort of hybrid race—half independent, half dependent—as to their bodily wants a race of self-supporting citizens, and as to their mental nourishment a race of paupers.

Mann went on to argue that since the masses had only recently been enfranchised, it was too early to make a serious extension of the existing "sectional—charitable" scheme of education. The views of more than half the population had not yet been ascertained. It would be well to give to those most affected an opportunity of expressing their opinions.

Mann's argument at first sight seems to concede that his national system was only a second best arrangement. The first best was complete self-help and laissez faire in education. The existing partial system of aid to the education of the poor meanwhile was third best. On closer scrutiny of his argument however this interpretation does not fit. The national system of universal State education that he was proposing appears in quite enthusiastic terms. It might after all be the best of all worlds. The tendency of the time, Mann observed, was towards a fusion of the classes wherever fusion was possible; and this was a tendency of which he utterly approved. The trouble with the existing type of sectional legislation was that it was an obstacle to this "social fusion" and would "petrify into permanence the existing class distinction."

This was a fairly new note in the nineteenth-century debate; it amounted to a separate and special case for State education. Indeed this case has only recently been subjected to close analysis.[7] But an argument for a state system that is based on the need for "social fusion" is quite distinct from the usual one which discusses the need to protect children against irresponsible or poor parents. Its advocates in the nineteenth century were saying that the primary need was not more schools but the socialization (nationalization) of existing ones. Mann urged that, in the age of heroic remedies, the Bill for promoting national education might, ". . . embrace within its scope all persons of the nation—providing the community with various grades of schools and colleges, rather than providing schools and colleges for various grades of the community." Even

7. See for instance A. C. F. Beales, Mark Blaug, Sir Douglas Veale and E. G. West, *Education: A Framework for Choice,* Inst. Econ. Affairs, 1967.

if such a project were to involve substantial costs the benefits would be sufficiently substantial. To stop short of such a scheme, Mann argued, might only involve double cost and labour hereafter ". . . for it would be vain to imagine that the country will be permanently satisfied with anything less than this. Years of local squabbling may intervene, but to this we may come at last."

Mann obviously had considerable "prophetic" vision. Hindsight of course allows us to be critical of his particular scheme. After a century of experience in America many people now question whether the "melting pot" function of a State school system may not be overdone. The warning of John Stuart Mill, Mann's contemporary, that a State system may result in a kind of "despotism over the mind" and a contrivance to cast more people in the same mould has had a new airing in an era of totalitarian and bureaucratic regimes. Mann's hope that "the community" could use the same schools seems to imply the desirability that each and every school could and should contain a cross-section of society. Social stratification by residence, however, has prevented this. The American and British resort to busing between schools districts and the controversy surrounding it shows that the policy of trying to use statutory means for "social fusion" is by no means unanimously accepted.[8]

Mann wanted the whole of the finance of education to be placed upon the central government. As it has transpired local governments share heavily in financial responsibility. As with most visionaries there was considerable optimism in many of his remarks. Admitting his scheme would be very costly he hoped that a reduction in spending on defence might supply the deficiency. This hope, of course, has subsequently been reflected in the projects of countless social reformers down to those who have devised new social programmes to be funded from money released from reduced defence expenditure.[9] Mann hoped that there would be plenty of scope for local energy and management of nationalized schools.

8. Mann does not seem to have thought through his ideas very carefully and it may be that we are reading too much into his commentary. He argued in a footnote to his Essay on National Education that although Parliament could provide the funds for primary, secondary and higher education, this need not prevent the existence of private schools. 9. Mann also wanted to nationalize all educational endowments and use them to finance the State system.

A better board of education could be expected if the electors had simply to enquire who are the best men qualified to govern. This would not happen, he argued, if the responsibility was thrown on local ratepayers who were more concerned to ask which candidate was most likely to keep down the rates. The risk of extravagance would be met eventually by the continuation of the Victorian system of "payment by results" supervised by a strong system of inspection. This last part of Mann's proposals certainly did not materialize and responsibility *has* been thrown on ratepayers. "Payments by results" was scrapped and inspection has not been nearly as rigorous as he wanted. Perhaps the most Utopian aspect of Mann's argument was his belief that the 1867 Reform Act had brought with it at last "pure democracy." The community's views would be faithfully represented in the House of Commons which would then in turn supervise and finance a perfectly functioning democratic system of education. Finally, there is no twentieth-century evidence that the low-income parent believes that he is paying for his "free education" through his taxes. Indeed, many observers now believe that the most important function of State education is to redistribute wealth. Those who use private schools "pay twice" and so redistribute in favour of State school users.[10] What Mann called "pauperization" is today called "redistribution."

There is no intention here to extend the debate that Mann started. Suffice it to record that his "social-fusion" argument was a new strand in late nineteenth-century discussions on education, a strand which was increasingly reflected in the reports of the Education Department. Several officials who supervised the construction of the new board schools after 1870 seemed more and more disposed to regard them as establishments that would not merely complement the existing voluntary system but would eventually replace it. This view is clearly reflected in the Annual Report of the Committee of Council of 1872–3. While insisting that the public system of elementary schools did not have sufficient accommodation to cater for the whole of the school-age population, it only barely recognized that there were other schools outside this system.

10. I. Preece, "The Laissez-faire System of Finance of Education," *British Journal of Education Studies*, 1969, p. 33.

> We are aware that there is a considerable number of schools, more or
> less efficient, which for one reason or another, do not seek annual aid,
> and are not, therefore, subject to periodical inspection. *But it may be
> anticipated, from various influences, these schools will decrease in
> number;* and it will therefore be asked, How is the deficiency in the
> number of aided, i.e. of public elementary schools, being supplied?
> (our italics) [11]

Among the "various influences" that were discouraging the non-aided
schools was the new competition from the public elementary schools.
This however was "unfair" competition not free market competition. In
the latter entrepreneurs enjoy access to available resources upon equal
terms. The schools set up by school boards enjoyed substantially favourable terms. By 1873 they were availing themselves freely of the power of
obtaining effectively, subsidized loans under security of the rates as provided by the Act. [12] In addition they were enabled to make big reductions
in their fees on the strength of the rates. The private school's struggle
therefore was similar to the attempt by merchants without a bounty to
compete with other merchants who had a considerable one. The competition was most severe for schools that were entirely outside the public system, i.e. that enjoyed no grants or subsidies whatever. There was
"unfair" competition also within the public sector. This took place between the new board schools (completely public) and the voluntary
schools who had traditionally relied on the government grants for new
buildings or extensions. The Forster Act told them that, after December 31st, 1870, no further applications would be received. Although
these schools received other government grants (for teachers and examination results) a bigger burden was now placed upon the pupils' fees.
But these were not allowed to exceed nine pence a week.

It has recently been observed that the financial conditions that these
schools had to meet after 1870, by comparison with those enjoyed by
the school boards, were so disadvantageous "as almost to constitute a

11. *Parliamentary Papers*, XXIV, 1873, p. xvii.
12. In 1873 loans had been issued for over one million pounds for the building of new
capacity in the public sector outside London.

sentence of lingering death upon the denominational system."[13] There
can be no doubt that many people hoped that this would be one of the
consequences of the 1870 Act and others who thought it was the secret
intention. Many of them no doubt shared the new sentiments of Horace
Mann. To them the need was not so much the further multiplication of
schools under the existing system but a change in the quality of schooling so as to achieve "social fusion." Obviously there were many types of
"national systems." Mann's system was not Gladstone's or Forster's. The
latter told Parliament when introducing his Bill ". . . we must take care
not to destroy in building up—not to destroy the existing system in introducing a new one." The variant of a "national system" discussed in this
chapter clearly was of a kind that *did* want to destroy the existing (heterogeneous) system of the 1870 Act. Ironically the board schools that
Forster offered the country in the marginal areas with their ability to
out-price their competitors provided his opponents, supporters of a homogeneous system, with their main chance.

13. H. C. Dent, "The Role of Central Government," *Trends in Education 1870–1970,*
Feb. 1970, Dept. of Education & Science, p. 33.

15 · W. E. Forster and Robert Lowe Versus the Birmingham League

As we showed in a previous chapter Forster's evidence of school deficiency in 1870 was deficient. Even his figures conceded that three-quarters of all children were already in school. And Forster himself would have been the first to stress to a twentieth-century audience that his Act of 1870 was intended primarily not to create education from scratch but simply to augment it. As he told Parliament, the object was to complete the existing voluntary system by filling up the gaps. *His* ideal was an heterogeneous national system.

Today, a century later, the situation is reversed. State schools provide most of the education whilst private provision fills the gaps. How do we explain the rapidity of the transformation? One answer lies in the type of administrative machinery that Forster set up, a machinery which seems to have gathered its own momentum and to have developed far beyond his original aspirations. Forster intended simply that the Government should make strict enquiries into educational needs in each area and only set up school boards in those areas where a significant deficiency was proved.

As it happened many officials were often over-ambitious in their reports of these needs. Gladstone himself could not stop them. He protested in 1873 that four-fifths of the children in his own constituency were already provided for and that for the remainder further provision in three additional infant schools was being organized. Why set up a

school board, he protested, which in comparison with voluntary arrangements already being made was of necessity cumbrous and costly?

At a time of rising population, the question soon arose on who should
provide the schooling for the net increase in children, the new school
boards or the voluntary system? Soon after 1870 the Education Department (not Parliament) took upon itself to establish the rule that where
school boards existed, however small, they had the first right to supply
the new deficiency. Even Forster, the author of the 1870 Act, could not
stop this administrative horse from galloping. He protested, at a meeting
in 1878, that those who ought to decide on new schools were those who
were willing to build them. The Education Department, Forster pro-
claimed: "would find that they had engaged in a most obnoxious business
which they could only transact with odium if they tried to take upon
themselves to decide whether any fresh call was necessary or not."[1] But
now out of office Forster was powerless. New board schools appeared
with increasing momentum throughout the country. Where excess board
school capacity was created, the boards were able to reduce their fees
and to drive out many private establishments. Many private schools indeed were forced into take-overs by the board school system and swelled
the number of board schools that the 1870 Act was subsequently claimed
to have "created."

Differential Effect?

As previously demonstrated the 1870 Act arrived at a time when a considerable amount of education was already available. In the late 1860s
most people were literate, most children had some schooling; and most
parents were paying fees for it. The progress that was already in train
would surely have continued had there been no Forster Act. By how
much did the new legislation step up educational progress still further?
What was its differential effect? The more the Government money to
finance board schools came from the rich the bigger the boost would
have been. The biggest part of tax revenue, however, came from the

1. Address to a Wesleyan Meeting, 1878.

working class, for the bulk of the revenue came from indirect tax payments such as customs and excise.[2] Progressive taxation was not introduced until the twentieth century.

All this suggests is that governments after 1870 increasingly did people's educational spending for them as Mann wanted. Much Government educational expenditure, in other words, did not make for a net increase in education, only a switching of power between those who controlled it.

This sort of observation and evidence certainly challenges the usual interpretation of the 1870 Act. The differential effect of that Act is difficult to estimate precisely; but it was a differential effect only. The socialization of existing schools in 1870 should not allow us to be misled into giving the excessive credit to Forster's Act that is usually accorded.

Onus on Parents

Although often described as the architect of the present system of education in England, Forster would have opposed it in the twentieth century in some very important respects. The first draft of his Education Bill was presented to the Cabinet in October 1869. In it he argued that in pursuing the objective of filling the gaps in education it was necessary that there should be the least possible encouragement to parents to neglect their duties, the least possible expenditure of the public money, and the least possible injury to existing efficient private schools.

Forster considered each of four plans which were at the time being vigorously mooted. The first was that of the Birmingham League and the one that foreshadowed our twentieth-century system. The League proposed that local authorities should establish non-fee-paying schools, that such schools should teach no religious dogma, and that they be built and maintained by rates and taxes (the rates paying one-third of the cost and the taxes the remainder). These schools were to be managed by the

---

2. Not all indirect taxes are regressive; their final incidence is often difficult to determine precisely. However, by the same token, we certainly cannot assume that most of the public education funds came from the rich.

ratepayers but to be inspected to a standard set by the central government. Mr. Forster objected to this plan; in his words it was "too logical a piece of machinery." Such a system, he argued, would quickly undermine the existing private schools. It would also relieve the parents of all the payment and destroy their necessary involvement in their children's education.

Aided Schools

Another of the four plans which Forster dismissed stood at the opposite pole. The National Educational Union wanted voluntary schools to be aided by increased Government subsidies. This, Forster asserted, would be insufficient to meet the problems of the impoverished areas. Forster finally accepted the plan proposed by Sir Robert Lowe. Its ruling idea was compulsory school provision if and where necessary but not otherwise. The country was to be divided into districts and officials in each district were to determine whether board schools were necessary. *This*, then, was the national system that Forster had finally in mind. This was certainly not our modern national system of State schools. Forster worked for a "system" only in the sense of a very efficiently and systematically organized patching-up job.

Forster's speeches make clear that his overriding objective was simply to secure for all children in the country access to good schools. His final plan was not designed to please any one class or party, and it certainly did not aim to superimpose a homogeneous standard throughout the land. In pursuing these aims Forster incurred the hostility of the doctrinaire radicals of the Birmingham League on the one hand and the Non-conformists on the other. He revealed the talents of the politician who seeks a shrewd workable compromise solution, certainly; but his speeches and actions were clearly those of the dedicated social reformer who looks first to the needs of children and who at the same time champions the role of the family.

Forster would be extremely uncomfortable with the crown which is put upon his head by some twentieth-century educationists. While he wanted to cover the country with good schools most of them were still to be based on the voluntary principle and to continue enjoying direct grants from the central government. It is ironic that exactly 100 years later in 1970, the Schools Commission recommended the scrapping of the English direct grant system altogether.

The Universalists

Two principles feature in the debate on social welfare provision in the twentieth century, the principle of "universality" and the principle of "selectivity." Most educationists today are, like Horace Mann, universalists—that is, wanting government provision for rich and poor alike. The principle which guided Forster was that of selectivity. In his own words, the object "is to complete the present voluntary system, to fill up gaps, sparing the public money where it can be done without, procuring as much as we can the assistance of the parents." His new board schools, which were to fill the gaps, were themselves a classic exercise in selectivity, that is an exercise in *discriminating* Government provision. While the direct grant system was doing a useful job in 1870, and was to be continued, it would not adequately cover the deprived areas of education. In Forster's words to Parliament: "Where State help had been most wanted, State help has been least given, and where it was desirable that State power should be most felt it was not felt at all."

Another important difference between the modern educationist and Forster is that he did not want free schooling. Even in his new board schools fees would be charged. If the schooling was provided free, he argued, other sections of the education system would begin to clamour also for enough State aid to make *their* education free. To relieve the average parent from payments for the education of his child would be mischievous and unwise. Generally speaking, the enormous majority of the parents were able, and would continue to be able, to pay the fees. In the case of the very poorest sections the school board was allowed to give what were called "free tickets" to cover the fees. "We do not give up school fees," Forster told Parliament, "and indeed we keep to the present proportions, namely, of about one-third raised from the parents, one-third out of public taxes and one-third out of local funds."

Parental Choice

Perhaps the biggest difference between Forster and most modern educationists lies in his vigorous defence of the principle of parental choice. His tenacity in defending this principle was demonstrated in the few months after the Act had been passed. His opponents in the Birmingham League had turned upon section 25 of his Act which made the provision for supplying poor parents with free tickets to cover school fees.

This provision brought out "the religious difficulty" in all its starkness. The practice of using local rates to provide parents with money to pay fees at denominational schools was savagely questioned. But the real issue, as Forster now saw it, was whether a poor parent who was unable to pay his child's school fees, was to be at liberty to choose between a denominational and secular school or was to be compelled to send the child to a school of the latter description—that is, to have "Hobson's Choice" only. He came down firmly on the right of the poor parent to choose between available schools. This indeed was the reply that he made in response to Mr. Dixon's Parliamentary attack in 1872.

Forster's Vision

Forster's championship of parental choice of school fees and of the direct grant system clearly separates him from most educationists a century later. Such differences are a matter of individual philosophy or taste. The task here has been to get the historical record straight. The claims of our modern system to a common ancestry with W. E. Forster must be severely qualified in the ways shown. Compulsory, Universal, Free and Comprehensive; of these four modern features of our present system Forster would have given his support to the first two only. He did not want a system that was what he called "too logical." Voluntary provision complemented by really efficient, but marginal, government aid and inspection—that was his vision. Education had not become, and Forster did not want it to become, the exclusive property of politics.

Part 4 · The Economic Realities of Intervention

16 · The Public/Private Displacement Mechanism: Did Education Grow Faster or Slower?

This chapter presents analysis and statistical measurement of the net effect of government intervention upon nineteenth-century British educational growth. By "net" effect is meant the stimulus to the public system minus the damage to private schools. It first applies hypotheses from the modern economics of bureaucracy for an explanation of the strategy of the growing Victorian Education Department. It documents the way in which its discretionary behaviour led to the "crowding out" of private schools. It goes on to present a simple economic model that illustrates the full potentialities of the "crowding out" effect and the consequences for total (public and private) educational expenditure. Finally it estimates the share of primary education in the national income 12 years after the national intervention: the Forster Act of 1870. It then compares this proportion with estimates for 1833 and 1858 and with estimates for other European countries and America. The total evidence is finally brought to bear on two questions: first, how did Britain's education effort in the "industrial revolution year" of 1833 compare with other European countries at similar income levels? Second, did education grow slower or faster in the remaining part of the century after the 1870 Act?[1]

---

1. The problem was outlined in E. G. West, *Education and the State*, London, 1970, Chapter 10.

The Complaint of Unequal Competition

It was openly recognized in the nineteenth century that the expansion of the public sector in education had an adverse effect on private schools. In 1859 for example Horace Mann observed that the expansion of government schools would mean that they would be "either destroyed by the unequal competition" or taken over by the public sector.[2] Whilst such displacement appeared to him as an inescapable fact of life, to others it was a subject of serious complaint. In his evidence to the 1834 Parliamentary Committee on the State of Education for that year, the Lord Chancellor, Lord Brougham, observed:

> It is probable that day schools for 1,200,000 at least are now supported without endowment, and endowed schools established for above 170,000 making, in all, schools capable of educating nearly 1,400,000 children. But if the State were to interfere, and obliged every parish to support a school or schools sufficient for educating all children, two consequences would inevitably follow; the greater part of the funds now raised voluntarily for this purpose would be withdrawn, and the State or the rate-payers in each parish would have to provide schools for 2,000,000 of children. . . . Now to establish and maintain such a number of schools, would be a most heavy expense . . . (it) would cost £2,000,000 a year.[3]

Eighteen years later, Gladstone expressed the same fear, and in similar terms. His reference to private effort, like Brougham's, included the fees willingly paid by parents of all social classes. These were covering one-third of the costs in the 1850s.

> It appears to me clear that the day you sanction compulsory rating for the purpose of education you sign the death-warrant of voluntary exertions. . . . Are we preparing to undergo the risk of extinguishing that vast amount of voluntary effort which now exists throughout the country?[4]

2. Evidence of Horace Mann to the Commission of Inquiry into the State of Popular Education in England (the Newcastle Report) 6th December 1859.
3. Report, pp. 144–5.
4. Gladstone's intervention in the Education Debate, House of Commons, 1856.

By this time, however, the displacement effect was not just a matter of conjecture. There was widespread evidence that it was already in fierce operation. The Newcastle Report of 1861 observed, ". . . the complaint that the Government grant enables the public (government) schools to undersell, and so ruin them, is very common amongst the teachers. . . ." The point was:

> . . . except in very favourable situations, the school fee cannot be raised much above the public school level, and that in consequence the private teachers bitterly complain that they find it difficult to earn a living. . . . They complain that the tendency of the interference of Government is to give a monopoly to a particular class of schools.[5]

A few years after the 1870 Act the board schools (the new "common schools") played the strongest of their (government provided) trump cards: their services were offered free. This "zero pricing" was an insuperable problem to large numbers of the independent schools, even those that were supported by endowments. The huge, but threatened, private sector of education consisted of two main parts, first the church schools —most of which were accustomed to receiving some amount of government aid prior to 1870; second, the completely independent schools whether religious or secular. The problem as it faced each will be examined in turn.

The Denominational Schools and the Displacement Effect

One explanation of the squeeze on the denominational schools can be offered in terms of the new economic theory of bureaucracy based on the hypothesis that members of any government department behave so as to maximize, and continually expand, its budget.[6] This is due partly to the fact that the heads of bureaus cannot keep the profits that accrue from efficient operation and thus have no incentive to operate efficiently. Also the size of personal salaries is geared to the degree of "responsibility" and this in turn is related to the quantity of resources supervised. Steady expansion of the budget therefore is the most conducive to promotion and salary advance.

5. Vol. 1, page 95.
6. W. A. Niskanen, *Bureaucracy and Representative Government*, New York, 1971.

In our context the theory can be used in a "weak" or a "strong" version. In the strong case the "public spirited" administrators will be dominated by the self-interested ones. Whilst the budget is predicted to expand in all instances it will do so to a greater degree in the strong case, for here there will be fewer scruples. For instance if the budget can be expected to expand faster with the gradual establishment of a *universal* system of public schooling that benefits the children of middle-income parents as well as the poorest, this system will be "pushed" by the "strong" bureau even if the poorest would do better in a smaller *selective* system wherein all the benefits went to them exclusively. Evidence relevant to this will be examined subsequently.

Another feature of the "strong" bureau theory is that it can be predicted that it will engage in promotional activities favouring its own services.[7] It will be increasingly jealous of rival bureaus and other competitors. It will also urge the need for "mergers," for "proper coordination," for "centralization," and ultimately for one exclusive monolithic body.

Finally, the theory predicts that bureaus will be prompted (a) to form alliances with labour and other supply interests; (b) gradually to attempt to exclude all rivals by means other than normal competition. In our context the rivals included private bureaus and competing private suppliers of education. The rival bureaus were the religious societies through which public money was normally channelled. The competing suppliers were the private schools and the teacher training (normal) schools. Theory would predict that, given discretion, the new Education Department would have deliberately hindered the efforts of these competitors. In proceeding to the evidence it will first be necessary to go back to the origins of the Department itself.

The Origins of the Education Department

From the commencement of government aid to education in 1833 down to 1839 the public money (mainly school building grants) was channelled through the National Society and the British and Foreign School Society.

---

7. In economic terms it is interested in shifting to the right the demand curve for its services. It is also interested in making the curve steeper (less elastic).

On 10 April 1839, an order in Council was issued directing the formation of a Committee of Council to administer the education grant which was at the same time raised to £30,000. (The Secretary of the Committee was to be, James Kay-Shuttleworth.) Preparation for this body seems to have been incubating for some time; for its first Minutes appeared only three days after its establishment. They announced that in future the New Committee of Council (the Education Department in effect) was to take over the administration of the building grants from the two religious societies (the rival private bureaus). The minutes were also aimed at the private teacher-training schools. They decreed: "that no grant be made now or hereafter for the establishment of normal schools (teacher-training schools), or of any other schools, unless the right of inspection be retained . . ."

The school was to include a model school, in which children of all ages from three to 14 might be taught. The general instruction was to be such as was common to all kinds and denominations of persons calling themselves Christians whilst periods were to be set apart for such peculiar doctrinal teaching as might be required for the religious training of those children wanting it.[8]

These proposals caused a public controversy in which the threatened private bureaus were active. A meeting of the National Society under the presidency of the Archbishop of Canterbury pointedly resolved that instruction in the truths and precepts of Christianity should be under the superintendence of the clergy, and in conformity with the doctrines of the Established Church. Subsequently, Parliament was prompted to censure the new Education Committee. These were the days when the parliamentary system suffered the defects of "delegated legislation"; that is the practice of excessive use of administrative orders in Council that made such serious changes as to be equivalent to statutory edicts.

---

8. Some insight into the pressure and the motives for setting up the Committee of Council for education can be gleaned from a letter from Lord John Russell to Lord Lansdowne dated February 4th 1839. The letter makes much reference to "Her Majesty's Commands." Among the first tasks of the Committee was to be the setting up of a normal school. Four principle objects were to be kept in view. 1. Religious Instruction. 2. General Instruction. 3. Moral Training. 4. Habits of Industry. (Reproduced in J. Stuart McLure, *Educational Documents* (1965).)

We shall see that, despite the Archbishop's resolutions, the Committee continued for much of the century to enjoy its discretionary powers and to avoid seeking the consent of Parliament on many fundamental changes. It is true that in the short run the Secretary of the Committee, Kay-Shuttleworth, was forced to devise new formulas in order to placate the adversaries. The Government however persisted with its new bureau and the Committee of Council virtually became the Education Department. It did do, incidentally, without direct Parliamentary authority; authority was obtained indirectly, namely by annual votes for the salaries of the vice-president and various Committee officials.

The professed government objective in setting up the Committee was to spread education over all parts of the country, even though, to a large extent, it was already so spread. The Committee proceeded to take full control of the annual education grant; at the same time Parliament's control over it was attenuated.[9]

The Initial Encroachments on Private Schools

The encroachment on the private school competitors followed that on the private bureaus and the teacher training colleges. The first method used was that of partial "takeover." The department was able to use its discretion to expand the public sector by relaxing the conditions for receiving government grants. Schools that could have managed without them were gradually given access to the public funds in exchange for their agreement to regulations and to inspections.[10] Next official statistics were produced by the Department alleging educational "deficiencies" after the 1840s. These "deficiencies" were based on an unexplained target school population of one in six of the total population, a target that as we showed in Chapter 3 was not reached by any other country and has still not to-

9. For several years after the initial controversy over the proposed normal school many promoters of new Church schools were reluctant to accept the Committee-controlled building grants. Considerable suspicion was abroad that the new government Department was seriously attempting to wrest from the church the whole educational function.
10. The Department conceded quite openly on such use of its discretion. See the evidence of R. Lingen in the Report of the Commission on Popular Education, 1861, Vol. 6, p. 15.

day. Such allegations of deficiencies nevertheless prepared the ground for further public growth.

The Committee in Council (hereafter the Department or Bureau) next made a successful bid for the main factor supply, the teacher interests. This was accomplished with the introduction, in 1846, of the pupil-teacher system into private schools, provided they would accept public supervision. An elaborate scheme emerged outlining the role of the pupil-teacher, the examination he had to pass, the amount of instruction to be given by the principal teacher, and the stipends to be payable by the Department. Payments were, in the mid-nineteenth century, relatively attractive. The pupil-teacher was paid £10 if he completed his first year satisfactorily. Increments of £2.5s. would follow in each of the next five years. One pupil-teacher was allowed for every 25 scholars in a school. Head teachers qualified to have their incomes augmented by a special Departmental grant dependent on the examination success of the pupil-teacher and the willingness of local voluntary effort to match the extra public expenditure. In addition, the Department allowed to head teachers £5 for instructing one pupil-teacher, £9 for two and £12 for three. Teachers would qualify for pensions after 15 years' teaching. The interests of the school masters and managers were thus engaged quite effectively; and this at a time when the teaching profession was becoming organized and on the brink of significant political influence. Some necessary conditions preparing for the growth of bureaucracy as outlined in the earlier model were clearly being fulfilled.[11]

An Education bureau that aspired eventually to monopolize education would be interested in reducing the ability of private agencies (including the Church) from filling the rest of the "gaps" in education. As it was very many of these gaps were slowly being filled without bureau assistance simply with the passage of time, with some Church aid, and with increases in family and other incomes. Educational deficiencies (defined so as to include a schooling of too short a duration) were concentrated in the lower income families and in the poorer areas generally. By the 1840s the hands of the Churches had become somewhat tied in this

---

11. In 1847 the Department made it compulsory for schools to use one form of trust deed, the penalty being the complete withdrawal of Government aid.

particular "poverty battle"; and a discretionary departmental ruling was again the cause. A condition for the receipt of government building grants was that an equivalent sum should be contributed by local proprietors or local voluntary help from persons living within four miles of the parish. The relative absence of necessary "volunteer wealth" in the poorer parishes meant that they were often quite unable to generate any public grants. When the more prosperous churches attempted to proffer assistance, the Department stopped them by laying down that they were not to be allowed to use any portion of the public grants to be transferred to poor neighbours. By 1870 the Government was able to make implicit criticism of the Church for not having provided enough schools in these parishes.[12]

The 1870 Act's Promises to the Church Schools

The few years after the 1870 Act were the most crucial to the expansion of the bureau "empire." After a steady stream of advice from his officials W. E. Forster used his legislation of 1870 to superimpose upon the existing government system of subsidies to largely private and usually church-connected schools, a new provision for public ("common") schools called "Board schools." It was these new establishments, which were to be supplied "where necessary" by "School Boards," that provided the main chance for Departmental expansion. Forster promised the subsidized private schools sufficient future finance against competition from the new publicly provided schools. The ultimate expression and detail of these promises however was left to the Administration.

During the Bill's passage through Parliament, it was eventually agreed that while the new School Boards were to be financed from new local rates (property taxes), they were not to be allowed the power of aiding denominational schools. To offset this disadvantage a compromise was reached whereby the Church schools were to receive an increase of the

12. Conformity with building rules was insisted upon by the Department in the 1840s. There were particularly precise regulations about the width of the rooms, ventilation and materials used. Later in the century new Departments found fault with earlier requirements and expensive changes were insisted upon.

grant from the *central* government instead of aid from the local rates as originally planned. The loose way in which the compromise was worded should be noticed. Gladstone, who first introduced it on 16 June 1870, confidently announced that this matter did not need positive legislation but could be handled later by a Council Minute.

Later on, Gladstone acknowledged that the augmentation would be "within a maximum of 50 per cent." Mr. Gathorne Hardy (June 16th 1870) thought that Forster ". . . ought to put on paper what it is proposed to do in reference to the Revised Code next year." Sir Massey Lopes (South Devon) asked, more pointedly, ". . . if the Government would insert in the Bill a provision with reference to the extent and the amount of the Government grants, so as not to leave them to the caprice and whim of the Education Department, more especially when they exercise such arbitrary and absolute powers?" Forster was unyielding. "What had been said was, that the Government looked forward to additional grants to schools not exceeding 50 per cent."

A few days later (June 28th 1870) Lord Robert Montagu proposed a motion which reflected even stronger distrust of the Department. The Prime Minister, he observed, had offered a compromise which involved concessions from all parties ". . . but it ought, like the others, to be made permanent, and put into the Bill. It was only just that they (the concessions) should be equally permanent and secure." Montagu warned that if the voluntary schools were eventually deprived of the maximum grant increase of 50 per cent, while they lost the other sources of income on which they relied, ". . . they would be starved out, and the Bill, would be a measure not to complete, but entirely to supersede the existing system." If the grant conditions were not put formally into one of the schedules of the Bill ". . . there would be a perpetual liability to change by the Education Department. . . ." Montagu's proposal had many supporters.

Attempting to settle matters, Disraeli finally intervened. In effect, he insisted, the whole thing was a matter of the promises of gentlemen; and the British House of Commons was above all a "gentlemanly" institution. After this Lord Montagu allowed his motion to be negatived.

Subsequent events showed that Montagu's fears were well founded. The eventual fate of the promised grant was as follows. It *was* raised

50 per cent—the grant for average attendance was raised from 4*s*. to 6*s*. and the grant on examination from 8*s*. to 12*s*. But the increase was only nominal. The Department so used its discretionary powers in changing the conditions of the grant that the full increase was impossible to obtain. First there were severe Departmental alterations in the conditions of examination. Half-time scholars had to put in 150 attendances instead of the previous 100—an increase of 50 per cent. Full time students had to attend 250 times instead of the previous 200—an increase of 25 per cent. Second, no attendance was to count unless two hours of secular instruction had been received. Third, the old condition that the grant should not exceed the amount raised by school fees and subscriptions continued to be strictly observed. That is, *the grant for any year could not exceed the annual school income derived from voluntary contributions, school fees, and any other sources other than the Parliamentary Grant*. This third condition (hereafter the "Parity Condition") was to play a critical part in the eventual financial difficulties of denominational schools.

It is important to understand that the original provision of Forster's Bill was that the new school boards were to be able to use the rate funds to assist the denominational schools as well as, where necessary, to set up their own.

Although this method was later dropped, the intention behind it, of equality of treatment, was apparently to have been preserved. Suppose however the first method had been persevered with and the denominational schools had received assistance from the local rates. Then under the Parity Condition this assistance would have been treated as money to be matched by the central Government Grant, the procedure adopted with the new Board Schools. Under the adopted second method however the private schools lost this advantage. The Board schools thereafter earned a bigger central government grant than the voluntary schools in so far as their matching income was bigger by local rate assistance. The 50 per cent additional grant was thus largely withheld from the poorer voluntary schools because they had little alternative income sources with which to match it. This situation not only led to severe hindrance to the continuation of church attempts to build new schools in the poorest "gap" areas (where they were concentrated); there were now new difficulties faced by existing voluntary schools when neighbouring board schools began to compete for students.

Whilst Gladstone mentioned the figure of up to 50 per cent grant increase for voluntary schools, the actual increase by 1874 had amounted to only half that. Church schools in that year received 11s. per head which was only about 25 per cent above the 1870 grant of 8s. 9d. per head. Eventually some political agitation was organized by the denominational school interests with the result that Lord Sandon's Act was passed in 1876. Although this Act did something to remove the financial plight of the church schools, two years later the Education Bureau confronted them with the biggest obstacle of all. The Education Bureau (the Department) now took it upon itself to establish the rule that *where school boards existed,* they had the first right to supply the deficiencies of the gaps. The gaps of course were a continuous phenomena, for the population growth was producing thousands of new students requiring new places. Where the school boards accepted the responsibility to supply these growing needs after 1887, as they invariably did, additional private school accommodation was officially deemed unnecessary. New proposed voluntary establishments were now *completely* ineligible for any subsidy, and this by *administrative* (bureau) decree.

From the voluntary school point of view, Lord Sandon's Act of 1876 had clearly come too late. Board schools had by then attained a substantial threshold and for two reasons. First the size of the gaps to be filled had been statistically over-estimated—often apparently with Departmental connivance.[13] Second, the fact of the denominational school's financial disabilities (aggravated if not caused by Departmental regulations) in the early 1870s, had put them at a severe disadvantage in the poorer areas compared with the board schools. A wide network of the latter was in existence by 1878. This was all that was necessary to allow them to carry out their final wave of expansion; and this under the pro-

13. See Joseph Nunn, "School Board Waste: Being an Enquiry into the fallacies upon which the London School Board propose to provide additional school accommodation for 103,863 scholars at a cost of which no estimate at present can be made." London, 1872. See also E. G. West, *Education and the State,* 1970, p. 151.

tection of the bureau's decree that existing school boards were to have the option of all further "gap-filling."

In absolute terms the number of voluntary schools built after 1870 still looks large to a twentieth-century observer. By 1886 over 3m. places had been added, and a half of them were due to voluntary agencies. This proportion, however, would have been much bigger had it not been for the failure to fulfil Gladstone's 1870 promises. But the important statistical feature to notice was the differential rate of growth. The school board's firm foothold by the late 1870s caused the public/private displacement to become progressive. As the board schools exploited their new monopoly rights of servicing the *new* populations in the gap areas, others competed on such unfair terms with voluntary schools even in the "non-gap" areas as to cause large numbers of these into school board take-overs. Whereas in 1879 voluntary schools were providing more than two-thirds of the school places in the country, by 1886 the proportion had fallen to three-fifths.

It is not the present purpose to enter the debate on the "rights" or "wrongs" of these historical events. Clearly it is open to majorities in the political process to declare that denominational or private schooling is socially undesirable. It has often been argued for instance (as Horace Mann did) that in the interests of "social cohesion" it is necessary to send all children to the "same sort of school,"[14] or to schools that have a "public quality."[15] The question that is relevant to this position here is whether political majorities through their democratic processes in the nineteenth century *did* articulate a desire for the change of the pre-1870 system. Since our answer has been in the negative, alternative explanations of the actual events are required. We have accordingly found

14. For a modern version of the social cohesion argument, see Mark Blaug's contribution to *"Education: a Framework for Choice,"* Readings in Political Economy, No. 1, I.E.A., 1967.

15. The phrase "public quality" must mean the quality of being controlled by the political process. To some people this in turn conjures up an education that is "neutral" in ideology, or religion. Yet "Secularism," "anti-denominationalism," "nationalism," and "Socialism" were all historically associated with the drive for publicly provided schooling; and these interests were just as much ideological as those that were being superseded.

those of the economics of bureaucracy. The verdict is that the evidence seems consistent with the hypotheses of this new subject. The denominational schools suffered considerable demotion yet, to repeat, there was *no explicit declaration* in the 1870 Act, or any other Act, that such a result was the primary policy aim. Indeed, when presenting his Bill, W. E. Forster went out of his way to emphasize ". . . we must take care not to destroy in building up—not to destroy the existing system in introducing a new one."

Profit Earning in the Private and Public Sector

The ability of the board schools, enjoying the aid of rate revenues, to lower their fees could be matched to some extent at least by the denominational schools; for often they could draw upon private endowments. The completely independent school on the other hand did not have such auxilliary aid with which to retaliate. Schools "run for private profit" were at all times in the nineteenth-century precluded from public subsidy; for the word "profit" seems to have been used pejoratively. Yet in the economic sense most private schools did not make profits. In the highly competitive conditions of the times, they were only just covering their costs.

"Profit-earning" in the economic sense was indeed more applicable to the public sector schools. The latter contained public employees who were more than covering their opportunity costs; in other words they were enjoying special rents ("profits") from working for the government.[16] Interestingly enough the phrases "profit-seeking" and "private adventure schooling" were used most commonly by bureau officials. It is arguable that, unconsciously, this practice could have served the purpose of distracting the attention from their own economic profits. There were of course two levels of bureaucracy, that of the local school board and that of the Central Education Department. The primary attention here is upon the latter. But its fortunes depended in the first instance upon the growth of the smaller public bureaucracies; for they were instrumental

16. *Newcastle Report*, 1861, Vol. 1, p. 95.

in reducing the share of the biggest competitor—the private schools. This event automatically raised the central budget, and the theory of bureaucracy argues that it is the steady growth of their budget that bureaucrats desire most because it increases their non-pecuniary benefits and their promotion prospects.

What were the consequences of intervention and bureau behaviour for total expenditure? Some recent empirical analysis by Professor Sam Peltzman seems relevant. He has demonstrated that, in twentieth-century higher education, it is possible for government intervention to lead to *lower* total levels of expenditure.[17] Two key circumstances in Peltzman's model are repeated in the environment of British primary education after 1870. First, a large initial base of privately provided education; second, the introduction of one particular method of government intervention, the "subsidy in kind" method. Under it those who choose public aid must accept a fairly homogenous quantity (£x) of education from government-provided institutions (e.g. the board school system). If a family wants a bigger quantity, after intervention, say £x + 2, it has to forfeit the public aid altogether. This provides the main key to the paradox. Many families may accept the "free" £x worth of public education even though they would purchase say £x + 1 worth in the absence of intervention. If the consequent reduction in their children's school expenditure is sufficiently large it could outweigh the increase on the poorest so that total expenditure declines.

Compare this "subsidy in kind" with "money subsidies" of the 1833–70 type. Under this method the government rebated a fraction of the amount charged at any school chosen. The subsidy allowed the direct payment (the fee) to be lowered. The lower fee could have been a uniform reduction of say one third of the original price of different schools. The 1s., 9d. and 6d. schools could then charge 8d., 6d., and 4d., per week respectively. This pre-1870 system of money subsidies permitted the family to choose amounts of schooling in excess of a uniformly fixed £x

17. Sam Peltzman, "The Effect of Government Subsidies in-kind on Private Expenditures: The Case of Higher Education," *J.P.E.*, February, 1973.

without forfeiting the public aid. If the socially desired minimum of £x was an education costing 4*d.*, a family that was already buying a 6*d.* education would not, as in the "subsidy in kind" method be tempted to *reduce* expenditure to 4*d.* Indeed it would be more likely to increase it to an 8*d.* education. For an extra expenditure of twopence (from 6*d.* to 8*d.*) it could contain an increased educational value of 6*d.* (from 6*d.* to 1*s.*). The family would do this by changing to a more expensive, 8*d.*-a-week, school that was receiving a subsidy of 4*d.*—one third of the total cost. The point is that since, in so acting, public aid is not forfeited, the family is more encouraged to increase its expenditure too; and this is not to the detriment of poorer consumers since factors will be encouraged from outside so as to cause an increase in the total supply of education.

An Economic Model of the Displacement Effect

To illustrate most of the possibilities we shall employ a highly abstract model of a community of eight equal size families (see Table 1). Assume there are no non-parents. Also assume three income groups earning 100*s.*, 200*s.*, and 300*s.* with 2, 6, and 2 families in each group respectively (column 1). Suppose that prior to intervention the poorest two families were purchasing a 10*s.* per year education each, the middle six a 20*s.* education each, and the wealthiest two a 30*s.* education each (column 2). The total "national" expenditure on education is therefore 200*s.* Now suppose the government makes available, at government schools exclusively, a free schooling worth 12½*s.* and there are no excess costs in so doing, no "costs of bureaucracy" for instance. The two poor families will obviously accept; their consumption increases by 25 per cent and they have no direct costs. The middle income, paradoxically, will be presented with an additional cost. If it persists with its 20*s.* education it will give up the right to receive a 12½*s.* one free of charge. A decision to forego this "gift" is an opportunity cost. It is conceivable that it will judge that the continuation of the private schooling not worth such cost. This is the assumption we make in Table 1 (column 4) where all six middle-income families opt for the "free" education. With respect to the two rich families

Table 1. Hypothetical Family Expenditure on Education Before
and After Government Intervention (Shillings)

	1	2	3	4	5	
Number of families	Income per family (shillings)	Value of each family's education purchased before intervention (shillings)	Total expenditure on education before intervention (shillings)	Value of each family's education consumption when available "free" (worth 12.5 shillings)	Total expenditure on education after intervention	
					public	private
2	100	10	20	12.5	25	—
6	200	20	120	12.5	75	—
2	300	30	60	30	—	60
Totals: 110			all 200 private		160 { 100 public + 60 private	

we assume that their intensity of preference for a 30s. schooling is in their case such as to cause them to consider the new opportunity cost (of foregoing the free government schooling) not sufficiently high to justify the transfer.

This is of course a hypothetical case only and we have yet to test it empirically. Before we do this, notice that it demonstrates some of the possibilities suggested in Peltzman's theory. First, it shows how some families could move to a lower-valued education, after intervention of the 1870 type. Second, in columns 3 and 5 we see that total "national" expenditure on education could fall (from 200s.) after intervention. Hereafter we shall call this the Peltzman effect. Third it shows how public funds might not be targeted on the poorer families that most need them. The total of public funds used is 100s. but only 25s. are reaching the 2 poor families.

Table 2. Hypothetical Distributions of Tax Burden
After Government Intervention

Total tax revenue required for public sector schools = 100 (from Table 1)

		1	2		3
			Total tax revenue from each income growth according to (a) a proportionate tax (b) a regressive tax		
No. of families	*Income per family (shillings)*		*(a)*		*(b)*
2	100	10	5%	25	12½%
6	200	60	5%	60	5%
2	300	30	5%	15	2½%
Totals 10		100		100	

The remainder is going to the middle income families who do not need them; for they can be relied upon to purchase 20s. Notice however that although the national expenditure on education falls, *the size of the public sector is increasing; and it is this increase that plays the dominant role in the economics of the "strong" bureau; the key maximand is the size of its budget, not national expenditure.*

Before proceeding to the evidence we shall discuss some further qualifications. In Table 2 we examine two different hypothetical allocations of the taxes necessary to finance the subsidy: (a) a proportionate tax on incomes (of 5 per cent); (b) a regressive tax which starts with the rate of 12½ per cent on the poorest 2 families.[18] In case (b) there is no redistribution of wealth in favour of the poor families. Each of them is now paying in taxes an amount that is equal to the value of their "free" education.

18. A regressive tax is defined as one in which the tax rate decreases as the tax base increases. Here the tax base is income and as it increases, going down column 3, the tax rate falls from 12½% to 2½%.

Recall that the original historical aim of intervention was to so expand it that there would be an improvement in national prosperity and in law and order. The first of these objectives calls for an expansion of educational expenditure beyond the non-intervention levels. In our model intervention can be inefficient or even counter-productive; the displacement effect can have the "perverse" result of *lowering* national expenditure. With respect to crime reduction, the Victorians were thinking mainly in terms of educating the poor. In our model the system is inefficient because much of the public money does not reach them but is "siphoned" away by the middle income groups. Moreover, insofar as the tax is sufficiently regressive (as in column 3 Table 2) poverty is not relieved because the poor are fully "paying for" their "free" education.[19] It is widely believed in fact that mid-Victorian taxes were regressive. Excise taxes played a big role and progressive income taxes did not exist. Household rates (property taxes), used after 1870, were also regressive.[20]

We have worked on the assumption of a given kind of subsidy, the "subsidy in kind." This is the post-1870 kind, the "free" board school provision. Things were not in fact so clear cut in the first few years because board schools continued charging some fees for quite a time. Moreover the older schools enjoying the pre-1870 money subsidies still dominated. The Peltzman effect is still possible however. Our previous model in Table 1 illustrates the extreme alternatives of free and public, or full cost and private. The results of the model are only modified in degree (not in direction) if we assume that an unusually low fee is charged at board schools. For instance in column 4 of Table 1 we could substitute a fee of 2s. for "free" provision and still get a lower national expenditure after intervention. The main requirement for this result is that the board schools have a significant *differential* subsidy advantage over others that they can charge lower and lower fees. We have already documented the origins of substantial financial advantages bestowed upon the board

19. Excise taxes are normally regressive largely because the poor consume a larger proportion of their income. Individual excises on luxury goods *can* be progressive; but these goods did not predominate among taxed commodities in the nineteenth century.
20. Ursula Hicks, *Public Finance,* 1947, pp. 289–91. Excise taxes are normally regressive simply because the non-wealthy consume a larger proportion of their income.

schools by the Education Bureau soon after 1870. By 1876 this advantage was enabling Birmingham schools to set a fee as little as 1*d.* per week.

The Evidence: The Share of Education in the British National Income after 1870

Histories of education invariably claim that the 1870 Act brought unprecedented progress to education. Their argument rests largely upon figures of an increased number of school places available in the public sector by the 1880s. Pauline Gregg, for instance, argues that, whereas in 1870 there was accommodation for just under 2m. compared with a requirement of 3½m., by 1886 the target had been passed because there were then over 5m. school places for a population of nearly 28m.[21] We have dealt elsewhere with the deficiencies of this kind or argument. Briefly they stem from failure to acknowledge the following five factors: First, the 2m. places in 1870 refer only to the publicly subsidized sector; second, because after 1870 the population and the national income were both growing, one would have expected an increase in private provision anyway; third, many of the "new" public sector places were simply transferred private schools that were "taken over" after 1870; fourth, the "required" 3½m. in 1870 was based on the "impossible" target of one sixth of the total population; fifth, and consistent with the last point, there was considerable excess capacity in school building by the 1880s—that is the number of school places available was much bigger than the number of pupils taught.

Economic historians prefer, as a more reliable measure, the total current expenditure per year on the numbers actually in attendance. We shall next make such computations for England and Wales, and then compare them with similar computations for America and European countries. We shall focus upon the year 1882 because this year was sufficiently distant from 1870 to allow the new "subsidy in kind" system in England to have settled down; second, it was two years after universal compulsion

21. Pauline Gregg, *A Social and Economic History of Great Britain; 1760–1950*, Harrap 1954, p. 513.

Table 3. School Population and Costs in 1882

Average	Voluntary Schools	Board Schools
Attendance:	2,069,920	945,231
School Costs:	£1 14s. 6¾d.	£2 1s. 6½d.

Source: Annual Report for 1882, Tables II and III.

was established; third, useful figures happen to be available in the Annual Report for 1882. Table 3 gives the 1882 school population in voluntary and board schools as reported to the Education Department by the Inspectors. The voluntary schools include those that were receiving the pre-1870 type "money subsidies"; the board schools were those providing the new all or nothing "subsidies in kind."

The table also includes the cost of maintenance of the schools, i.e. salaries of teachers, books, repairs of buildings and furniture, lighting and heating. These figures underestimate the costs because they exclude interest charges. The 1882 Annual Report indicates (p. 29) that interest payments paid on loans came to about one fifth of the costs shown in Table 3. Strictly it is necessary also to impute interest on capital owned by the school board. In 1882 this would not have been large. To cover this point we shall assume that interest (paid out and imputed) accounted for one fourth of the costs shown in the Table. This would bring the annual costs for board schools up to about £2 12s. The voluntary school costs similarly adjusted come to about £2 3s. 3d. If we multiply these revised costs by the attendance number of Table 3 we arrive at a total cost of £2,457,601 for board schools and £4,476,202 for voluntary schools—a total of £6,933,803.

To this figure must be added about £2m. for the non-inspected (independent) schools. Elsewhere we have estimated the average costs of these to be £3.12s. with about 550,000 pupils.[22] This brings the total expenditure to £8,933,803. We must still add something for Sunday Schools.

22. See West "Educational Slowdown and Public Intervention in 19th Century England," *Explorations in Economic History*, Spring 1975.

Although these had passed the peak by this time, we shall assume that every day-scholar attended Sunday School. If we value this schooling on the same basis as our estimate for 1833[23] we obtain a generous figure of about £1m. This brings the total expenditure on primary education up to about £10m. The gross national income was approximately £1,074m.[24] If, as in our 1833 estimate, we deduct Scotland's share we have £940m. for England and Wales. Our estimate of £10m. educational expenditure consequently reaches a proportion of 1.06 of the 1882 national income. This is bigger than Albert Fishlow's estimate for the UK in 1880 of 0.9 per cent, but quite consistent with it. The difference is because our figure refers to England and Wales only and it includes Sunday Schools. Applying our same methods for the year 1858, we arrive at a figure of 1.10 per cent of gross national income.[25] For the year 1833 we have previously obtained a figure of 1 per cent of national income.[26]

Judged on such a basis, therefore, the 1870 legislation had brought no progress by 1882. Certainly our estimates have included several approximations and there may be room for some further marginal adjustments.[27] More important, if education was a "strongly superior good," its income elasticity of demand would have been above unity. This means that for every one per cent increase in private income the private increase in educational expenditure demanded would have been more than one per cent. If we assume this then even if the share of education in GNP remained constant between 1858 and 1882, the 1870 legislation would have

23. E. G. West "Resource Allocation and Growth in Early Nineteenth Century British Education," *E.H.R.*, 1970, pp. 68–95.
24. B. R. Mitchell and Phyllis Deane, *Abstract of British Historical Statistics*, C.U.P., p. 366.
25. Our 1958 estimate is derived from school figures from the Newcastle Report for that year. The population figures and national income estimates were taken from Mitchell and Deane, *op. cit.*
26. E. G. West, *E.H.R.*, 1970, p. 87.
27. It is debatable whether the costs of the central administration of the public system in 1882 should be included in a comparison with the completely private system of 1833. We have omitted them. The School Board administration of 1882 cost about $\frac{1}{4}$m. No *substantial* adjustment is required on account of changes in the population structure. The share of the 5–14 year olds in the total population was .229 in 1840, .222 in 1860, and .229 in 1880.

reduced the amount of money going into it compared with what private expenditure without legislation would have attained. Clearly much depends upon the facts about income elasticities in the nineteenth century.

Some rough estimates of elasticities in England and other countries may be obtained from Table 4. The evidence in this table suggests that England and Wales had an income elasticity only just above unity between 1833 and 1858. A useful comparison after that might be obtained from other countries as their incomes (column 3) increased above $108 per capita (the English level of 1858). Judged on the figures alone the income elasticities for continental countries are very high indeed. Most of the increased educational expenditure in these countries however was government sponsored. This makes it difficult to distinguish private preference from bureau pressure. For America we do have a separate measure of private expenditures (in Albert Fishlow's article, *op. cit,* column 3 minus column 2 in his Table I). Between 1860 and 1880 private expenditure increased by above 66 per cent and the income over the same period increased by 26.5 per cent. This indicates an income elasticity of over 2. As a qualification we should note that such a figure becomes less representative the lower the proportion of private sector total education. In 1860 and 1880 in America it was 43 per cent and 23 per cent respectively.

Table 4 also affords a new comparison of nineteenth-century "effort" at similar rates of per capita income. Column 5 adjusts for population structure. It is assumed that out of two countries with the same ratio of education to GNP the one with the smaller proportion of children in its population is making the biggest educational effort. Column 5 accordingly divides the share in GNP with the share of children in the population. This is equivalent to expenditures per child divided by GNP per capita. The first striking fact from Table 4 is that, at per capita constant dollar incomes at or below $100, England's performance was over twice as good as that of France, and better than that of Germany.[28] This means

---

28. The Italian performance seems impressive. It is likely however that measurement of Italian national incomes is the least accurate since there is a higher element of domestic agricultural production that was not included; and a higher national income would reduce the Italian achievement figures in columns 3 and 4.

Table 4. Share of Education in 19th-Century National Incomes:
An International Comparison

	1	2	3	4	5
	Prevailing policy towards school control, attendance and finance	*G.N.P. per capita current dollars*	*G.N.P. per capita constant dollars (1890–99) = 100*	*Share of educational expenditure in G.N.P.*	*= Col. 4 divided by share of children in the population*
England and Wales 1833	Completely private i.e., no government subsidy. Fee paying. No compulsion	$104	$84	1.00%	4.36%
England and Wales 1858	Predominantly private and church aided; but some schools subsidized and inspected. No compulsion.	$134	$108	1.10%	4.95%
England and Wales 1882	One third of pupils in board schools. Compulsion. Fees much reduced in board schools.	$174	$151	1.06%	4.63%
United States 1860	Common School system predominantly local finance. Fees a significant element in several states. Typically little compulsion.	$147	$137	0.80%	3.20%
United States 1880	Fees largely abolished. About half the states have compulsion.	$186	$159	1.10%	4.53%
United States 1900	Compulsory and free nearly everywhere. Increasing centralization.	$204	$202	1.70%	7.63%
France 1860	Centralized, compulsion and free.	$107	$104	0.40%	2.30%

(*continued*)

Table 4. (*continued*)

	1	2	3	4	5
	Prevailing policy towards school control, attendance and finance	*G.N.P. per capita current dollars*	*G.N.P. per capita constant dollars (1890–99) = 100*	*Share of educational expenditure in G.N.P.*	*= Col. 4 divided by share of children in the population*
France 1880	Big public effort after the war defeat of 1870.	$139	$125	0.90%	5.14%
France 1900		$156	$156	1.30%	7.78%
Germany 1860	Centralized, compulsory and free from the early	$100	$120	1.00%	4.20%
1880	century.	$120	$122	1.60%	7.34%
1900		$138	$133	1.90%	8.75%
Italy 1883	Over 80% public. Local government respon-	$81	$80	0.98%	4.88%
1898	sibility mainly, but increasing central government share.	$86	$82	1.39%	6.50%

Sources:

Gross National Income

England and Wales: B. R. Mitchell and Phyllis Deane, *Abstract of British Historical Statistics* (Cambridge, 1962), p. 366.

United States, *Historical Statistics of the United States* (Washington DC, Government Printing Office 1960), p. 139.

France, *Annuaire Statistique De La France Retrospectif* Ed. 1961, p. 20.

Germany's figures are for *net* national income. W. S. Wotinsky and E. S. Wotinsky, *World Population and Resources* (N.Y. 1953), p. 386.

Italy, *Indagine statistica sullo sviluppo del reddito nazionale dell'Italia dal 1861 al 1956* (Roma 1957).

Where the per capita calculation was not available it was estimated with the relevant population census. All dates, pounds converted to dollars at one to five, marks at four to one, francs and lire at five to one. (These ratios correspond approximately to the exchanges reported in the *Economist* over this period.)

Estimates for G.N.P. at constant prices were based on G.N.P. deflators in E. H. Phelps Brown and Margaret Browne *A Century of Pay* (1968). The figure for England in 1833 was obtained with a combination of wage and price indices in B. R. Mitchell and Phyllis Deane, *op cit.*

(*continued*)

Table 4. (*continued*)

Population: Share of 5–14 years olds.
  England and Wales: B. R. Mitchell and Phyllis Deane, *op cit.*, p. 12.
  United States: *Historical Statistics*, p. 10.
  France: *Annuaire Statistique Retrospectif*, p. 5.
  Germany: Statistik des Deutschen Reichs 1833 Band LVII
  1903   "   150
  Italy: Vera Zamagni, *Lo sviluppo economico*, in Gianni Toniolo Italiano 1861–1940, p. 187.

Share of Education in National Income
  England and Wales: 1833, 1858, 1882, as stated in the text.
  United States, France, and Germany: Albert Fishlow, "Levels of Nineteenth Century American Investment in Education," *Jnl of Economic History*, 1967, p. 432.
  Italy: Vera Zamagni, *op cit.*, Table 3. Figures reduced by the figure for education "superiori" to leave Elementarie and Secondarie.

that the share of education in GNP in the "industrial revolution year" of 1833 in England and Wales was greater than that of industrialising Germany in 1860 and very much better than that of France in 1860. This is all the more interesting in view of the absence of English government intervention (see column 1) compared with the newly established public systems in the European countries.

Second, there is a modest improvement in England's effort by 1858, and this is accompanied by the system of "money subsidies" first introduced in 1833. England's effort in 1858 relates to an income of $134. America did not approach this effort until she had an income of $186 (in 1880). On the other hand at income levels similar to England in 1858 ($130–140 per capita), France caught up in education achievement (in 1880), and Germany was considerably in advance (in 1890).

These results seem consistent with Niskanen's theory of bureaucracy. Because the continental countries by the mid-nineteenth century had mature bureaucracies and England did not, the theory would predict that the former would have a greater expansion. Although the expenditures are higher in these countries, marginal net benefits would have been smaller; that is the marginal value of the service will be less than the marginal cost. Niskanen concludes that a full bureau will supply up to twice that of a competitive industry faced with the same demands and cost functions. This suggests that we can, at one extreme, discount the "bureau effect" by dividing the observed figures by two. If we do this for

Germany in 1900, the educational effort figure of 8.75 (column 4 Table 4) becomes 4.375. This is not far off the figure of 4.63 for England in 1882. Bearing in mind that her per capita income in that year was 26 per cent bigger than Germany's of 1900, and also that we are applying Niskanen's most extreme prediction, these results would appear to strengthen the impression that by 1882 England had fallen below her potential in educational supply. This belief of course is also prompted by the drop from 4.95 to 4.63 in the English ratios between 1858 and 1882 (column 4).

It may be asked why the "Peltzman effect" does not also show up in the case of America. In several states in 1860 the charging of parental fees (rate bills) was certainly a feature of the common school system. There was also a significant tradition of private schooling. Between 1860 and 1880 most of the common schools became "free." (In New York State for instance fees were abolished in 1867.) This event would present many families with the same opportunity cost that was described earlier when England introduced the all or nothing "subsidy in kind" in 1870. On similar application of the displacement hypothesis it would have been rational for many American families to have switched to public education even where this was of somewhat lower resource value to the one they were accustomed. One answer is that already in 1860 the relatively homogenous common schools were accounting for 57 per cent of education. In England in 1860 government aid accounted for less than 33 per cent, and this was distributed largely to the more heterogenous private and parochial schools. England's public intervention in other words was still one of "money subsidies." It was the sudden change from this system to one of "common schools" after 1870 that probably induced the "Peltzman effect." Another answer could be that in America there *was* a substantial switching by the middle class from private to public (as in the Peltzman theory), but that this was just offset by the increase in the education of low-income groups. On this reasoning, with other things equal, although there would be positive growth in the share of education in GNP it would be at lower levels and rates than those in continental Europe where the private school base was much smaller.

In Peltzman's model of "in kind" subsidies the *direction* of expenditure on the education of the poor is always positive. The *degree* of additional spending on the poor, however, depends upon the amount of switching into "free" education by the middle class. It might be tempting to argue that, because the marginal social rate of return was greater for poorer than for richer individuals, the Peltzman effect in nineteenth-century England might have been deliberately planned as an efficiency measure. With more going to the poor and less to the middle-income groups the switch to "free" state schools could have raised the GNP. We shall call this the "social engineer's argument." Its logic is questionable. First, nothing is said about the tax source of the subsidy; regressive tax sources could have made a big difference to the argument. Second, if a switch of emphasis towards the poor was required, one should ask whether the pre-1870 method could not have accomplished it at less cost. It can easily be shown that it could. In terms of Table 1, if instead of a "free" education worth 12½s. a flat subsidy of 5s. were given for the schooling of the low and middle groups, expenditure on the poor would expand to 15s. and total public expenditure would fall by 60 per cent. And any system of means tests applied to the pre-1870 system would have stopped the "leakage" to the middle class and allowed more for the poor. We still need an explanation therefore why the change in the method of intervention occurred. In the absence of a better one, the theory of bureaucracy seems acceptable.

Another and even more important objection to the "social engineer's" argument is that it implicitly contains a "dictator" model of government. In it the "dictator" (planner) uses coercion with the single-minded aim of raising GNP. This however does not conform to reality. In a democratic society, policy is geared, not to the wishes of a "dictator," but to those of the median voter. Policies that do not meet *his* preferences will not be adopted because they will fail to obtain a majority. The median voter's attitude to policy will depend on the tax "prices" he will have to contribute. We have seen that progressive income taxes were not operative in the nineteenth century. If we assume proportional taxes then the median voter expects to pay his full share—just as he does when he purchases through the market. Let us also make the usual assumption that demand for education is a positive function of income. Consider next that because of the usual pattern of income distribution *the median voter's income is less than the mean income.* It follows that when education is collectivised through the political process there will be less total expenditure on it than previously. This is the initial effect before the growth of a full bureaucracy. When the latter eventually matures the "Niskanen effect" operates in the opposite direction.

This extra model of the "economics of politics" provides an additional potential explanation of our post-1870 data on English education. It is a general explanation that could well complement the others. On its own however it would seem to be insufficient to explain why the post-1870 "in kind" subsidy method was adopted; only that once a collectivized and "free" education was adopted the proportion of expenditure to the GNP would decline. The bureau strategy that we have documented seems a much more persuasive explanation of the switch in methods of intervention. And in a democracy the bureau, as well as the median voter, has important influence in the outcomes. Moreover as the bureaucracy eventually reaches full monopoly powers it is able freely to encroach upon the median voter's consumer surplus and cause him to pay more than he would on the market. In England this latter became a twentieth- rather than a nineteenth-century phenomenon. In 1882 the public sector accounted for not more than one half of total expenditure. There remained therefore much scope for the operation of the Peltzman effect. There was much "ruin" left in the private sector; and it was this "ruin" that seems to have been the main reason why the strong *public sector* growth did not mean strong *national* growth.

17 · Legal Compulsion:
Logic and Reality

To explain the significance of the introduction of legal compulsion in education in the nineteenth century it is necessary first to explore the economic implications of the principle. The impact of compulsory education upon a family is proportionate to the effect upon its current real income. This in turn depends upon whether compulsion is accompanied by an education that is simultaneously made "free" or "partly free." Strictly there is a distinction too between compulsory *education* and compulsory *"schooling"*; the former can be obtained outside schools— in which case it is called "informal education." Table 1 shows the possible combinations:

Table 1.

	Compulsory Education	Compulsory Schooling
Full cost: Fee paying	1	4
Partially subsidized: Fee paying	2	5
Full subsidy: Free	3	6

Numbers 1, 2 and 3 in the diagram were implemented by the British Education Act of 1876. The political economists Adam Smith, Thomas

Malthus, James Mill, J. M. McCulloch, John Stuart Mill, Henry Fawcett and Stanley Jevons were in favour of Numbers 1 and 2. Smith especially was concerned less about where people obtained their education than with the results. Compulsory education of course requires a different kind of policing, or set of incentives, than does compulsory schooling. John Stuart Mill advocated the incentive of public examination:

> Once in every year the examination should be renewed, with a gradu-
> ally extending range of subjects, so as to make the universal acquisition
> and what is more, retention, of a certain minimum of general knowl-
> edge virtually compulsory. Beyond that minimum there should be vol-
> untary examinations on all subjects, at which all who come up to a
> certain standard of proficiency might claim a certificate.[1]

In addition Mill adopted Bentham's principle that examination pass certificates were to be the price payable for the right to vote.[2] Subsidized education (items 2 and 3), as distinct from subsidized schooling, today takes such forms as free public libraries, subsidized museums, radio, television, theatre and literature.

Numbers 4 and 5 in Table 1, which refer to compulsory, but not fully subsidized, *schooling,* were implemented in certain areas by the English Act of 1870. School districts were given the optional power to pass by-laws to make schooling obligatory up to certain ages. The legislation was generalized in 1880 when all areas were obliged to have by-laws. Item No. 6, "compulsory and free," was the ideal espoused by the British National Education League (The Birmingham League) led by Joseph Chamberlain in the late 1860s and early 1870s.[3]

Whilst we have referred so far to direct compulsion, indirect compulsion is almost equally as important. This is usually effected by child

---

1. *Liberty,* 1962 edition (Fontana), p. 2.
2. Henry Brougham also incorporated this idea in his educational proposals to Parliament in 1837.
3. The full objectives of the Birmingham League were Compulsory, Free and Non-sectarian. These aims were strongly held by a wide group of individuals in the nineteenth century ranging from George Dixon, Robert Applegarth and Jesse Collins to Charles Dickens. Henry Fawcett, Professor of Political Economy in Cambridge, eventually broke with the League on the question of fees. J. S. Mill might have joined if free schooling had not been insisted upon.

labour laws and these in turn involve separate features. The laws usually prescribe minimum age requirements for employment. Sometimes however they confine themselves to regulation of hours and conditions of work. Another possibility is the insistence upon documentary evidence of education before permission to work is granted. The British 1876 Act again provides an example. It stipulated that no child might be employed between the ages of 10 and 14 without a certificate from H.M. Inspectors. The certificate had to show that its bearer had passed a certain standard examination in the three Rs or had made a given number of attendances at any elementary school certified by the Inspectors as efficient.

Compulsory and Free Versus Compulsory and Full Cost Fees

The form of compulsion that would seemingly make the biggest immediate encroachment upon family real income is that associated with full cost payments (items 1 and 4 in Table 1). This is not inevitable however. Whilst the subsidies certainly appear to the beneficiaries as unambiguous cost reductions, this impression stems from partial equilibrium considerations only. General equilibrium analysis requires a fuller picture including the identification of those who are obliged to pay the taxes that supply the subsidies. It is possible that a family may pay in taxes nearly the same amount as it receives in education benefits. Certainly it should not be forgotten that all families pay taxes; indirect taxes are universal and many of them are regressive; household rates (property taxes)—which are a common source of educational revenue—can be an especially disproportionate burden on poor and large families either directly or indirectly through rents that are higher because of rates. We have shown that in 1869 the English educational statistician Horace Mann believed that making individual families pay fully and consciously for their "free" education through national (not local) taxes was the correct policy aim. His system would, at least at first sight, be *equivalent* to item 4 in Table 1. The parent would pay the full cost—but directly through taxes.

Mann's argument is best understood in the perspective of life-time tax contributions. In some periods parents may be receiving educational and other subsidies in excess of the taxes they are currently paying. Non-

parents meanwhile will also be contributing taxes for educational purposes. Over a life-time however tax payments could equal the benefits.
Some have argued that tax revenues can therefore be regarded as a common pool from which each member of society can draw at the period of
his child's schooling. At other periods of adult life—before marriage and
in middle and old age—the individual can be regarded as paying taxes in
anticipation of "free" educational services expected or for services received in the past. One reply to such an argument is that it would be a
coincidence if taxes paid over a lifetime just matched benefits received.
Moreover, where capital markets exist the system may be unnecessary.
Parents can then always borrow to finance their children's schooling and
the requisite loans can be repaid over the parents' lifetime. The advocates
of the "tax pooling" system usually imply that capital markets do not exist
or that if they do they suffer from serious "imperfections." The tax pooling system to them is a kind of collectivized system of installment paying
that is necessary in an area where private markets do not work effectively.

From modern economics we are aware that Mann's system of "free"
education that is not free (because everybody pays for himself through
his taxes) is not necessarily the equivalent to direct (fee) payments, however much of the policy intention might be to make them the same. There
are two main reasons. First, where capital markets do exist (and there is
no easy proof that they don't)[4] the imposition of a collectivized "installment system" is beneficial at most only to those families that take advantage of it. A "free" and compulsory system would be a loss to those who
would not voluntarily choose more education. Some would be worse off
and others better off therefore compared with "non-compulsory" private
markets. It is helpful to keep separate the two issues "compulsory education" and "simulated capital markets." For those who believe there are
serious capital market imperfections, the direct policy arrangement
might be to establish a public loan system. Those who wish to purchase
more education can then do so. If the main concern is with the "need"
to compel families to have more education then compulsion *per se*, i.e.
direct coercion, is required.

4. High rates of interest in such markets do not necessarily show that they are imperfect. These rates may reflect the real risk involved.

The second reason why "collectivized installment purchase" through taxes will be different from direct purchase, relates to differences in incidental costs of using each system. If the transaction costs of purchasing through the market are less than those from purchasing through the political process, other things equal, there is an extra burden on family purchases of education (and vice versa). The transaction costs of "compulsory purchase" can for instance be particularly high to an individual family if the system also involves public provision of government-run schools. This is partly because the individual preferences of the family might be less efficiently met. For instance it may prefer eight hours' arithmetic teaching per week and only receive four hours in a public system. The remaining four hours would have to be purchased privately outside school hours. Subjects may be forced upon it that are not preferred; other subjects that are preferred may be absent. In the extreme case of disagreement with a public system the family will be forced to purchase fully private schooling and will so "pay twice" for education.

Transaction costs can rise to critical levels where costly public education bureaucracies are established to administer a system which is compulsory and "free"; and we have already referred to the new "economics of bureaucracy" that predicts that the *primary* aim of the senior officers in a bureau is to maximize not public welfare but the size of the bureau's budget.[5] The transaction costs to families for information can grow considerably when it is provided mainly by education bureaux. The developed bureau, according to the modern theory, will sponsor research and information concerning the output of the service for which it is responsible. It will ensure however, that this information is sufficiently self-serving to avoid any risk of spoiling the cumulative development or preservation of its own monopoly.

Special Nineteenth-Century Circumstances

Having examined basic economic aspects of compulsion we now turn to some special nineteenth-century circumstances. In the era of nineteenth-century social reform there was genuine and growing concern for chil-

5. W. A. Niskanen, *Bureaucracy and Represented Government,* New York, 1971.

dren who were deprived—in all senses—not just at the level of education. All kinds of public policies were devised to discriminate in favour of such children and these included measures to protect them from malnutrition, parental cruelty, poor housing and clothing. Laws were so operated as to discipline irresponsible parents selectively. Since it was rarely suggested that the delinquent families were in the majority, these *discriminatory* measures were usually considered sufficient. Those parents who were coerced by the law to improve their standards of treatment to their children, relating to feeding or clothing for instance, were in effect subject to compulsion—but it was what we shall call *selective* compulsion (i.e. compulsion applied to a selected minority of parents after they had shown evidence of irresponsibility). The case of education developed differently; here the law applied what we call *universal* compulsion. This was *not* a matter of selecting the delinquent families for special attention; here compulsion applied to *all* families automatically. At first sight there seems no difference between the two types of compulsion. Universally applicable laws, it will be argued, should not affect responsible families since they will already be doing what the law wants them to do. Further investigation however shows there was an important difference.

In Britain just prior to universal compulsion (in the 1860s) there was, as we have shown, a near universal system of private fee-paying schools and the majority of parents were using it. In 1870 it was thought necessary to *complement* this system with a few government schools (Board schools) in those areas where there was proved insufficiency. In 1880, universal compulsion was legislated. It was next argued that since it was wrong for the government to force parents to do something that they could not afford, education should be made "free." Free schooling should be available however to the majority of parents who were previously paying for it as well as to the minority that the legislation was ostensibly aimed at. Free schooling of course required full subsidization. It was next argued that only the new government sponsored (board) schools could fully qualify for such treatment. Private schools that were run for a profit should not be aided because this practice would subsidize profit makers. (This anti-profit principle was incorporated into every piece of nineteenth-century legislation.) Most of the remainder of private schools were connected with the churches. It was contended that it would be wrong to treat these as favourably as the Board schools because that would be using Catholic taxpayers' contributions to subsidize Protestant schools and vice-versa. The result was that the new Board schools originally set up to *complement* a private system eventually *superseded* it; the Board schools accomplished this by subsidized "unfair" competition which increasingly asserted itself.

Many, if not most, of those who originally advocated compulsion were supporters of voluntary church schools. In the particular way in which compulsion was enacted (*universal* as distinct from *selective* compulsion) there were however significant effects upon the majority of parents who did not need it. For them it became in effect *compulsion to change from one school system to another;* as private schools went out of business the Board schools often provided the only alternative. This new (collectivized) system was associated with a growing educational bureaucracy and a protection-seeking teaching profession that was among the strongest of nineteenth-century agitators for universal compulsion. For these reasons it is possible that *universal* compulsion eventually led to *less* total education in real terms, or in terms related to family preference, than would otherwise have resulted—bearing in mind that education is a normal good[6] the supply of which would have increased "voluntarily" following the increases in income and population that actually occurred after 1880.[7]

---

6. A "normal" good in economics is one whose consumption increases with increases of income.

7. In developed economies the subject of compulsion comes to the public's attention primarily when there is a question of raising the compulsory leaving age. The emphasis now switches from the need to compel minimum educational attainments (such as literacy) to the need to extend the time served in school. Whilst this is still possibly compatible with motives of "protecting young people against under-preparation for the more sophisticated needs of twentieth century occupations" an increasing number of people now believe that it is also consistent with other explanations. Extended compulsory schooling, it is now suggested, is really required to provide employment for an expanded and politically articulate teaching profession, to protect unionized adult workers from competition from younger workers, and to reduce the embarrassment of governments that face already swollen figures of teenage unemployment—unemployment that is (in America) often the consequence of minimum wage laws. Extra com-

It will be seen that in terms of our Table 1 (page 245) political and economic pressure groups can shift provision from compulsory *education* (the first column) to compulsory *schooling* (second column) and to push from item 1 (full fees) through consecutively to item 6 (free schooling). It should also be clear that *universal* compulsion can not be treated in isolation but has to be seen as one of a set of simultaneously determined equations.

The previous points can be sharpened by a further application of economic principles. In the absence of compulsion a "voluntary" education level establishes itself up to the point where the family demand for it equals the marginal cost. We can consider demand for schooling either as a consumer good or an investment good. Here we shall treat it as an investment. The family's individual demand curve for education, DD in Figure 1 (page 253) can be viewed as a line showing successive marginal rates of return at different investment levels. The marginal rate of return is the ratio of the monetary return from an additional unit of education over the cost. The demand curve will slope downwards especially because of the rising opportunity cost of time as more units of human capital are required. There will also be falling marginal productivity of educational resources owing to "fixed" mental and physical capacity of the educatee. The position of the whole curve (as distinct from its slope) will be determined by the individual's ability to produce human capital.

The supply curve SS in Figure 1 is expressed as a line joining relevant interest rate costs and will normally slope upwards. The costs will be low at first because they relate to available family funds having a low opportunity cost. As more education is purchased subsidized funds at below market rates may be used up to a point. Beyond this the individual has to use funds from private capital markets at the highest interest rates.[8]

Before compulsion the family will purchase voluntarily O.V. school-

---

pulsory education often means to young people not more education but longer education; but since their frustration can not so easily express itself politically there is little they can do. This is so even though they prefer more education—but further education that is provided at a place of work.

8. W. M. Landes and L. C. Solmon, "Compulsory Schooling Legislation: An Economic Analysis of the Law and Social Change in the Nineteenth Century," *Journal of Economic History,* March 1972, Sec. III. Gary Becker, *Human Capital and the Personal Distribution of Income,* 1967.

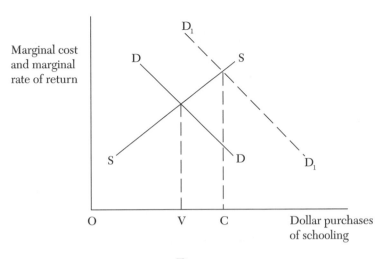

Fig. 1.

ing. Suppose the new legislation now is of type 4 in Table 1 and compels the family to have O.C. schooling but does not make it "free." On the assumption that the law was fully enforced there would be an increase of V.C. schooling and the family's supply curve S.S. would only be applicable to the right of C. Suppose next that legislation of type 5 or 6 is adopted and after schooling is made compulsory it is provided "free" or is heavily subsidized from taxes that do not fall immediately upon parents. This will reduce considerably the direct costs to the individual of producing human capital invesments and will thus increase the marginal rate of return. In Figure 1 the demand curve would shift to the right and become D_1D_1. As we have drawn it, the result is that the compulsory and the new voluntary levels of schooling coincide.[9]

This last point is of considerable importance and hitherto has been overlooked in economic analysis. The important implication that it contains is that it is possible that the socially desired optimum level of O.C. can be attained solely by price subsidies. Where this is so, compulsion is not necessary. If compulsion is insisted upon, society is involved in

9. Child Labour laws could have a similar effect. The probability of penalties for employing young people will reduce the employers' demand for their services. This will cause their potential wages to fall. In turn this means that the opportunity cost of a young person's time would fall and the marginal rate of return from education would rise. (Landes & Solmon, *op. cit.*).

unnecessary policing costs. The only individuals who would have an interest in compulsion would be the potential members of the inspectorate; and the economics of bureaucracy would suggest that senior members of a potentially expanding bureau would have no incentive in divulging this point.

Reference has already been made to the nineteenth-century argument that where schooling was made compulsory the State had an obligation to see to it that poor parents could pay the necessary fees. This principle goes back as far as the Report on the Hand-loom Weavers in 1841, which was largely written by Nassau Senior. It appears on page 123:

> It is equally obvious that if the State be bound to require the parent to educate his child it is bound to see that he has the means to do so.[10]

In his *Principles* published seven years later, John Stuart Mill similarly argued:

> It is therefore an allowable exercise of the powers of government to impose on parents the legal obligation of giving elementary instruction to children. This, however, cannot fairly be done, without taking measures to insure that such instruction shall always be accessible to them either gratuitously or at a trifling expense.[11]

Mill's basic case for the establishment of compulsion rested on his belief that the voluntary principle had failed to supply sufficient instruction.

> . . . I shall merely express my conviction that even in quantity it is (in 1848) and is likely to remain altogether insufficient. . . .[12]

Notice that this was not an appeal to systematic evidence. National data was not available until the 1851 Census Report on Education in England and Wales. This revealed in fact over 2 million day scholars. Mill was arguing from impressionism—from a "conviction." He had a very firm opinion that: "The uncultivated cannot be competent judges of cultivation." The voluntary principle failed because ". . . the end not being desired, the means will not be provided at all. . . ."[13]

---

10. *Parliamentary Papers*, 1841, Vol. X.
11. *Principles*, 1909, Ashley Edition, p. 954.
12. *Ibid.*, p. 955.
13. *Ibid.*, p. 953.

If Mill and his supporters had received the correct evidence they might not have been so hasty in recommending *universal* compulsion. Careful reflection would have shown that it was difficult to distinguish between parental "negligence" and parental indigence. Countless observers in the nineteenth century condemned parents for their *irresponsibility* and then, after compulsion was established, urged that the fees should be abolished to enable them to overcome their *poverty*. The only sure way to disentangle these issues is to subsidize the fees first; only then, after a suitable time lag, will the real preferences of parents reveal themselves. In terms of our Figure 1 it is necessary to discover by how much the "voluntary" demand curve moves to the right after subsidization. Furthermore one should add to the total amount available for subsidy the funds that would otherwise be spent on policing a compulsory system.

Empirical Studies

Hitherto historians of education have been unanimous that the evidence shows that compulsion did significantly increase attendance in the 20–30 years after the legislation. Their usual arguments however are inadequate. There are four reasons. The first relates to the point just made. Among the other things that happened in addition to compulsion was the steady reduction of fees. This reduction works in the direction of expanding the demand for schooling (provided that the subsidies do not come entirely from extra taxes on the beneficiaries). Second, the per capita national income was increasing during the 20–30 years after compulsion. This means that, provided education was a normal good (with a positive income elasticity of demand) the voluntary demand for it even as a consumption good would have increased anyway. It is true that the opportunity costs of education (foregone earnings) would have increased and this would have worked in the opposite direction. Still other forces were pushing in favour of expansion however. There was for instance a secular decline in loan interest, a circumstance that tends to increase the incentive to invest in more schooling. Again the secular fall in morbidity rates must have had a similar influence.[14]

14. Gary Becker, *op. cit.*

Third there was a steady expansion of population. Growth of voluntary attendance in absolute terms would have occurred for this reason alone. (Several historians do acknowledge this point.) Fourth, many observers have quoted figures of increased enrolment following compulsion at *public* (state) schools. Much of this increase however was, as we have seen, the result of a switching from private schools because the public schools were increasingly forcing others out of the market by the use of heavily subsidized fees.

In their (1972) regression analysis of nineteenth-century compulsory legislation in the U.S. Landes and Solmon found that in 1880 the average level of schooling was greater in states with compulsory laws than in states without them when other independent variables, such as state income, the number of foreign immigrants, population density, etc. were held constant. They emphasized however that it was not possible to conclude from this that a compulsory legislation was the *cause* of higher levels of schooling. The possibility remained that differences in schooling between states with and without compulsory laws pre-dated these laws. Further investigation revealed that this in fact was the case. They concluded that school legislation was definitely not the cause of higher schooling levels.

> Instead these laws appear to have merely formalized what was already an observed fact; namely, that the vast majority of school age persons had already been obtaining a level of schooling equal to or greater than what was to be later specified by statute.[15]

In Britain the nineteenth-century data is less accessible and more fragmented. Compulsion was initiated by thousands of local school boards when they were set up after 1870. One has the strong immediate impression that in the short run there was some significant influence. But there were different circumstances between Britain and the U.S. In many parts of America universal free education was established before compulsion. For instance in New York State the Free Schools Act finally abolished fees (parental rate bills) in 1867. The New York Education Act establishing compulsion was passed seven years later. In Britain compulsion came

15. *Ibid.*, Section IV.

first and the trend towards heavily subsidized fees and eventually zero prices came *after*. The causal connection between compulsion and enrolment is therefore more difficult to elicit in the British case, because the move towards free schooling could have been a strong influence in expanding enrolments. A stronger *apparent* effect of the compulsory legislation in Britain might therefore be explained in these terms.

Enforcement Costs

Our analysis so far has assumed that compulsion is fully enforced. In practice enforcement is a variable and its success is proportionate to the resources devoted to it. After the nineteenth-century legislation, truancy did not cease completely; and it has not done so to this day. Minimum school laws impose an expected penalty depending on the probability of being caught and the probability of legal proceedings. This cost will vary in subjective terms depending on personal disutility from non-compliance and on risk aversion. If "too much" compulsion is enforced there is the danger of large scale parental "rebellion" and the law is brought into disrepute.

In a paper read before the British Association in the 1870s a Professor Jack questioned the wisdom of the authorities in Birmingham in being so proud of their above-average attendance increases. These were obtained, he protested, with especially stringent enforcement measures. Whereas the average attendance increase in Glasgow, after compulsion was adopted in that city, was 25 per cent per annum, with prosecutions of one in 20,000 of the population, in Birmingham the average increase was 31 per cent and the prosecutions one in 200. Joseph Chamberlain however retorted that Birmingham was *not* being tougher than Glasgow. In Scotland, he argued, although there were fewer convictions they were more severe. The actual amount of the Glasgow penalty was in many cases 40s. whereas the extreme amount of penalty in England was 5s. including costs. The fear of the heavier Scotch penalty was thus an even bigger deterrent. But the most interesting part of Chamberlain's reply was his argument that the biggest cause of increased attendance in Birmingham was the drastic reduction of school fees. The Birmingham school board was exceptional in these reductions. It has lowered fees in many cases to one penny whereas the typical board school fee was 3*d*. Chamberlain discovered (in modern terms) an inelastic demand for education:

> As regards the boys' and girls' schools in which the penny fee has been adopted, the result has been very remarkable, and to some of us, at all events, very satisfactory. Wherever the fees have been reduced the total amount of fees received in a given period after the reduction has exceeded the total amount of fees [originally] received . . . in other words, the reduction of fees in every case has trebled the attendance . . . I can only say that my experience since I have sat upon this Board confirms me in the opinion that if we could have universal free schools in England, as they exist in America, France, Sweden, Norway, Denmark and many other countries, we should reduce the necessity of compulsion to a minimum, even if we did not do away with it altogether.[16]

Compulsion and the Economics of Politics

The findings of Landes and Solmon that school legislation in the U.S. did not cause higher schooling levels in the nineteenth century leave us with an obvious problem. Why was such an elaborate administration for universal compulsion set up if its achievements were so small? As a preliminary to an attempt to answer this question let us consider first another example of "individual failure": inadequate feeding or individual malnutrition.[17] Suppose that two people out of a community of one thousand cannot be trusted to feed themselves or their children adequately and that such irresponsibility is regarded as a social detriment. What is the most viable policy for a politician whose behaviour is constrained by vote maximization? If a *universal* degree of compulsion is to be established this could involve substantial policing costs including the costs of in-

16. Joseph Chamberlain, "Six Years of Educational Work in Birmingham," an address delivered to the Birmingham School Board, 2 November 1876, pp. 19–20.
17. The following illustration and parts of the subsequent argument are taken from my *Economical Education and the Politician.* Institute of Econ. Affairs Hobart Paper 42, London, 1968. This work develops the argument especially in the context of the forthcoming raising of annual leaving age in Britain.

specting and checking not only the eating habits of the two delinquents but also that of the other 998. Compare this situation with one wherein say about 450 out of the 1,000 are likely to be delinquents. At first sight it may appear that the case for *universal* (as distinct from selective) compulsion is less substantial in the first situation with 2 "delinquents" than in the second with 450. When political considerations enter however, the position appears more complex. Making nearly half of the electorate do something they have no wish to do is clearly a policy which stands to lose more votes than one which coerces only two people.

The result seems paradoxical. Other things equal, compulsion is more "profitable" to the government the smaller the minority to be compelled. Yet the needs of the children of a small minority of "irresponsible" parents may be met more efficiently if the paternalistic powers of government were concentrated on them, and not diffused over wide areas where they are not needed. Ideally compulsion should be selective not universal. Where *universal* compulsion is too readily applied the authorities may shelter themselves too comfortably from pressures to improve facilities. Where there is no compulsion to stay on at school in the sixteenth or seventeenth year the suppliers of formal education (the schools) are in competition with informal, but efficient alternative forms of education such as apprenticeships and learning on the job. The obligation constantly to "lure" young people into additional schooling is to put constant pressure upon schools and teachers to be imaginative and efficient. Conversely the protectionist instinct of schools leads them into alliance with governments to support compulsion. This hypothesis was previously put forward in an article in 1967[18] where it was concluded that in the U.S. context:

> Especially since public money was distributed to the schools and their staffs in proportion to the numbers in attendance, we should expect that the kind of agitation that would next have been undertaken (after fees had been successfully abolished) by the income maximizing teachers, managers and the officials, especially those of average or less than

18. E. G. West, "The Political Economy of American Public School Legislation," *Journal of Law & Economics*, 1967.

average ability, would have been a campaign for an education that was compulsory by statute.[19]

The historical evidence in America supported the hypothesis:

> Serious agitation for compulsory attendance by Bureau officials and teachers, built up very soon after the success of the free school campaign of 1867.[20]

Landes and Solmon now conclude that their findings are also consistent with this sort of explanation.

> On the demand side, two forces would be at work to increase the demand for compulsory legislation. First teachers and school officials are likely to favour and promote legislation that compels persons to purchase their product; namely schooling. As enrollment and attendance rates rise and the length of the school year increases, the number of teachers and school officials also increases. Along with a growth in their number, we expect an increase in their power to influence legislators to support a compulsory law. On the supply side. . . . With a growth of schooling levels, the number of parents opposed to the enactment of the law would obviously decline.[21]

There is similar evidence in English history. Almost without exception the nineteenth-century Departmental School Inspectors wanted compulsion.[22] Matthew Arnold, School Inspector for the Metropolitan district of Westminster, was no exception though he gives this impression at first sight. In 1867 he announced that compulsion was not appropriate to England. "In Prussia, which is so often quoted, education is not flourishing because it is compulsory, it is compulsory because it is flourishing. . . . When instruction is valued in this country as it is in Germany it may be made obligatory here. . . ."[23] This objection obviously related

---

19. *Ibid.,* p. 124.
20. *Ibid.,* p. 124.
21. Landes & Solmon, *op. cit.,* 1972.
22. See especially the annual reports to the Education Department of W. J. Kennedy (1872), Mr. Waddington (1872), Mr. Bowstead (1871), Rev. F. Watkins (1872), Rev. F. F. Cornish (1882), J. G. Fitch (1882), G. H. Gordon (1882).
23. Matthew Arnold's Report for 1867.

only to the question of timing; compulsion should be established when everybody, or nearly everybody, prized culture so much that voluntary instruction would be universal. The question why the "means" of universal compulsion should be applied after the "ends" had already largely been obtained was not raised by Arnold. It was in the interests of his fellow inspectors and his Department that it was not. But despite his doubts about direct compulsion Arnold was a strong advocate of *indirect* compulsion. This, in 1867, was the better expedient:

> The persevering extension of provisions for the schooling of all children employed in any kind of labour is probably the best and most practicable way of making education obligatory that we can at present take.[24]

Besides the Inspectorate and the Education Department the proprietors of schools also advocated compulsion. Whilst the voluntary school managers objected to the setting up of board *schools* that were able to compete unfairly, they were not opposed to the setting up of school *boards* (as the Act allowed) to organize compulsion and finance to help the poor pay the voluntary school fees. Mr. Bowstead in his report testified to this attitude:

> It by no means follows that, if once such a supply of voluntary schools were secured, the same objections would continue to be raised to the establishment of school boards. On the contrary there is among school managers, both lay and clerical, a very strong desire to be armed with the powers conferred upon school boards by the recent Statute.[25]

If compulsion does cause (or prolong) lethargy among monopoly suppliers of schooling the reform will be perverse. This point was grasped a century ago in America. When, in 1871, the school suppliers of education in New York State were lamenting their loss of income because of "early leaving" the Superintendent protested:

> It is palpable that the prominent defect, that calls for speedy reformation, is not incomplete attendance, but poor teaching . . . I speak of the needed improvement in the particular mentioned, in comparison with

24. *Op. cit.*
25. Mr. Bowstead's General Report for 1871.

compulsion, as a means of securing attendance; and I contend, that, before sending out ministers of the law to force children to school, we should place genuine teachers in the school room to attract them . . . the improvement in question should be made before resorting to the doubtful experiment of compulsion. It cannot be done suddenly by legislation.[26]

The Superintendent's proposal however was defeated. The influence of the teachers' political lobby was too strong for him.

It is consistent with the hypothesis of political "profit (vote) maximizing" that politicians under pressure from, or in alliance with, the supply interest groups, will have an incentive to make the electorate believe that the size of delinquency is greater than it really is. One way of fostering such illusion is by making each separate parent think that, in confidence, compulsion is not intended for *his* particular children; for this would indeed be a reflection on the parent in question and the politician does not want to alienate him. The politician will be on better ground if he suggests that compulsion is perhaps really needed for some of his (unspecified) neighbours who are less obviously reliable. Indeed it is possible that in such a way the more compulsion that is established the more the "good" individual families may believe that "bad" families exist. By such a process, the status of the politician grows in proportion as that "the average parent" deteriorates.

Normative Welfare Economics

So far we have employed positive economics which proceeds by prediction and the testing of hypotheses with the facts. In contrast, normative economics is concerned with what "ought" to be rather than with what is. Traditional normative analysis has been rooted in the welfare economics of Pareto which assumes that each individual is to count and that each is the best judge of his own interest. A Pareto optimum *point* is one where any change from it will harm at least one person in society. A

26. Annual Report of the New York Superintendent of Public Instruction, 1871.

Pareto optimum *move* is one that benefits at least one person and harms nobody.

In one sense if we take the family to be the basic unit, and if the new laws are to "bite," the establishment of compulsion will not pass the Pareto criteria because it will injure some individuals; it will not be a Pareto *move*. It is possible however to achieve a given level of schooling without injury if simultaneous compensation is paid. If compulsion is accompanied by the introduction of "free" education, the financial benefit of the reduced education costs to the family may provide this compensation. The family could rationally vote for such a move (although there is still considerable fiscal illusion concerning which taxpayers pay for what). The direct expenses of education (the fees) are not the only costs however. In some cases indirect costs, notably in the shape of the loss of foregone earnings, will be critical. Whilst the social benefits are positive, the private benefits might be negative especially for low achievers.[27] In all these cases it will be necessary to compensate the family not only with education subsidies but also with income replenishments. It should be emphasized that where compulsion *is* accompanied by appropriate compensation it no longer has the implications of strong coercion.

If the beneficiaries receive education subsidies that are not financed through taxes upon themselves, normative welfare economics must explore the possible motives of those in society who voluntarily vote to have funds transferred away from them for the education of others. One common explanation is that the consumption of education by one person— "a" enters into the utility of several other persons comprising Group B. In other words there are interdependent utility functions. Another explanation is that education provides external benefits to Group B. These externalities however are never specified very precisely and there is a dearth of supporting evidence. Usually writers confine themselves to a *presumption* that they exist and give one or two possible illustrations.

27. W. Hansen, B. A. Weisbrod and W. Scanlon, "Schooling and Earnings of Low Achievers," *AER*, Vol. LX, No. 3, June 1970, p. 417. See also the subsequent comments by Barry Chiswick, Stanley Masters and Thomas Ribich and the reply by Hansen *et al.*, *AER*, Vol. LXII, No. 4, September 1972, p. 752.

The most popular example is that an educated child will be more law-abiding. This proposition as it affected the early nineteenth-century Britain was critically examined in Chapter 10. As it affects the twentieth century the same proposition has been examined empirically elsewhere[28] and it has been shown that the evidence does not support it.

Compulsion as a Constitutional Provision

An avenue through which compulsion, in the more conventional sense of coercion, can be partially reconciled with the (near) unanimity voting is by way of what, in normative economics, is called the "constitutional approach." Each individual is treated as a choice-maker in his selection from basic sets of constitutions and legal frameworks. Every individual is now a decision-maker not only in the market place and the ballot-box but also in the setting up of the basic constitution which lays down the ground rules within the chosen democratic system. Imagine a new community settlement of young immigrant adults wherein no children had yet been born and no constitution had yet been laid down. Each adult would now have to consider not only his future private utility of having children but also the potential disutility from the "undesirable" behaviour or appearance of the neighbour's children. Since the neighbour will be in the reverse position (fearing the potential disutility from one's own children) a constitutional rule may be agreed to laying down the conditions in which the privileges of parenthood shall be conferred. One of these conditions could be that each would supply a given minimum of education, food, clothing and so on, from his own resources. If society depended exclusively on these conditions to protect children and to provide sufficient external benefits, then no subsidies, income transfers, or price reductions would be necessary for any of the goods and services mentioned. Because of the anticipated legal responsibilities adults would be discouraged from marriage or parenthood until such a time as they could afford to bring their children up in conformity with the minimum constitutional standards previously laid down. Paretian optimality would

28. E. G. West, *Education and the State,* second edition, 1970, ch. 3.

now be achieved by a preliminary and unanimous agreement to abide by the chosen democratic rules. Compulsion would still be a principle in education, but it would be compulsion of parents to purchase education, like other necessities, in the upbringing of their children. Education in this case would be positively priced.

Clearly we have now isolated two polar cases. The first is the circumstance of constitutional compulsion wherein the adult is previously contracted to full responsibility for prerequisite levels of consumption of externality-generating goods.[29] The second is the opposite where the community accepts full responsibility and supplies these goods free of charge together with compensatory income transfers where necessary. In the second case "compulsion" is of an emasculated kind.

Does the "constitutional explanation" hold good? Conceptually there is a problem of infinite regress—of knowing which individual preferences to respect: those at the constitutional stage or those where the individual wants to rebel at some subsequent period. Again in the real world we observe piecemeal plans and a combination of devices. While families are expected adequately to clothe their children, children's apparel is not, as is education, made free to all; neither are there (with respect to clothing) any universally compulsory laws fully equivalent to those related to education. True there are "child abuse" laws requiring minimum standards of consumption of food and clothing. As distinct from the way education is customarily provided however, no financial benefits exist to supplement the operation of these laws directly although welfare or child assistance subsidies probably have that effect. Nor are there typically subsidies for the housing of children, and certainly rarely to the extent of making accommodation universally free. Parents usually expect that they have to face obligations to purchase food for their offspring at positive prices. School lunches are often subsidized, it is true, but rarely are they so fully subsidized as to allow consumers to enjoy zero prices. School lunches moreover are not subsidized on non-school days. It is evident that some rough conformity with the polar cases or

29. Externality-generating goods are those that simultaneously provide private *and* *public* benefits.

normative welfare principles previously outlined does appear here and there. The principles upon which mixtures of these cases appear are however quite obscure.

The next chapter, which probes deeper into the late-nineteenth-century dialogue, will reveal some long forgotten advocates of the "constitutional" approach as just explained. It will show particularly how the principle of compulsion was crucially connected with that of making education "free" and how the "constitutionalists" tried to stand their ground—but failed.

18 · Free Education: Who Benefited?

Although this book concentrates on the Industrial Revolution, the fullest understanding of events demands some attention to the simultaneous emergence of an intellectual revolution on the question of who should control or supply education. Whereas to a large extent the Industrial Revolution was a free market phenomenon, schooling was quickly becoming a non-market operation. Since it is not possible to separate clearly the two revolutions, the next few chapters will discuss the simultaneous quest for a "national system" by prominent writers of the period and the new implications for proposed changes in public finance.

Compulsion having been established in England and Wales, attention was, as we have seen, increasingly focused upon the question whether or not, and to what extent, the government should assist parents in covering the necessary costs of additional schooling. Two polar positions were taken up that correspond to those outlined at the end of the previous chapter. First, completely free schooling for all, the principle championed by the Birmingham League. Second, the opposite principle of full cost fees—the "constitutional approach." This latter position was held by Mrs. Helena Fawcett and her husband Henry Fawcett, Professor of Political Economy at Cambridge.[1]

Mrs. Fawcett strongly believed in compulsion but believed that the

---

1. He was Alfred Marshall's predecessor in the Cambridge chair and an associate of John Stuart Mill.

remission of fees could have a pauperizing effect; it should be avoided wherever possible, she insisted, because it amounted to a system of out-door relief. When pressed she did make some practical concessions. Thus where compulsion was established there could be *some* remission of fees in one or two cases; but even here government must resign itself to the consequent "pauperization"; and the stigma of pauperization, she insisted, "ought" to attach to the favoured parents. Clearly a Malthusian in economics, her views were shared by her husband, Henry Fawcett. He pointed out that the latter class of parent would be earning the lowest subsistence income level. Government could impose compulsion upon many of such parents without providing education free because the pay-ment for schooling would come not out of their pockets but would be made up in their wages.[2]

Sir Charles Dilke, spokesman for the Birmingham League, protested that Helena Fawcett's reasoning was the "*reductio ad absurdum* of some of the coldest principles of science to degrade the people in order to suc-cessfully maintain an economic theory."[3] It was, argued Dilke, the se-lective remission of fees, which Mrs. Fawcett and her supporters were resigned to, that was closest to outdoor relief; a *universally* free school system could not be so regarded. Children whose fees were remitted were placed "in a miserable position towards the others and their parents lowered in the moral scale by having to solicit the favour of exemption, but these degrading effects will be permanent, and will cling for ever to the system." Jesse Collins, the Secretary of the League, argued similarly that separate treatment of the poor would create class distinction in school life, and ". . . by ticketing a certain number of children with the badge of poverty, would subject them to annoyance and ill treatment cal-culated to destroy that self-respect which it should be the first object of education to foster."[4]

Those among the middle classes who, like the Fawcetts, were opposed

2. Winifred Holt, *A Beacon for the Blind,* 1926, p. 119.
3. Sir Charles Dilke, Report of the Third Annual Meeting of the National Education League held in Birmingham 17 and 18 October, 1971.
4. Jesse Collins, *Remarks on the Establishment of Common Schools in England,* 1872.

to free schools for the poor were accused of being hypocritical. Do they really mean what they say, asked Edwin Chadwick, ". . . or do they decline to avail themselves of free education for their own children by endowments whenever they can get it? Have not the higher classes extensively invaded and appropriated the provisions of endowments in the universities and public schools left for the poor and middle classes? Have not the middle classes in the metropolis and throughout the corporate towns invaded and, wherever they could, appropriated the educational endowments left in charity for the very poorest beneath themselves?"[5]

Henry Fawcett was a strong defender of the practice of directing endowment benefits to the "talented"—i.e. mainly to the middle classes. His speech on the Endowed Schools Act Amendment Bill on July 20th, 1874, which was a defence of the recently published report of the Schools Inquiry Commission, clearly revealed this position. The Commission had recommended the transfer of much endowment finance away from poor schools in order to give more prizes to those who "could best benefit from higher education."[6] Fawcett would probably have replied to Chadwick that subsidies to the most talented would not have a debilitating (pauperizing) effect. The qualifications necessary to apply for *higher* education scholarships included by definition evidence of hard work. The main justification at this higher level of education, Fawcett would have insisted, was that the policy of subsidizing merit met the needs of the State; it was conducive to national prosperity and progress. But he could not deny that middle class individuals who received the endowment "prizes" used them also to secure bigger private incomes for themselves. Clearly this weakened his argument against free schooling for the poor.

It was national benefits (as distinct from private benefits) that the Birmingham League also pointed to in their argument for free schools. This was brought out most graphically in Sir Charles Dilke's further discussion

---

5. Edwin Chadwick, "National Education: A letter thereon to the Lord President of the Council," 1870, p. 37.
6. "The Schools Inquiry Commission most emphatically insisted on the importance of devoting school endowments to reward merit, instead of applying them to indiscriminate gratuitous education." Fawcett's speech, 1874.

of Mrs. Fawcett's arguments. Mrs. Fawcett had contended that if one was to provide free education then one should provide free clothes and free food on the same reasoning. This was a false analogy Dilke protested. When the State interferes to save the child from lack of food, it interfered to protect the life of a citizen who was incapable of protecting his own. State interference here was justifiable from the point of view of the *individual.* Free (and compulsory) education on the other hand was justifiable from the point of view of the *State.* "The State suffers by crime and outrage, the results of ignorance. It interferes, therefore, to protect itself." And on what grounds in particular? It was the old argument that education reduces crime. To be poor was to be crime-prone and so the poor had to be educated out of this condition. If Mrs. Fawcett was degrading the people in order to successfully maintain an economic theory, so it seems was Dilke and the Birmingham League in order to maintain a political one. It was the League's philosophy nevertheless that predominated; its arguments had great influence in securing the eventual abolition of fees. It is interesting that whilst to the average twentieth-century observer the predominant rationale of free schooling is the necessity to redistribute income and to protect the poor, the historical reasoning produced to support it in the nineteenth century was the need to protect the property of the rich and the middle classes (against the disorderly poor).

Just as important as Law and Order, it was argued, was the need for National Defence. Dilke flatly asserted that ". . . education comes far nearer to drill than it does to clothes. Drill, or compulsory service of all citizens in time of emergency may become a state necessity."[7]

Jesse Collins argued similarly that

> the policy of the country on critical occasions, involving war or any other calamity, has to be determined by the people, and it is of the greatest national importance that they should be fitted by education to exercise an intelligent judgement on any subject submitted to their decision . . . all are taxed for the maintenance of the Army, Navy and Police, because all share in the benefits these institutions are supposed to

7. Dilke, *op. cit.,* p. 157.

afford, and would have to share in the loss and inconvenience result-ing from their non-existence; and by the same rule all should be taxed for the support of schools because all share in the increased wealth, se-curity, and general advantages resulting from the education of the people, and have also to share the expense and danger of crime and other results of ignorance.[8]

The argument so far however had not really destroyed the analogy of education with food and clothing. A half starved, half clad population would be just as useless in defence as a half-educated one. Joseph Cham-berlain added another argument that seemed more consistent: whilst food was a necessity for existence, education was not a necessity at all.

> Human nature, which was almost perpetually hungry, might be trusted to supply itself with the elements of bare existence; but human nature could not be trusted to supply itself with instruction, of which a great many human beings had, unfortunately, a very low opinion.[9]

One missing element in Chamberlain's theory was attention to the prob-lem of how such an "irresponsible" population could be relied upon to vote for politicians like himself who wanted to compel them, now that democracy had largely arrived (with the 1867 enfranchisement). It was not just a question of "educating our masters"; there was the problem of politically persuading the "masters" to elect their "mentors." Next, one should pay attention to Chamberlain's accusation that educational irre-sponsibility applied to "a great many human beings." A great many more, that is the majority of families, had proved that they did have a high opin-ion of education. In 1869 most parents were buying it directly, most fami-lies were already sending their children to school without being com-pelled, most school leavers were literate, and most of "our masters," in other words, were already being educated of their own free will. The argument for compulsion therefore applied at most only to a margin of families.

8. Jesse Collins, *Remarks on the Establishment of Common Schools in England,* 1872.
9. Joseph Chamberlain, "Free Schools" address to the Birmingham School Board, 18 June 1975.

The Birmingham League supporters meant something more in their arguments however. The "human nature" that "could not be trusted to supply itself with instruction" was really at fault because it could not supply itself with the *right sort of instruction*. It had allowed itself to be given an education that was typically connected with religious organizations—especially of Anglican persuasion. The Birmingham League was an expression of the newer secular nationalism of the nineteenth century and included many individuals that the twentieth century could now describe as "false optimists." The system of compulsion that they had in mind included compelling people to change from sectarian to secular (or non-sectarian) schools. They realized that this could not be accomplished by direct means; other groups had to be reckoned with. The High Tories, for instance, believed that only an education controlled by the established church could be effective in improving morality and decreasing crime. But the League was more astute than its opponents. Its external political pressure for Board schools was no doubt welcomed by the education bureau since its interests were the same. And once established, the Board schools, as we have seen, began to price many of the church schools out of the field largely because of financial advantages bestowed by Departmental discretion. The League complemented these activities with its argument that church schools should not be able similarly to be supported by public funds because that would involve the objectionable practice of subsidizing religions. People should pay for their religious instruction separately.

The Reverend F. S. Dale protested in 1875 against the campaign of the Birmingham League for universally free schools. He did not oppose the *selective* remission of burdens upon the poor but complained that the League's desire for *universally* free schooling (in the new Board schools) was a desire to undermine the 1870 Education Act and destroy existing schools. "Free schools were part of yet a greater scheme, when the Church of England should be thrown over." [10] Jesse Collins, on behalf of the League, made the following candid reply (which is here in reported speech):

10. Meeting of the Birmingham School Board, 18 June 1875.

With regard to Mr. F. S. Dale's assertion that the free system would close the voluntary schools—denominational schools was the best name—he quite admitted, and he thought they ought not to deny, that, insofar as they were sectarian institutions, or remained for sectarian purposes, the free system would kill them. It was the pure Darwinian theory—the fittest only would survive. If education was the object, then the free scheme got them out of all their difficulties, because they could not deny that by the free system under the School Board, a better education would be given than could possibly be given by the voluntary schools, on account of their precarious income. . . .[11]

Edwin Chadwick also supported compulsory attendance provided it was at the right (i.e. the "nationalized") schools. He urged that the small sectarian schools did not provide the appropriate *secular* curriculum: "The experience is now accumulating of the great disadvantage of the small separate schools." In the large schools subsidized or established or controlled by governments there were the "superior" attractions "of gymnastic exercises, the drill, elementary drawing, music, *military fêtes* and parades, to which the small sectarian could not obtain. . . ."[12] Free education—but in schools specially selected by the authorities (not the parents)—was therefore the order of the day.

Although it may come as a surprise to readers today, the emphasis by contemporary educational "reformers" on the militaristic function of the new English state schooling in the 1870s was seriously intended. Moreover it was sedulously adopted as official policy. Military Drill became a recognized "subject" and was incorporated in the Departmental Code of 1871. The Annual Report for 1882 observed (p. 12):

It further appears from the reports of the inspectors that *military drill,* which (as distinguished from the ordinary school drill practised in every good school) was first recognized by the Code of 1871, is systematically taught to the boys attending 1,157 day schools. A short

11. Birmingham School Board meeting, 18 June 1875. The "survival of the fittest" analogy was obscure; in the Darwinian scheme it was not a matter of subsidized animals surviving the non-subsidized, or the heavily subsidized surviving the weakly subsidized.
12. Edwin Chadwick, "National Education: A letter thereon to the Lord President of the Council," 1870.

Manual of Elementary Military Exercise and Drill, which has been
adopted in army schools for soldier's children, has been placed by the
Controller of the Sanitary office on the list of War Office publications.
This manual may be found useful in civil schools, and will shortly be
procurable (price 2*d.*) through the ordinary channels of trade.

Our review of the late nineteenth-century debate has clearly brought the
special circumstances of politics well into the picture. From simple normative economics it is conceivable that the public could unanimously
elect to live in a constitution that provided compulsory, free, and secular
schools that were primarily designed to insure military protection and
domestic order. Each individual would then express his own preferences
ex ante. Compulsion could thus be reconciled with the tradition of respect for individual preference that the welfare economics endorses.
The argument is stronger however the nearer the system is to unanimous
or near unanimous consent. The most elementary reference to the historical record encourages doubt whether there was anything like a popularly articulated preference for the system that evolved. The positive
economics of politics (especially the politics of pressure groups) seem to
explain more than the normative economics of voluntary constitutions.

It has been shown that historically compulsion was closely interrelated
with the issue of "free" schooling. Both compulsion and free provision
were introduced in such special ways as to suggest that the general public were more manipulated than consulted. There is in fact no known English record of direct consultation of individual families to discover their
opinions on compulsion in the late nineteenth century. There *is* such a
record concerning their views as to the desirability of "free" education.
This was contained in the most intensive nineteenth-century survey of
education by the Newcastle Commission. It reported in 1861:

> Almost all the evidence goes to show that though the offer of gratu-
> itous education might be accepted by a certain proportion of the par-
> ents, it would in general be otherwise. The sentiment of independence
> is strong, and it is wounded by the offer of an absolutely gratuitous
> education.[13]

13. 1861 Report, Vol. I, p. 73.

Such evidence is not good enough for Jesse Collins, the enthusiast and propagandist for America-type common schools, and Secretary of the Birmingham League. The following sentiments he expressed on the eve of the League's establishment show clearly that the intention was to "guide" or pressure the public:

> It is frequently urged that the public mind is not yet ripe for such laws as free public schools would necessitate, and that it is unwise to legislate so much in advance of public opinion. The public mind is more easily led in a right direction than Government sometimes wish it to be, and in this instance, if fairly tested would probably be found fully under the idea of a National system of compulsory, unsectarian education . . . and this reveals the necessity for the immediate formation of a Society, National in its name and constitution, refusing all compromise, but adopting as its platform—*National, secular (or unsectarian) education, compulsory as to rating and attendance, with state aid and inspection, and local management.* The action of such a Society would be similar to that of the Anti-Corn Law League, and its success is certain; by lectures, by writing, by agitation in every town, it would give direction and voice to the fresh and ever-increasing interest felt by the people in this matter.[14]

Whether "fresh and ever-increasing interest" was eventually felt by the people has never been demonstrated. Certainly the politicians did find vote support in their programs of free and compulsory education but that is not necessarily the same thing. What the discussion has revealed is that compulsion in education can mean many things and can be applied in several ways and with a variety of consequences. The strongest nineteenth-century motivation behind the politically expressed "need" for compulsion in Britain was a desire to compel the majority to secularize, "politicize" and collectivize, their education. To do this compulsion had to be universal. Selective compulsion could certainly meet problems caused by a minority of delinquents or poor families; but this would not reduce the power of the church and the free choice of schools by the

---

14. Written in 1867 this passage is contained in Jesse Collins': *Remarks on the Establishment of Common Schools in England,* 1872, pp. 46–7. The italics are in the original.

majority of parents. The Birmingham League grasped the fact that an attack on parental choice and religious influence could be accomplished by *universal* compulsion if this in turn was coupled with universally free education. "Free" education, they argued, applied predominantly to secular (or non-sectarian) schools exclusively.

Normally a case for aid to families for education does not automatically amount to a case for zero priced tuition. Full cost fees may still be desirable but the desired aid can take the form of explicit grants, scholarships or tax exceptions, all of which can be used to pay the fee at the chosen school. Wherever aid to families is given in the form of zero priced tuition fees, the parents have less influence on the activities of the schools and their preferences are ranked much lower than otherwise. Conversely where the aid is in the form of grants and scholarships, or tax allowances, the parents who pay for tuition fees have a greater role in determining which institutions shall be rewarded for superior performance.

> Recognition of these differences in effect explains why some people have asserted the Administrators and Members of State Universities and Colleges, which are currently financed by direct legislative appropriation, have sought from self-interest, rather than educational interest, to maintain the impression that zero tuition is the only feasible or sensible means of aid to Students,—in order to replace Student influence and control over the Colleges while retaining the influence of the Politicians.[15]

Where there are full cost tuition fees, there is competition among schools to attract students. Where public funds are given to families in the form of grants spendable on education, parents can pay the full cost fees and so make the system work. Under it the energies of the schools are devoted less to negotiations with school boards, public treasuries or legislators and more attention is made to classroom behaviour of instructors. Producers usually conclude that they are better judges of the appropriate quality for the consumer. "This tendency is especially rewarding if the producer can thereby obtain a sheltered competitive position in the production of the goods. He would tend to produce a quality and quan-

---

15. Armen A. Alchian, "The Economic and Social Impact of Free Tuition." Center for Independent Education, Wichita Collegiate School.

tity in a style related more to that which enhances his welfare and less to what Students and Parents prefer." [16] The full cost fee system removes his power to do this.

Legislators similarly conclude that they are better judges of quality. It is not surprising that they also tend to favour free schooling; for their power over educational institutions and families is reduced where the fee approaches full cost. State Inspectors of Schools can similarly be expected to favour zero prices. They are employed indirectly by legislators and have to fall in line with their wishes. Moreover the more that parents are deemed to be the judges of their best interests, the less need there is for official inspectors. It was in the latters' interest to be disparaging about the quality of the fee paying private schools. The Inspectors' reports in fact do show considerable disdain for them. The choice of the name "private adventure schools" was probably no accident. The Annual Report of Inspector Fitch for 1869 is revealing:

> And in just the proportion in which the Managers shift the responsibility of payment on the parents, I regret to find symptoms of increased subservience to parental whims on the part of the teachers, and a prospect, that even in the inspected schools some of the worst faults of the lower class in private adventure schools may be reproduced. [17]

Although Matthew Arnold saw some virtue in fee paying, his views relate to a narrow context. Arnold thought that some fee was better than none because it established a principle and caused parents to take some interest in their schools. Thus a fee of 2*d*. or 3*d*. would achieve this end. On the other hand, "Parents who pay 6*d*. per week for the instruction of their children are apt to criticize nicely, though not always judiciously, the institution where that instruction is given. They desire this and that for their child, and they object to this and that, and, being not very reasonable persons, they greatly embarrass a teacher. They are exceedingly apt, for instance, to object to the employment of their children as monitors, on the ground that teaching takes them away from learning. . . .

"The teachers independence is diminished, because, when his salary is principally or entirely derived from the school pence, the favour of the

16. Alchian, *op. cit.*
17. *Parliamentary Papers,* 1870, XXII, p. 322.

parents becomes of the greatest importance to him; hence it arises that the children of these schools, though disciplinable, are often not well disciplined, owing to the Master's fear of offending parents by a strictness which may appear to them excessive."[18]

In his report for 1871 Inspector Watkins complained that parents in Yorkshire were attaching too much priority to the quality of a teacher and too little to the quality of the buildings. "It will be needful that all *efficient* schools be registered and publicly recognized as such, or some parents will continue to send their children to the miserable places where so many of them go now, and will represent them to the enquiring officer as 'at school.' But their statement must not be accepted. It certainly will be very difficult at first to convince parents of its unreality, especially in cases where the instruction of a School is efficient, but the premises are unsatisfactory. It will be very difficult to convince a Yorkshire father that the School is not *'efficient'* when his child is getting on very well in it."

Inspector Brodie in his report for 1872 claimed that the great majority of "private adventure schools" were wholly inefficient. His patronizing tone matched that of Fitch. "It was impossible . . . not occasionally to sympathize with some of the teachers in these schools, the history of whom was sad enough; it was impossible also not to respect the motives of several parents for sending their children to these schools in preference to the inspected ones; for exhibiting often ignorance and prejudice, they at least equally showed parental care and thoughtfulness very pleasing to find. Questioning some of the Mothers why they prefer private adventure schools they variously answered me 'better taken care of there,' 'looked after separately,' 'don't get infectious diseases,' 'don't get so rough,' 'don't learn bad language.'"

To many Birmingham League supporters free choice of parents was objectionable where this led to the selection of Sectarian teaching or to the rejection of schools that emphasized "desirable" and new subjects such as "drill." Edwin Chadwick observed that "parents of the middle class now naturally and properly object to sending their children to the same schools with other children who are filthy. Elementary Schools, as

---

18. Matthew Arnold's General Report for the year 1852.

at present conducted, we have shown to be mostly centres of children's epidemics. . . ."[19] But characteristically he declared that this problem would be removed the moment there was proper provision of lavatories and sanitation.

Chadwick recognized the argument that payments to the teachers by fees gave them the motive of exertion to keep up attendance. To him, however, the fee system would lead to too much respect to family choice; there would be too little voluntary choice of the large schools that were in his opinion so very economical and which provided the new and essential subjects of gymnastic exercises, music and military parades. He advocated payments by results but results that were determined not by the parents but by the administrators. Schools would be awarded direct grants by the administrators according to the number who passed one thorough "leaving" examination, "which I have since learned is the practice in Germany."

Fee Paying and the 1870 Act

There were several provisions in the 1870 Act to enable poor families to send their children to school. First a School Board could start a free school when there were special circumstances, that is, when a locality was in great poverty. The Education Department and the School Board had to be convinced however of its necessity. Up to 1873 no applications were made to sanction such free schools. Second, School Boards were given powers as Managers of their own schools, to remit the fees where they felt the parents were too poor to pay them. This was felt necessary in order to give them the same powers as other managers. Third came the 25th section, eventually much disputed. This gave power to the School Board to pay the school fees in voluntary schools provided that they were inspected and declared efficient. It was because the 1870 Act allowed (permissive) compulsion, and because Forster was of the view that it was impossible to compel a parent to send his children to school if he were too poor to pay the fees, that he inserted the 25th Section.

19. *Op. cit.*, p. 8.

We showed above that an argument for aid to families for education does not by itself imply zero pricing of schools. A full cost service can be continued and the aid can be given in the form of grants to parents. Section 25 of the 1870 Act reflected this method; and there was no opposition at the time of its passing. Objection came only after experience with it. The chief complaint, made by the Birmingham League, was that public funds were being used to subsidize denominational schools. Another objection was that the Boards of Guardians were better than School Boards to ascertain whether a parent had the right or not to assistance.

The intention of the 1870 Act was not only to fill the gaps in school provision but to get the children into the schools. Where the gaps in buildings did not occur and the existing private or church schools had ample accommodation, the payment of fees for the poor was felt to be the only way in some cases to get the children into them. Let the poor parent choose the schools to his liking and the School Board would then pay the fees. The Birmingham League in effect wanted to remove this parental preference. Forster, in defence of his scheme, asked: "Is it wise or prudent, then, to have this difficulty in compulsion—that you will say to the parent who is too poor to pay the fees that he shall have no choice of school for his child, according to convenience of locality, to say nothing of conscience or other preference, but that he must send his child to that school only which we prefer? . . . there is not merely the conscience of the ratepayer to consult, but also the conscience of the parent, which is necessary to interfere with as little as possible . . . surely where there is a choice of schools we ought to allow of its exercise."[20] The main intention of the Act therefore was not to subsidize voluntary schools but simply to prevent parents having reasonable excuse for not sending their children to school.

Notable among the towns that made full use of the 25th section were Salford, Manchester and Stockport. The official survey of the Salford region immediately following the 1870 Act showed that there were no gaps to fill; there was indeed an actual surplus of accommodation. Although describing himself as not of their party politically, the Inspector of the

20. Forster's speech in the Commons, 17 July 1873.

District Mr. Brodie, in his general report for 1872, felt he had to come to the defence of the Salford School Board in view of the "very hard things" that had been said about it. "These charges mainly are, that they will allow no Board school to be built; that they will not take over any denominational school for conversion into a Board school; that they have not worked compulsion fairly or wisely; that they pauperize many parents by paying fees needlessly whether parents can and ought to pay; and that they pamper the existing denominational schools by sending board pupils to them and paying fees for them." Mr. Brodie insisted that there was no need for further building in Salford and therefore no need for a special Board school to take the children of the poor. He maintained that the School Board had acted "with much practical sagacity, duly caring for the interests of the ratepayers as one side, and on the other really doing a good deal to get the children to school and promote their regular attendance." By 1872 the Salford School Board was paying for about 1/10th of the children who were attending voluntary schools in the Borough—about 1,900 children in all. "As to pampering existing schools, the children must, I presume, go to those which exist, and as in every case the parent or guardian may choose a school for the child where no hardship or grievance seems to arise. *Nor can the School Board pack favourite schools with their pupils.*"[21]

The "hardship" imposed on public ratepayers of supporting denominational schools was largely imaginary and at most infinitesimal. These schools were supported from three sources, the Government grant, schools fees, and voluntary contributions. The school fees contributed just over a quarter of the total contributions. If a Board paid in a poor locality as much as 1/5th of the total fees, the rates even in this extreme case would bear only 1/20th of the cost of such a school.

The number of cases where parents were helped by the 25th Section of the 1870 Act dwindled as time went on. This was partly due to the political hostility that was organized by the Birmingham League but also to a technical change that was made in 1877. In that year the duty of paying the school fees for the non-pauper children was transferred from the

21. Annual Report of Mr. Brodie, 1872.

School Board to the Poor Law Guardians. There was a definite stigma attached to the receipt of any help from the latter authority—whatever its nature. Inspector Cornish in 1882 observed: ". . . of course it does not matter to the ratepayers through what agency the money is paid, but it makes a good deal of difference to the parents, and, on that account, many of those who knew the poor best deplored the change when it was made." What seems to have been needed, and what was not provided, was an agency that was independent of both the School Board and the Poor Law Guardians. This kind of independent body could have specialized in providing funds to cover schools' fees without prejudice and without incurring stigma costs to the poor parents and their children. Such an agency indeed was advocated by the Newcastle Commission in its report of 1861; but the Commission did not recommend compulsion so its argument for the agency did not appear as urgent.

The abolition of fees took a long time. Twelve years after Forster's Act of 1870 they were still providing substantial amounts towards costs. The lowest were to be found in the Board schools and in the Roman Catholic schools where 2d. to 3d. was typically charged. The Board schools contained about one third of the total school attendants. Most of the rest were still in voluntary schools where fees up to 9d. per week were charged. The highest (6d. to 9d.) were levied in the British and Wesleyan schools and in some Church schools. In the majority of Church of England schools they varied between 3d. and 6d.[22] There was an average attendance of about two million in the voluntary schools and one million in the Board schools. According to David Wardle the initial effect on the introduction of compulsion was actually to increase the trade of private schools in the Nottingham area. ". . . many parents were prepared to pay a fairly high fee to avoid sending their children to Board schools. The period from 1870 to 1890 was a prosperous period for the cheap private school, and in 1891 there were 43 schools in the town with about 1,000 children."[23] Evidently it was not the building of new and substantial buildings by the

22. General Report for the year 1882 by H.M. Inspector, J. G. Fitch.
23. David Wardle, *Education and Society Nineteenth Century Nottingham*, 1971, p. 169.

school boards by itself that caused the main damage to voluntary schools. But excess capacity in the Board schools soon caused embarrassment to the authorities. They were then forced to play their strongest card—the severe reduction of school fees. "The abolition of fees in Board schools in 1891 was the death blow to the private schools, which then became a very expensive luxury. By 1895 there were (in Nottingham) only 24 schools with 489 children and the number continued to decline until 1898 when there were thirteen schools with 270 pupils."[24]

With the coming of zero price tuition and the new appearance of one or two large Board school establishments in a locality, parental choice became restricted and slowly suffered through lack of exercise. The predominant controlling power quietly passed to the authorities, the teachers, and the inspectors. The suppliers of school services then became more interested in giving their main attention to requirements addressed to them from above, in a growing hierarchy of public control. Even Inspector Fitch began to show signs of disappointment: "Among the younger generation of schoolmasters and assistants, I find a good deal of professional ambition and a keener interest in what may be called educational politics. There is also considerable zeal about the grade of their certificates and about obtaining from South Kensington special certificates for drawing and science. A small but increasing number of the more ambitious is also to be found reading from the degrees of the University of London. But much of this mental activity is directed mainly to the passing of examinations, and when the status so desired is once secured the young teacher is still apt to consider his equipment complete." This was in the 1880s, the period of H. G. Wells' Mr. Lewisham. The days of the amateur teacher were clearly over. He was replaced by the new professional, a person whose whole lifetime was often spent within the classroom. That there were costs as well as benefits from the new order was now lamented: "It is one of the saddest results of any reform of

24. David Wardle, *ibid.* In his last report the now elderly (and changed?) Matthew Arnold tried to stem the tide. People valued more favourably and used more respectfully what they pay a price for "but the advocates of free education seem never to have heard of it." See his Annual Report for 1882.

official machinery and regulations that it tends to diminish the necessity for independent and spontaneous exertion on the part of the teachers. As the legal requirements approach more nearly to a high ideal they become more easily accepted as final and sufficient, and many teachers who were capable of better things are found fastening their whole attention on the best means of complying with this or that regulation of the Code, and of securing the maximum grant."[25]

But education was "free." The politicians and the Birmingham League had won. Who could go back now?

25. Annual Report of J. G. Fitch, 1882.

19 · Education and Industrial Growth: Did Victorian Britain Fail?

The relationship between education and industrial growth is unexpectedly complex. Demonstrated correlation is one thing; proved causation is another. In our case the data does not readily lend itself to sophisticated treatment. Ideally what is required is evidence on the stock of education embodied in the nineteenth-century labour force and its rate of increase. There are serious problems even with lagged correlations between education and national income. This is because a multitude of other variables are potentially relevant. In view of all these considerations the aim of this chapter has to be a modest one. It attempts to clarify, and possibly remove, some important misconceptions about basic and relevant facts that prevail in the conventional histories. These are connected with the alleged stagnation of education during the early Industrial Revolution and with the belief in a slowdown of productivity after 1870, a slowdown for which, it is argued, inadequate education was partly responsible.

Our evidence in previous chapters has refuted the hypothesis that the Industrial Revolution brought educational stagnation. In the Scottish towns of the Industrial Revolution, for instance, there was a most remarkable expansion of mainly private schools, an expansion that the non-industrial areas did not match. The highlands in particular provided a very strong contrast. The rural lowlands certainly enjoyed reasonable standards and it was there that the parochial school system was at its best. Even so, the evidence of the Factory Commissioners in 1834 suggests that the rural lowlands were not the pace-makers; they were only just keeping up with educational provisions in the towns. Throughout Britain literacy attainments were generally bigger in the towns than elsewhere. The rich variety of institutions outside formal schooling found in England and Wales was especially to be seen in the industrial areas and included Sunday schools, Mechanics Institutes, night schools, public libraries and philosophical societies. And the detailed testimony is in previous chapters.

It is interesting meanwhile to place the facts of the British case in the perspective of cross section studies of national incomes and educational attainments across a number of countries in the twentieth century. In 1963 M. J. Bowman and C. A. Anderson[1] examined the 1950 literacy rates of eighty-three countries and compared them with their respective national incomes of 1955. They concluded that a 40 per cent literacy rate is a necessary condition for per capita incomes to exceed $300, and a 90 per cent rate for incomes of above $500. In Britain in 1840, according to R. K. Webb,[2] something like two thirds to three quarters of *the working classes* were already literate. The varied sources of evidence that we have examined in this book would also support this statement. It is interesting too to place such facts next to the results of C. A. Anderson's historical study of countries like the United States, France and Russia. He concluded that a 40 per cent literacy rate can be regarded as a general threshold level for economic development.[3]

The broad measures of nineteenth-century attainment in Britain therefore easily pass the test of these recent findings about the amount of education required as a necessary condition for rapid development. The relationship with economic growth however calls for a demonstration, not just of the attainment of a threshold, but of a continued expansion beyond it. We believe that our earlier chapters demonstrate substantial growth in education especially in the first half of the century. This returns

1. M. J. Bowman and C. A. Anderson, "Concerning the role of education in development" in M. J. Bowman *et. al.*, *Readings in the Economics of Education*, UNESCO, Paris, 1968.
2. R. K. Webb, "The Victorian Reading Public," in *From Dickens to Hardy*, Pelican, 1963.
3. C. A. Anderson, "Literacy and schooling on the development threshold: some historical cases" in C. A. Anderson and M. J. Bowman (eds) *Education and Economic Development*, 1965 (Aldine).

us to the problems of holding other variables constant. More important even where strong correlation is proved there remains the question of the precise mechanism whereby education helps economic growth.

Despite the many years of belief in the ability of education to produce national prosperity, we are still very ignorant in our understanding of why people with more schooling are in a bigger demand and enjoy bigger earnings. As W. L. Hansen recently put it:

> It is clear that, in general, employers offer higher pay to more highly educated workers, but our knowledge of what elements of ingredients of school make people more productive is scanty. . . . Is it what they have learned in school, as measured by test scores? Or is schooling valuable for the patterns and modes of thought and behaviour it develops in people? Or does schooling merely serve as a screening device that identifies the more able, highly motivated young people in our society?"[4]

In Mark Blaug's subsequent exploration he has delineated three alternative explanations:[5]

1. The "economic explanation,"

2. The "sociological explanation,"

3. The "psychological explanation."

The economic explanation amounts to the proposition that education helps to supply scarce and useful skills; the second—the sociological explanation—is that education disseminates social values and recruits people into a ruling elite of society; the third, psychological, explanation is that education simply screens people according to their abilities.

The Economic Explanation

The first argument implies that the *marginal product* of education is positive. This normally occurs because of two reasons (a) a higher demand curve for educated labour, (b) a supply of it that is more restricted than

4. W. L. Hansen, ed. *Education, Income & Human Capital*, New York, 1970.
5. Mark Blaug, "The correlation between Education and Earnings: What does it signify?" *Higher Education*, 1972. The next three pages are indebted to this article.

uneducated labour. The proposition that the supply is restricted is an empirical generalization and one that certainly applies in the twentieth century. The supply of more educated people in all countries is today smaller than the supply of less educated people. One of the reasons is related no doubt to educational costs. These include not only fees, books, and other material, but also foregone earnings. The restriction of the supply of educated labour will vary with variations in these costs. It is interesting that there were some dramatic reductions in the *direct* costs of education in the nineteenth century. These came notably in the form of large-scale economies in school enterprises (the monitorial school was one example). Moreover, with an increase in incomes during the early nineteenth century, charitable bodies were able to afford bigger subsidies that reduced the direct costs of education still further. Some indirect costs however moved in the opposite direction. With increasing average earnings, the foregone earnings element in education costs increased especially. It is this element that is implied in the frequent reports that parents were inclined to take their children away from school early in boom years especially in the regions where the wages of young people were high. Altogether therefore the movements of *total* cost were ambiguous.

The trend on the demand side however was distinctly one of increase. A minimum consumption of education developed a taste for more. Many of those who left school early continued on a part-time or on-the-job basis. A necessary condition for the expansion of the demand for education was the prevalence of adequate competition in factor and product markets. The higher marginal product of educated labour could not have "registered" if employers were not sensitive to their costs and revenues, or, in other words, if they were not strongly motivated by the desire to maximize profit (or avoid losses). Increasing competition would have encouraged such behaviour; and it seems a reasonable generalization that competition was expanding in our period. Moreover, the growth of education had reciprocal effects on competition. Education is an agency for rapidly diffusing information. The bigger the quantity of printing media available and the larger the number of people who are literate the bigger the knowledge of alternative job offers throughout labour markets; the greater indeed is the mobility of all factors. With such inter-acting processes barriers between non-competing groups are (and were) gradually broken down. There was increasing spread of information concerning different income earning possibilities and job opportunities. The secular downward trends both in interest rates and morbidity rates must also have helped to make educational investments more attractive.[6] This is not to say that workers developed a *sophisticated* knowledge of human capital valuation. It is sufficient to note that they probably made rough "benchmark" approximations that would have worked in the direction of such valuation.[7]

Today "excessive" education requirements are used to restrict entry to many occupations and professions. This was much less true in the nineteenth century when many professional organizations were in their infancy. Today in many countries there is a big proportion of the total educated labour force employed in the public sector at administered pay scales. These are based upon paper qualifications according to routine and often non-economic rules. This was not the case in the early nineteenth century. It was more true to say then that the private sector set the rate of pay for the public sector; this being so the chances were that workers were being paid nearer to their "genuine" marginal product; and as we have seen this condition must apply if the "economic explanation" that education helps to supply scarce skills is to be fully applicable.

One must avoid giving the impression that education is *the* key to economic growth. In this proposition, there is, as we have shown, growing skepticism. Empirical studies in the 1970s have certainly shaken our confidence in it.[8] All that is being argued here is that it is reasonable to assume that in the nineteenth century education played *some* part in economic growth. And on the importance of such "threshold effects" of education we have the support of the economist Alfred Marshall. In his

6. G. Becker, *Human Capital*, Chicago 1964.

7. For a recent example of how individuals in the underdeveloped economy act in this way see M. Blaug, R. Layard and M. Woodhall: *The Causes of Graduate Unemployment in India*, 1969.

8. O.E.C.D. (1970) "Occupational and Education Structures of the Labour Force and Level of Economic Development," Paris; O.E.C.D., P. R. G. Layward *et. al. Qualified Manpower and Economic Performance* (1971) London, Alan Vain the Penguin Press; Ivar Berg, *Education and Jobs: The Great Training Robbery* (1970) New York, Praeger.

Principles of Economics, first published in 1890, he urged that even a few years of schooling could make a big difference because the young person could later transfer some of his elementary skills acquired in school to all kinds of problems in the factory. His competence would be so raised as to encourage him to make himself learn many other things.

> It is true that the children of the working classes must very often leave school, when they have but learnt the elements of reading, writing, arithmetic and drawing. . . .
>
> . . . But the advance made at school is important not so much on its own account, as for the power of future advance which a school education gives.
>
> . . . a good education confers great indirect benefits even on the ordinary workman. It stimulates his mental activity; it fosters in him a habit of wise inquisitiveness; it makes him more intelligent, more ready, more trustworthy in his ordinary work; it raises the tone of his life in working hours and out of working hours; it is thus an important means towards the production of material wealth; at the same time that, regarded as an end in itself, it is inferior to none of those which the production of material wealth can be made ready to subserve.[9]

The Sociological Explanation

Briefly this "explanation" is that clever or middle class children obtain more schooling than lower class or less clever children simply because they have superior opportunities to obtain it. In its most rigid form, this means that every class keeps its place in the hierarchy however much average income increases. Even in this sense nevertheless the sociological explanation cannot deny that average income increases can be a result of more education. People can maintain their social differentials but enjoy real increases of individual and national income at the same time. In fact the "sociological explanation" is inadequate to demonstrate why there are fine variations in income earning within social groups themselves. As Blaug argues: "more generally, in under-developed countries where some children do not attend school at all, and others start working at the

9. Alfred Marshall, *Principles of Economics,* Eighth Edition, 1961, pp. 173 and 175.

age of 10, 12, 14 and so on, we have to explain why positive earnings differentials emerge even for an additional sixth, seventh and eighth year of education. If graduates earn more because they are 'leaders of men,' are we expected to believe that this also applies to high school graduates and even to primary school leavers?" [10]

The Psychological Explanation

The third proposition, "the psychological explanation," has received special attention in the economics of education since the 1970s. The argument is as follows: As the structure of occupations becomes more and more complex and pyramids of responsibility become larger, the job of hiring personnel to fill posts within a firm or industry becomes more of a problem. Employers have found in educational attainments a rough and ready proxy for screening the best candidates. Many of those who believe that this psychological explanation is the only meaningful one conclude that the net contribution of education to national output is actually negative. This is so, they argue, because once students catch on to the habit of employers using educational credentials as surrogates for the requisite attributes for jobs, they will be urged to invest in more education to obtain a competitive advantage in the labour market. Much of this educational escalation however is of no net benefit to society. ". . . to put it slightly differently, the fact that more educated people earn more simply means that they 'exploit' the less-educated: Since educated labour is paid more than its marginal product, 'rural labour' must be paid less." [11]

How does this argument apply to education during the nineteenth century? The costs of the "educational escalation" just explained begin to be borne only after a substantial economic and educational level has been attained. At the stage of development in the early nineteenth century, the argument is much less applicable. Some screening of job applicants does constitute a "genuine" industrial cost. Managements have to use time and resources in hiring people. Educational attainments, at least initially, will be a useful rule of thumb that will reduce the transac-

10. Blaug, *op. cit.*, p. 70.
11. Blaug, *op. cit.*, p. 71.

tion costs of hiring. It is more likely therefore, that education was of more positive value in our period. Furthermore in those days there was considerable in-plant training and employers could have treated school credentials as a guide to the selection of people best able to profit from it—as an index of trainability. The psychological explanation moreover does not apply to vocational education. The commercial and industrial revolutions of the nineteenth century created the demand for office workers whose vocation required formal literary attainments. In this case formal schooling is a direct and obvious agent of development. Again teaching was an expanding "industry" and this also demanded formal education. Basic mathematical skills were required as a prerequisite for further training within factories which were adopting more complex machinery. In short there is a strong *a priori* case for a proposition that education *was* directly conducive to economic growth in the period on the psychological case alone.

It is interesting that the case we have been putting is one that modern historians applied to the later nineteenth century. Referring to the late sixties James Murphy for instance argues:

> . . . competition from abroad in trade and industry was demonstrating the weakness of a nation unable to base a system of secondary, technical and commercial education under firm foundation of a national system of elementary education.[12]

Similarly Eric Rich: ". . . England's manufacturing supremacy seems to be challenged by other nations whose technical schools were said to be better. . . ."[13] These views are partially a reflection of those of contemporaries. W. E. Forster made a reference to the urgent needs of educating the country to meet competition. With the Report by Fearon and Fitch on Leeds, Liverpool, Manchester and Birmingham fresh in his mind, he argued: "upon the steady provision of elementary education depends our industrial prosperity. It is of no use trying to give technical teaching to our artisans without elementary education; uneducated

12. James Murphy, *Church, State and Schools in Britain,* Routledge 1971, p. 46.
13. Eric Rich, *The Education Act 1870,* 1970, p. 75.

labourers—and many of our labourers are utterly uneducated—are, for the most part unskilled labourers, and if we leave our workforce any longer unskilled, notwithstanding their strong sinews and determined energy, they will become over-matched in the competition of the world." [14]

Many had been disturbed by the results of the international exhibition held at Paris in 1867. After the triumph of the 1851 exhibition, when Britain had taken most of the prizes, it came as a shock to learn that the British products now (in 1867) received only a meagre number of awards. At a time of growing nationalism and the decline of Britain's share of foreign trade, there was a feverish search for simple and immediate solutions. More scientific and technical education in addition to expansion of general education was one that was seized upon by most parties.

How far, in retrospect, can we agree with the economic diagnosis of the "cure"; the reality of the "disease" should first be investigated. There was certainly a consensus among economic historians up to recent years that economic "slackening" did occur after 1870 and was borne out by the statistics. The general verdict included three main aspects: output grew too slowly because of a sluggish demand; too much was invested abroad because British capital markets were functioning inefficiently; and productivity slowed up because of poor industrial leadership.

Those who held that the climacteric occurred in the 1870s and would, at first sight, be led to believe that the education of the 1870s (under Forster's Act) was deficient. One must however allow for lags. Most skilled workmen, entrepreneurs, and others employed in the 1870s would have had their schooling in the 1860s or before. But if the education of the 1850s and 1860s was critically deficient the arguments of the strongest advocates of the 1870 Education Bill were considerably validated.

Much depends therefore on the timing of the slowdown; a different picture emerges if it turns out that it did not occur in the 1870s. Many have too readily taken the fact of failure as proven and have concentrated on reasons why Britain failed. Recently there has been considerable conflict about the interpretation of the available facts. There have been two major sources of evidence: First the Hoffmann index of industrial output;

14. W. E. Forster, First Reading of the Education Bill, 17 February 1870.

second, the statistics of national income. D. J. Coppock drew attention in 1956 to the fact that these two sources gave contradictory results.[15] The index of industrial output grew slower than the index of national income. It is the index of industrial output, the Hoffman index, which places the climacteric in the 1870s; the national income figures place it in the 1890s. C. Wilson in 1965 described the whole issue as a "conundrum to which no satisfactory answer has been given."[16]

The last word on this subject seems to have been E. H. Phelps Brown and Margaret Browne (1968) and McCloskey (1970). All three date the slowdown around 1900.[17] McCloskey emphasized that the Hoffman index does not include the output of every sector. It is a non-random sample and the missing sectors might well have been growing faster than the others. The production for instance of soap, bicycles and retailing which were not included were in fact growing rapidly in this period. The index moreover measures gross, not net, outputs; it is not an index of national income originating in industry. McCloskey's argument is that the reasons for the slow rate of growth output was connected with binding resource limitations and not so much with faltering demand. If there had been faltering export demand, he argues, there would have been, after 1872, increasing unemployment as actual output fell more and more behind potential output. Yet unemployment after 1872 was low. Using national product estimates, McCloskey shows that there was in fact a rapid growth of real product from 1870 to 1900 and a sharp deceleration afterwards. The sustained growth of productivity in the 70s and 80s and 90s that his figure reveals, indicates that the conviction of contemporaries that they were falling behind the productivity expansion of Germany and the United States was mistaken. Productivity growth in the United States was in fact of the same order of magnitude as in the United Kingdom. McCloskey concludes:

15. D. J. Coppock, "The Climacteric of the 1890s: A Critical Note," *Manchester School,* XXIV (1956).

16. C. Wilson, "Economy and Society in Late Victorian England," *Economic History Review,* 2nd series, XVIII (1965).

17. Donald N. McCloskey, "Did Victorian Britain Fail?," *Economic History Review,* 2nd series, XVIII, 1970. E. H. Phelps Brown & Margaret Browne, *A Century of Pay,* 1968.

The case for a late Victorian failure in productivity, then, appears weak. Indeed the failure, to be precise, was Edwardian. . . . there is, indeed, little left of the dismal picture of British failure painted by historians. The alternative is a picture of an economy not stagnated but growing as rapidly as permitted by the growth of its resources and the effective exploitation of the available technology.[18]

Observers living in the 1870s who complained of the danger of economic failure did not of course employ evidence of national aggregates of output, labour and capital. Such statistics were not available. Their case rested typically on international comparisons of productivity in specific industries. Here however, their information was often impressionistic and confused. Lyon Playfair, an ex-professor of chemistry and a well respected Member of Parliament and who had served upon the international juries of both the 1851 and 1867 exhibitions, was responsible for the most influential testimony on the economic danger. In an urgent letter to Lord Taunton who was at the time Chairman of the Schools Inquiry Commission, a letter which seems to have impressed Parliament and alarmed public opinion, Playfair said there was unanimity of convictions at the Exhibition that the main cause for Britain's decline was that France, Prussia, Austria, Belgium and Switzerland possessed good systems of industrial education and that England did not.[19]

In particular, attention was drawn to the impressive Prussian system and its relationship to the success of the German chemical industry. Continuous agitation led to the setting up in 1868 of a Government Select Committee "to enquire into the provision for giving instruction in theoretical and applied science to the industrial classes." The findings of this Committee cannot be said to have been unanimous but certainly they put the matter into a perspective which seems to have been subsequently ignored:

> Although the pressure of foreign competition, where it exists, is considered by some witnesses to be partly of a superior scientific attainment of foreign manufacturers, yet the general result of the evidence

18. McCloskey, *op. cit.*, pp. 458 and 459.
19. Playfair's letter is reproduced in the *Journal of the Society of Arts,* 7 June 1867, Vol. XV, p. 477.

proves that it is to be attributed mainly to their artistic taste, to fashion, to lower wages, and to the absence of trade disputes abroad, and to the greater readiness with which handicraftsmen abroad, in some trades, adapt themselves to new requirements. It is owing to one or more of these favourable conditions rather than to superior education or technical skill, that lace-makers of Calais and the locomotive manufacturers of Creuzot and of Esalingen, are competing with this country in neutral markets, and even at home; Mr. Cochrane states that the lower rate of wages alone enabled the factory at Anzin to furnish him with pumping and winding engines, constructed according to his own design but of excellent workmanship, for his own collieries in Northumberland and Durham.[20]

In retrospect it is interesting to speculate how much such changes were simply the product of dynamic changes in an economy that was experiencing overall expansion. The extension of the franchise in 1867 had undoubtedly made Governments politically sensitive to the "needs" of those industries and their employees that were suffering strong and, perhaps, healthy pressures of competition. This would be especially the case where threatened industries or firms were so geographically concentrated as to coincide with political constituencies.

Britain's poor showing at the 1867 Exhibition in Paris was, in retrospect, a very superficial indicator of economic growth despite the contemporary conviction of contemporaries such as Playfair, Chadwick, and Forster. Where communications are well developed growth rates do not in any direct way depend upon inventions made within its boundaries. In certain circumstances some countries indeed may grow faster by waiting for and copying the best inventions of others. Japan would not have scored highly in the late-nineteenth-century international exhibitions, but few would argue that this fact would symbolize Japanese stagnation. One must question moreover the confidence of a small panel of judges (composed of university professors such as Lyon Playfair) to have assessed successfully the full *economic* significance of the exhibition entries. Consumers have the biggest part to play in any final assessment; and this involves trial and error and the passage of much time. Many en-

20. Select Committee on Scientific Instruction, 1868.

tries may have impressed the panel with their scientific ingenuity or complexity. Others may have had aesthetic appeal to them personally. Such individual assessment of quality can be quite distinct from assessment of commercial potentiality.

More questionable still is the assumption of a direct connection between education and invention. Consider Playfair's complaint that Belgian iron girders were being used in a building in Glasgow. The Belgian's success was, he thought, strongly connected with their use of science in the analysis of the chemical properties in iron ore and limestone. The Royal Commission on Scientific Instruction (1868) was, among other things, set up to investigate this question directly. In its findings it went a long way in refuting Playfair's argument. The Commission found that it was not scientific superiority but the *patent laws* which accounted for the use of Belgian girders in Glasgow. The Belgian chemical process was in fact common knowledge among English businessmen. They were prevented from using it however because, although the patent was in the hands of only one English producer, the law did not compel the patentee to exploit his patent himself. Others in Britain wanted to produce in the Belgian manner but were thus prevented from doing so by legal, not scientific, obstacles.

As for scientific advances in steel, it was an Englishman, not a German, whose invention was of most consequence. Sydney Gilchrist Thomas, who discovered how to make steel out of phosphoric ore in 1875, was an English Police Court Clerk and had conducted his experiments in the backyard of a small suburban house. This invention redounded to the advantage not of the English but of the Germans for it created a gigantic steel industry which would not have been possible without it. The Germans were able to use the invention not because they had impressive state schools, but simply because the invention enabled them at least to exploit their own ores, which were phosphoric.

Conclusion

We conclude that in the early nineteenth century there is no evidence to show that education did not play a significant part in the industrial progress. Education expansion accompanied industrial growth in the towns in England, Wales and Scotland. The extraordinary literacy attainments in the towns testifies to the success of educational endeavour among all industrial classes during the period. Whilst this in itself only shows a correlation between education and industrial growth, there are several reasons for arguing some significant causation also. Meanwhile the belief that educational deficiency was an important obstacle to prosperity in the latter half of the nineteenth century, has been shown to stem from confusion and misinformation. First, the evidence does not convincingly show that growth rates did in fact slow down significantly. Second, education in fact expanded vigorously during this period. Belief that this was not so has been encouraged by the acceptance hitherto of erroneous statistics of education. Those figures which were supplied, increasingly by the Education Department in the nineteenth century, were both partial and selective. Nineteenth-century education was of a small magnitude of course if judged from present-day standards; but so also was national output. Even by twentieth-century standards, however, the rates of growth of education and industrial output were impressive. None of this is to argue that education was *the* main cause of economic expansion in the nineteenth century. The main conclusion here is that, despite the widespread belief to the contrary, education expanded significantly during the periods examined; and at least on a priori reasoning, there is a fair presumption that it significantly assisted economic growth throughout. There was an Educational Revolution as well as an Industrial Revolution; and both were interrelated.

Bibliography

Nineteenth-Century Parliamentary Papers

Hansard: Vol. VIII, Col. 884. 1807 Whitbread Bill.
Vol. IX, Col. 538. 1807 Whitbread Bill (Revised).
Journal of the House of Commons: Vol. LXII, pp. 699–790, opposing petitions 1807.
Hansard: N.S. Vol. II, Brougham 1820.
Hansard: Vol. XV, Col. 760 (Salford) 1833.
Vol. XVI (Brougham recantation) 1833.
Vol. XX (Roebuck's speech) 1833.
Journal of the House of Commons: Vol. LXXXVIII.
Parliamentary Paper: No. 62, 1835 (Kerry Return).
Hansard: Vol. XXXIX, Cols. 458–59.
Hansard: 19 April 1847.
Report of the Select Committee on the Education of the Lower Orders; 1816 First, Second, Third and Fourth Reports.
1818 First, Second, Third and Fourth Reports.
Extracts from Information Received by the Poor Law Commissioners, 1833.
Report of the Poor Law Commissioners, 1834.
Report of the Select Committee on Education in England and Wales, 1835.
Report of the Select Committee on Education of the Poorer Classes, 1838.
Report to the Secretary of State from the Poor Law Commissioners, 1841.
Report of the Commissioners of Inquiry into the State of Education in Wales, 1847.
Census of Great Britain, 1851, England and Wales, Report and Tables (1854).

Report of the Royal Commission on Popular Education (7 Vols.) 1861 (New-castle Commission Report).

Schools Inquiry Commission (for 1858) 1861, Vol. I.

Schools Inquiry Commission: Vols. IV, V, and VI, 1868.

Report from the Select Committee on Scientific Instruction, 1868.

Hansard: Parliamentary Debates, X, Cols. 139–66.

    30 July 1833.

    House of Lords, 21 May 1835.

Minutes of the Committee of Council on Education, 1840–1841; Appendix III, p. 138.

Seventh Annual Report of the Registrar General, P.P. 1846 (727) XIX, 245.

Parliamentary Paper, Vol. XII, 1820, 341–49.

    Vol. XX, 1834.

Articles in Nineteenth-Century Periodicals

Economic Journal: 1891, J. S. Nicholson, "The Living Capital of the United Kingdom."

Literary Journal: 1806, 2nd Series, Vol. II.

Westminster Review: 1813, Art IX.

    1826, Vol. VI (Oct.).

Encyclopaedia Britannica: 1818, Article by James Mill.

The Jurist: 1833, Article by John Stuart Mill.

Edinburgh Review, 1813, Vol. XXI, p. 216.

    1827, Vol. XCI, pp. 107–32.

Journal of the Statistical Society of London, 1839–1841.

Journal of the Statistical Society of London, Report of the Inspector of Factories on the effects of the Educational Provisions of the Factories "Act." Alfred A. Fry, 1839.

Journal Statistical Society, London, III, 1840.

Education Committee of the Statistical Society of Bristol, J.R.S.S., Vol. IV, 1841, p. 252.

Manchester Statistical Society Report on the State of Education in Bury in 1835 (1836).

Manchester Statistical Society's Report on Hull, Journal Statistical Society, London, IV (1841), 158, 159.

Manchester Statistical Society on the State of Education in Rutand, Journal of Statistical Society, London, II (1839), Table II, p. 307.

Manchester Statistical Society on the State of Education in the Borough of Salford in 1835 (1836).

Manchester Statistical Society on the State of Education in the Borough of Manchester in 1834, 2nd ed., 1837.

Moral Statistics of the Highlands and Islands of Scotland. Compiled by Inverness Society for the Education of the Poor in the Highlands, Inverness, 1826.

Journal of the Statistical Society of London, II, 1839, Fry, Alfred, A.: *Report of the Inspectors of Factories on the effects of the Educational Provisions of the Factories Act.*

Articles in Twentieth-Century Periodicals

Becker, G. S.: Proceedings, L. 1960. "Underinvestment in College Education," *American Economic Review.*

Buchanan, J. M.: "Politics, Policy, and the Pigovian Margins," (Feb) 1962, *Economica.*

Buchanan, J. M. and Stubblebine, W.: "Externality," Nov. 1962, *Economica.*

Coase, R.: "The Problem of Social Cost," *Journal Law and Economics,* 1960.

Coppock, D. J.: "The Climacteric of the 1890's. A Critical Note," *Manchester School*, XXIV, 1956.

Fletcher, Laaden: "Payment for Means or Payment for Results. Administrative Dilemma of the 1860's." *Journal of Educational Administration and History*, June 1972.

Forbes, Duncan: "Scientific Whiggism; Adam Smith and John Millar," *Cambridge Journal*, Vol. VII, 1954.

Hurt, J. S.: "Professor West on Early Nineteenth Century Education," *Economic History Review*, XXIV, d. 1971.

Landes, W. M. and Solmon: "Compulsory Schooling Legislation: An Economic Analysis of the Law and Social Change in the Nineteenth Century," *Journal of Economic History*, March 1972, Sec. III.

McCann, W. P.: "Elementary Education in England and Wales on the Eve of the 1870 Education Act," *Journal of Educational Admin. and History*, June 1971.

McCloskey, Donald N.: "Did Victorian Britain Fail?" *Economic History Review*, 2nd Series, Vol. XXIII, 1970.

MacFie, A. L.: "The Scottish Tradition in Economic Thought," *Journal of Political Economy*, Vol. II, 1955.

Niskanen, W. A.: "The Peculiar Economics of Bureaucracy," *American Economic Review,* May 1961.

Peltzman, Sam: "The Effect of Government Subsidies in-kind on Private Expenditures: The Case of Higher Education," *Journal of Political Economy,* Feb. 1973.

Perkins, H. J.: "The Origins of the Popular Press," *History Today,* VII (1957).

Preece, I.: "The Laissez-Faire System of Finance of Education," *B. J. Ed. Statistics,* 1969.

Sanderson, Michael: "Education and the Factory in Industrial Lancashire 1780–1840," *Econ. History Review,* 2nd Ser. XX (1967).

Schultz, T. W.: "Literacy and Education in England 1640–1900," *Journal Past and Present,* No. 42, Feb. 1969.

Solmon, A.: "Adam Smith as a Sociologist," *Social Research,* Feb. 1954.

Weisbrod, B. A.: "Education and Investment in Human Capital," *Journal of Political Economy,* LXX, 1962, plus (supplement).

West, E. G.: "The Political Economy of American Public School Legislation," *Journal of Law and Economics,* Oct. 1967.

Wilson, C.: "Economy and Society in Late Victorian England," *Econ. History Review,* 2nd Series, XVIII, 1965.

Books and Pamphlets

Adams, Francis: *The Elementary School Contest* (1882).

Adamson, J. W.: *English Education 1789–1902,* Cambridge (1930).

Adamson, J. W.: *A Short History of Education,* London (1919).

Alchian, Armen A.: *The Economic and Social Impact of Free Tuition,* Centre for Independent Education, Wichita Collegiate School (1967).

Altick, Richard D.: *The English Common Reader,* University of Chicago Press (1957).

Anderson, C. A.: *Literacy and Schooling on the Development Threshold: Some Historical Cases,* C. A. Anderson and M. P. Bowman (eds), Education and Economic Development, 1965 (Aldine).

Armytage, W. G.: *Four Hundred Years of English Education,* Cambridge (1964).

Arnold, Matthew: *Reports on Elementary Schools 1852–1882,* London (1908).

Ashby, Sir Eric: *Technology and the Academics,* London (1958).

Barnard, H. G.: *A Short History of English Education,* London (1947).

Barnard, R. C.: *A History of English Education from 1760,* London, 2nd ed. (1961).

Baumol, W. J.: *Welfare Economics and the Theory of the State* (1952).

Becker, Gary: *Human Capital*, Chicago (1964).

Bentham, J.: *The Works of Jeremy Bentham* (Edited by P. Bowring), II Vols. (1843).

Bentham, J.: *Church of Englandism and its catechism examined*, London (1817).

Bentham, J.: *The Book of Fallacies*, London (1824).

Bentham, J.: *Collected Works*, 1843, XI, 81.

Berg, Ivan: *Education and Jobs—The Great Training Robbery* (1970).

Birchenough, C.: *History of Elementary Education in England and Wales* (1920).

Birchenough, C.: *History of Elementary Education in England and London*, 3rd ed. (1938).

Blaug, M.: *Education—a Framework for Choice: Readings in Political Economy No. I*, I.E.A. (1967).

Blaug, M.: *The Economics of Education in English Classical Political Economy: A Re-examination in Essays on Adam Smith*, Clarendon Press, Oxford, 1975.

Bowman, M. J. and Anderson, C. A.: *Concerning the Role of Education*, in M. J. Bowman, *et. al.*

Bowman, M. J. and Anderson, C. A.: *Readings in the Economics of Education*, UNESCO, Paris (1968).

Bryson, G.: *The Scottish Inquiry of the 18th Century*, Princeton (1945).

Chadwick, E.: Pamphlets: *Speeches to the British Association for Advancement of Social Science*, 1857, 1863, 1864, 1869.

Chadwick, E.: *National Elementary Education*. Delivered at a meeting of the Heads of Training Colleges and School Teachers, 15 Feb. 1868.

Chalmers, T.: *Political Economy in Connection with the Moral State and Moral Prospects of Society* (1832).

Chamberlain, Joseph: "Free Schools" Address to B.S.B., 18 June 1875.

Chamberlain, Joseph: *Six years of Educational Work in Birmingham*. An address delivered to the Birmingham School Board, 2 Nov. 1876.

Chambers, J. D.: *Nottinghamshire in the Eighteenth Century* (1966).

Churchill, Winston: *Lord Randolph Churchill*.

Collins, Jesse: *Remarks on the Establishment of Common Schools in England* (1872).

Collins, Philip: *Dickens and Education* (1965).

Connell, W. F.: *The Educational Thought and Influence of Matthew Arnold*, International Library of Sociology and Social Reconstruction, London (1950).

Court, W. H. B.: *A Concise History of Britain* (1967).

Cummins, I.: *Helvetius* (1935).

Cummins, I.: *James Mill on Education* (1959).

Cummins, I.: *A Manufactured Man* (1960).

Cummins, I.: *Useful Learning* (1961).

Curtis and Boultwood: *An Introductory History of English Education Since 1800,* London, 4th ed. (1966).

Curtis, S. P.: *History of Education in Great Britain,* London, 6th edition (1965).

Deane, Phyllis: *The First Industrial Revolution,* 1965.

Deane and W. A. Cole: *British Economic Growth 1688–1959,* Cambridge University Press, 1962, Table 75.

Dent, H. C.: *The Role of Central Government; Trends in Education 1870–1970,* Dept. of Education and Science, Feb. 1970.

Dicey: *Law and Public Opinion in England,* 2nd ed. (1914).

Dobson, J. L.: *The contribution of Francis Place and the Radicals to the Growth of Popular Education 1800–1840,* Unpublished Ph.D Thesis, King's College, Newcastle.

Elliot, H.: *Letters of John Stuart Mill,* 2 Vols. (1910).

Fay, C. R.: *Adam Smith and the Scotland of His Day* (1956).

Finer, S. E.: *The Life and Times of Sir Edwin Chadwick,* London (1852).

Fletcher, P.: *Summary of the Moral Statistics of England and Wales* (1849).

Friedman, M.: *Capitalism and Freedom,* Chicago (1962).

Giffen, Sir Robert: *Economic Enquiries and Studies* (1890).

Godwin, W.: *Enquiry Concerning Political Justice and its Influence on Morals and Happiness,* London (1796).

Gregg, P.: *A Social and Economic History of Britain 1790–1950,* London (1954).

Hadow Report: *The Education of the Adolescent,* 1927.

Halery, E.: *The Growth of Philosophic Radicalism,* London, 1928 ed.

Hanson, W. L. (ed.): *Education, Income and Human Capital,* New York (1970).

Harrison, J. F. C.: *Learning and Living 1790–1860: A Study in the History of the English Adult Education Movement,* London (1961).

Hartwell, M.: *The Industrial Revolution* (1971).

Hayek, F. A.: *The Constitution of Liberty,* London (1960).

Holt, Winifred: *A Beacon for the Blind* (1926).

Jewkes, J.: *The Sources of Invention,* London (1958).

Kay, Dr. J.: *The Moral and Physical Condition of the Working Classes,* London (1830).

Kay, Dr. J.: *The Social Condition and Education of the People in England and Europe,* Longman Brown (1850).

Knight, Frank, H.: *Risk, Uncertainty and Profit* (1921).

Leader, R. F.: *The Life and Letters of J. A. Roebuck,* Bush, London (1897).

Lehmann, W. C.: *John Millar of Glasgow,* London (1960).

Lowe, R.: *Middle Class Education: Endowment or Free Trade?* London (1868).

McCulloch, J. R.: *Principles of Political Economy.* A discourse delivered at the opening of the City of London Literary and Scientific Institution (1825).

McCulloch, J. R.: Edition of A. Smith's *The Wealth of Nations* (1828) Note XXI. The Scottish System of Parochial Education.

MacDonald, J.: *Scotland's Shifting Population 1770–1850,* Glasgow (1937).

McLachlan, D.: *English Education under the Test Acts,* London (1931).

MacLure, J. Stuart: *Educational Documents, England and Wales 1816–1968,* Methuen (1965).

Malthus, T. R.: *An Essay on the Principles of Population,* London (1798).

Mann, Horace: *Letter to S. Whitbread* by Malthus (1807), "National Education," *Transactions of the National Association for the Promotion of Social Science.* Bristol Meeting (1869) London, Longman's Green Reader and Dyer (1870).

Marshall, Alfred: *Principles of Economics,* Eighth edition (1961).

Mill, J. S.: *Principles of Political Economy,* London, 1848.

Mill, J. S.: *Essay on Liberty,* London, 1859, ed. Fontana (1962).

Mill, J. S.: *Dissertations and Discussion, 3 Vols.,* London, 1867.

Mill, J. S.: *Autobiography of John Stuart Mill,* London, 1873, Columbia University Press.

Millar, J. S.: *Historical Review of the English Government,* London (1803).

Mitchell, B. R. and Phyllis Deane: *Abstract of British Historical Statistics,* Cambridge (1962).

Montmorency, J. E. G. de: *State Intervention in English Education* (1902).

Murphy, James: *Church, State and Schools in Britain,* Routledge (1971).

Niskanen, William A.: *Bureaucracy and Representative Government,* New York (1971).

Northcote, Sir Stafford: *Twenty years of Financial Policy 1842–61,* London (1862).

Paine, T.: *The Rights of Man* (1791).

Pakenham, Lord: *Cause of Crime,* London (1958).

Porter, G. R.: *The Progress of the Nation* (1912).

Rich, Eric: *The Education Act* (1870).

Roberts, D. W.: *An Outline of the Economic History of England* (1962).

Rudé, George: *The Crowd in History 1730–1848,* John Wiley & Sons (1964).

Sadler, M.: *The Half Time Question,* London (1892).

Schultz, T. W.: *The Economic Value of Education,* Columbia University Press (1963).

Schumpeter, A.: *History of Economic Analysis,* New York (1955).

Scott, W. R.: *Adam Smith as Student and Professor,* London (1937).

Senior, N.: *Suggestions on Popular Education,* London (1861).

Simon, B.: *Studies in the History of Education 1780–1870,* London (1960).

Simon, B.: *Education and the Labour Movement 1870–1920,* London (1965).

Smith, A.: *An Enquiry into the Nature and Causes of the Wealth of Nations,* Bk. V, 1776.

Smith, Frank: *A History of English Elementary Education,* London (1931).

Smout, T. C.: *A History of the Scottish People 1560–1830,* Charles Scribner & Sons (1969).

Spencer, H.: *Social Statics,* London (1850).

Stephen, L.: *The English Utilitarians,* 3 Vol., London (1900).

Stone, Lawrence: "Literacy and Education in England 1640–1900," *Past and Present,* No. 42, Feb. 1969.

Stuart, M.: *The Education of the People. A History of Primary Education in England and Wales in the Nineteenth Century,* London (1967).

Sutherland, Gillian: *Elementary Education in the Nineteenth Century,* The Historical Association, London (1971).

Thornton, W. T.: *Over Population and its Remedy* (1846).

Tocqueville, Alexis de: *The Old Regime and the French Revolution,* Part III.

Vaizey, John: *The Costs of Education* (1958).

Vaizey, John: *The Economics of Education,* London (1962).

Vaizey, J. and Sheenan, John: *Resources of Education* (1967).

Vincent, W.: *The State and School Education 1640–1660,* London (1950).

Wallas, G.: *The Life of Francis Place,* London (1897).

Wardle, D.: *English Popular Education 1780–1970,* Cambridge (1970).

Wardle, D.: *Education and Society in Nineteenth-Century Nottingham,* C.U.P. (1971).

Webb, R. K.: "Working Class Readers in Early Victorian England," *The English Historical Review* (1950).

Webb, R. K.: "The Victorian Reading Public," in *From Dickens to Hardy,* Pelican (1963).

West, D. J.: *The Habitual Prisoner* (1963).

West, E. G.: *Education and the State,* 2nd ed. (1970).

West, E. G.: *Economics, Education and the Politician,* Hobart Paper 42, I.E.A. (1968).

West, E. G.: In: *Education, a Framework for Choice.* Readings in Political Economy I, I.E.A., 1967.

West, E. G.: "The Political Economy of American Public School Legislation," *Journal of Law and Economics* (October 1967).

Wiliams, R.: *The Long Revolution,* London (1961).

Index

Note: Page numbers in *italics* indicate figures; page numbers followed by *t* indicate tables; page numbers followed by *n* indicate footnotes.

Absence/absenteeism:
  admissible reasons for, 26, 26*n*, 27–28
  in agricultural areas, 38–39, 93–94
  causes of, 58
  opportunity costs of, 38–39
  statistical adjustment for, 118, 118*n*–119*n*
  See also School attendance
Absence of schooling:
  misleading estimates of, 106*n*–107*n*
  school-age base and, 16*n*–17*n*, 23
Accommodation of students, 235, 280
Act of 1696, 83
Adams, Francis, 136*n*
Adamson, J. W., 41*n*
Adolescents in school population, 10*n*, 10–11
Adventure schools:
  Growth of in Scotland, 85*t*, 85–86, 91–92

quality of education in, 89–90, 278
self-interest of school inspectors and, 277, 278
Agricultural areas:
  absenteeism in, 38–39, 93–94
  report on employment in, 107
Alchian, Armen A., 276*n*, 277
Altick, Richard D., 5, 5*n*, 46*n*, 47, 49, 49*n*, 79*n*, 88, 107, 110
America. *See* United States
Anderson, C. A., viii, xii, 48, 48*n*, 49, 55, 66, 286, 286*n*
Anglican Church, 272
Applegarth, Robert, 246*n*
Archer, M. Scotford, 36*n*
Argyll Commission (1867), 93, 98
Armytage, W. G., xvii, 41*n*
Arnold, Matthew, 139, 202, 202*n*, 260, 260*n*, 261, 277, 278*n*, 283*n*
Ashley, Lord, 12
"Associationist" psychology, 159
Attendance. *See* School attendance
Autobiography (Mill), 186, 186*n*

Balfour, G., 84*n*, 96*n*, 97*n*
Barnard, H. C., 41*n*

This book is set in New Caledonia, an Adobe font. Caledonia was designed for the Linotype machine by W. A. Dwiggens, a skilled calligrapher who wrote widely on design matters. It is a transitional face, based on the refined serifed typefaces of the late eighteenth century.

This book is printed on paper that is acid-free and meets the requirements of the American National Standard for Permanence of Paper for Printed Library Materials, z39.48-1992. ∞

Book design by Louise OFarrell,
Gainesville, Florida
Typography by G&S Typesetters, Inc.,
Austin, Texas
Printed and bound by Sheridan Books, Inc.,
Ann Arbor, Michigan